GOING PUBLIC

What Writing Programs Learn from Engagement

Edited by

SHIRLEY K ROSE
IRWIN WEISER

UTAH STATE UNIVERSITY PRESS
Logan, Utah
2010

Utah State University Press
Logan, Utah 84322

Cover design by Barbara Yale-Read

Library of Congress Cataloging-in-Publication Data

Going public : what writing programs learn from engagement / edited by Shirley K Rose, Irwin
Weiser.
    p. cm.
  Includes bibliographical references and index.
  ISBN 978-0-87421-769-8 (pbk. : alk. paper)—ISBN 978-0-87421-770-4 (e-book)
  1. English language–Study and teaching (Secondary)–United States. 2. Language arts (Secondary)–
United States. I. Rose, Shirley K. II. Weiser, Irwin.
  LB1631.G6156 2010
  428.0071'2–dc22
                                    2010000768

CONTENTS

INTRODUCTION
WPA as Citizen-Educator

Shirley K Rose
Irwin Weiser

We locate the work of this volume in the context of three conversations: 1) the recent public engagement movement in higher education, particularly as this movement serves to address and respond to calls for colleges and universities to be more accountable to the broader public; 2) recent interest in exploring perspectives on public discourse/civic rhetoric among scholars of rhetorical history and contemporary rhetorical theory; and 3) the service-learning movement in higher education, in particular the ways in which college and university writing programs have contributed to this movement.

The 1990 report authored by Ernest Boyer, *Scholarship Reconsidered: Priorities of the Professoriate,* and the 1999 report of the Kellogg Commission, *Returning to Our Roots: The Engaged Institution,* are frequently credited with initiating the discussion of "engagement" in the higher education community. These two documents have subsequently become touchstones for exploring relationships between higher education institutions and the communities they serve. The Kellogg Report articulated a central commitment, expressed as follows: "Embedded in the engagement ideal is a commitment to sharing and reciprocity. By engagement, the Commission envisions partnerships, two-way streets defined by mutual respect among the partners for what each brings to the table" (9). It is to this ethic of reciprocity that our title for this volume refers, as our contributors give accounts that describe, evaluate, and theorize what they have learned from their work with their engagement partners. Further, the Kellogg Report defined shared goals and criteria for assessing engagement efforts:

> The engaged institution must accomplish at least three things: 1. It must be organized to respond to the needs of today's students and tomorrow's, not yesterday's. 2. It must enrich students' experiences by bringing research and

engagement into the curriculum and offering practical opportunities for students to prepare for the world they will enter. 3. It must put its critical resources (knowledge and expertise) to work on the problems that the communities it serves face. (10)

As these definitions of engagement indicate, the concept of engagement we and the authors whose work follows are focusing on here is distinct from another current context in which that word is used—the work of the National Survey of Student Engagement (NSSE). NSSE and its related surveys gather "data to identify aspects of the undergraduate experience inside and outside the classroom that can be improved through changes in policies and practices more consistent with good practices in undergraduate education" (*nsse.iub.edu/html/about.cfm. Accessed 8-20-2009.*) Its questions are designed primarily to learn more about students' engagement in their academic programs and in their colleges and universities. Although some of the metrics used in the NSSE may reveal something about students' engagement in community activities (e.g., community and volunteer work, internships, and capstone courses), the emphasis of NSSE is on how these activities contribute to effective undergraduate education more broadly—in particular how students' engagement contributes to their persistence and retention. In this volume, however, we are considering how writing programs develop curricular engagement activities that are consistent with the "commitment to sharing and reciprocity" expressed in the Kellogg Report. Philosophically, engagement seen in this sense becomes an underlying principle of higher education, not simply a contribution to student success, as we explain in what follows.

In the last decade or so, as the discussion of community engagement and public scholarship in higher education has expanded its reach and deepened the articulation of its philosophical foundations, conceptions of college and university faculty work have begun to change. Though the traditional divisions of faculty work into research, teaching, and service constitute a still-familiar triad, many universities and colleges are strategically revising the rhetoric that sharply distinguished among the three elements and contributed to a division of labor among faculty. In addition to this older rhetoric, higher education faculty and administrators are developing new descriptions of their work that emphasize integrating these elements and articulating rationales that argue for the contributions their work makes to the public good. In his chapter for this volume, Jeff Grabill has described this kind of development at Michigan State University, where faculty have worked together to craft a document articulating their shared vision of the scholarship of outreach (Michigan State University). Likewise, faculty at Syracuse University have developed a position statement regarding their responsibilities for contributing to what they have described as a "scholarship in action" (Syracuse University). At Purdue University, a land-grant institution, we have participated in revisions of tenure and promotion guidelines in order to include specific language describing expectations for contributions to the scholarship of engagement. At Arizona State University, where Shirley now works, mission statements for colleges and schools frequently mention "use-inspired research," as opposed to "curiosity-inspired research"—a choice of terminology intended to make the same distinctions once made by the terms "applied research" vs. "basic research," but to do so without privileging one type of inquiry over another in terms of its priority, value, or importance. Employed to describe community engagement projects, among others, the term "use-inspired research" conveys the expectation that these projects will be knowledge-making work.

This redefinition of expectations for faculty work undoubtedly has implications for how our roles as writing program administrators and writing program faculty are defined as well. The work presented in this volume provides a glimpse into the ways writing program faculty across the country, at a variety of institutions with diverse missions serving diverse communities and student populations, have begun to re-conceive their roles as they enact their commitments as citizen educators. Though our collection features the work of writing program administrators and faculty, many of the issues addressed are shared by faculty and administrators involved in engagement-focused projects across the disciplines.

Some recent movements in higher education such as corporatization and globalization have met with resistance from writing program faculty, who view many of the outcomes of these movements as sometimes in conflict with the educational goals of their writing programs; however, the engagement movement has been received much more positively by writing program faculty. Engagement initiatives typically take a direction in which writing program faculty are more eager to move because these initiatives provide them with an opportunity for articulating the ways in which their writing programs' goals and purposes not only align with, but also significantly contribute to achieving these larger institutional goals and commitments.

Much of the discussion of engagement has served to rationalize the increasing interdependencies between higher education institutions and industry, and those developments often seem to have had little impact on undergraduate curricula. However, when colleges and universities turn their attention to developing engagement-focused curricula, their writing programs often become the potential scene or location for the resulting institutional initiatives. The move to involve writing programs is sometimes prompted by a recognition that the typically high enrollments in writing courses promise higher impact relative to administrative effort and other institutional support. Sometimes it is prompted by a hope that because writing courses often provide a critical introduction to academic work, they are an ideal location for executing an ideological turn in conceptions of the relationships between that academic work, citizenship, and professional life.

The chapters in this collection address issues arising from the changing expectations for college and university writing program faculty as institutions of higher education become increasingly invested in engagement with their stakeholder communities and focus greater attention on providing evidence of their accountability to the public. These changes in the larger higher education landscape impact college and university writing programs and their leaders because these programs are typically located where students make the transition from community to college (in first-year composition) or from college to community (in professional writing) and because these programs are dedicated to developing literacies that are most critically needed in communities.

As engagement work emerges as an expectation for faculty work and institutional commitments, writing program faculty need to understand and be prepared to locate their writing programs in relationship to these efforts. Public engagement initiatives have the potential to transform our understanding of the "service" role of writing courses from that of "serving" other academic programs to "serving" a much more broadly defined public. While many writing faculty find engagement values theoretically and ideologically compatible with their own, they may find the demands of an engagement-based program unfamiliar, requiring a new rhetoric: developing awareness of new audiences, turning attention in different directions, and discovering new sets of arguments for curricula.

Many administrators of post-secondary writing programs are already developing curricula that involve students in writing and literacy engagement activities that take their work public, both within their institution and outside its boundaries. In this collection, we present discussions of what several writing program administrators have learned from their work as designers, developers, coordinators, and advocates for public engagement projects, promoting activities that extend student writing beyond the individual classroom and making student writing a public rhetorical act. What we offer here is not intended to be a handbook or guidebook—it is too soon for that, as this new ground for arguing for writing program designs and goals is still mostly unexplored. Rather, we present these essays as an assemblage that illustrates the emergence of a new conception and definition of the pragmatic work of writing programs, informed by a new rhetoric and renewed rhetorical theory as well as by new conceptions of disciplinarity and professionalism. Some of the engagement projects wherein this pragmatic work takes place provide grounds for new arguments and rationales for curricula and suggest new terminologies; others implicitly or explicitly employ classical rhetorical theories. These projects are often the grounds upon which conflicts over changing conceptions of faculty work are played out. The ethic of reciprocity and shared knowledge-making that helps secure the success of many engagement projects may also threaten conceptions of professional and disciplinary identity that are located in the exclusive possession of special expertise.

While there have been a number of books and articles published describing and theorizing service-learning, community literacy programs, and other kinds of community-focused projects, most focus on the formal and/or informal curricular elements and address administrative issues primarily from that perspective if at all. *Going Public* is the first collection of essays to focus on the evolving roles and responsibilities of writing program faculty who have made commitments to lead their programs into engagement and the development of civic discourse. In developing an understanding of this evolution,, we have been influenced by such work as Paula Mathieu's *Tactics of Hope: The Public Turn in English Composition* (Boynton/Cook 2005) and Christian Weisser's *Moving Beyond Academic Discourse: Composition Studies and the Public Sphere* (SIUP, 2002); and, as our title demonstrates, we are influenced by Peter Mortensen's 1998 *CCC* article "Going Public" (50.2: 182-205). More recent work such as Jeff Grabill's *Writing Community Change* (Hampton

Press 2007) and Linda Adler-Kassner *The Activist WPA* (Utah State UP 2008), as well as Eli Goldblatt's *Because We Live Here* (Hampton Press 2007), Anne Feldman's *Making Writing Matter* (SUNY Press 2008) and Linda Flower's *Community Literacy and the Rhetoric of Public Engagement* (SIUP 2008) has also served to move our thinking in this direction.

We do not attempt here a survey or overview of writing programs' engagement projects, nor do we offer an historical sketch that might account for the changing role of writing instruction in colleges and universities with commitments to community engagement over the last century and more, nor do we speculate about why and how these engagement projects have emerged and evolved over the past decade. That project has been admirably carried out by Elinore Long in her volume for Parlor Press's Reference Guides to Rhetoric and Composition series, *Community Literacy and the Rhetoric of Local Publics*. Instead, in the chapters that follow, contributing authors present a range of perspectives on what we can learn when writing programs go public: from how we understand the writing program's role in the institution and community to learning from specific literacy communities, to understanding an institutional culture, to maintaining the core functions of our programs while finding ways to extend our reach, to viewing engagement as both a way of teaching and a way of conducting research. Some chapters offer a broad conceptual focus; others are more focused on particular programs, courses, or curricula. Some chapters emphasize the impact of a writing program focused on community engagement, where much of the writing is being done by people who are not enrolled at the university, while others emphasize how the writing students do for classes encourages civic awareness and participation. As the two of us read and discussed these chapters together, we began to hear how the voices from these multiple perspectives resonated with one another, each of their differing emphases providing a new understanding of how writing programs have embraced engagement as a way of defining the work of their faculty and students.

A fundamental principle of 21st century engagement programs involving college and universities is that all parties contribute to the production of knowledge. 20th century outreach programs emphasized the application of university-developed knowledge to solving problems in business, industry, and agriculture. Service-learning curricula focused on what students learned from their experiences of providing voluntary services to community programs. But contemporary engagement programs are typically driven by different values and vision, with expectations that both sides of the engagement partnership—the university or college and the community agency or entity—not only will contribute expertise and other resources but also will garner new knowledge and develop new resources. Similarly, as the contributors to this collection demonstrate, engagement activities are often the occasion for seeing our usual practices in a new light. Engagement activities provide a perspective from which to view our programs that allows us to see and understand aspects of our programs that we might otherwise never have recognized, to reconsider some practices we might never have questioned.

For college writing programs involved in community engagement activities, these new expectations that everyone is both knowledge-producer and knowledge-consumer can sometimes result in a seismic shift of the grounding assumptions about the writing program's purpose. Authors of the essays assembled here have all addressed that shift to some extent, giving an account of what they have learned about writing and about writing program administration from their programs' involvement in engagement work.

Other writing program faculty can certainly learn from these engagement projects. We learn about ways to improve the success of engagement programs from the trials and errors as well as from effective practices and activities described in these essays. But we also learn from our contributors' discussions of new insights about writing program design that have resulted from their participation in engagement work and of new understandings of their universities that they have gained from their work with their communities. These are lessons that have applied to other program activities as well. For these WPAs, engagement activities have been both an occasion for learning and a catalyst for change. Thus we call particular attention to not only what these programs can teach us about effective and successful engagement designs and activities, but what they can teach us about effectively leading and directing our writing programs' other work as well.

As Jeff Grabill writes in the opening chapter, "What a writing program does... helps determine what it is" (16). From his involvement in engagement work, Grabill has learned to re-envision the role of the writing program he helps to lead, replacing a traditional vision of the writing program as a "service" with a vision of the writing program as a center for intellectual activity. The focus of traditional humanities disciplines on the intellectual work of individuals obscures their practitioners' dependence upon the institutional infrastructures that support that work and allows them to ignore any activity that contributes to the maintenance of that infrastructure. This then leads them not only to devalue but also to resent any activity that distracts them from their focus upon their individual work. Making the infrastructure—and the dependence upon that infrastructure—more visible makes the potential of the writing program more visible as well. In his "Infrastructure Outreach and the Engaged Writing Program," Grabill explains how Michigan State University's documents articulating a view of the community-based work of outreach as intellectual work rather than service helps to make the writing program's work more visible. He argues that "Writing programs are already places where research happens and places for compelling engagement. The writing program of the future might more consciously and strategically 'center' these activities" (xx).

Michael Norton and Eli Goldblatt also credit community engagement activities with helping writing program administrators to see their writing programs anew. From their review and analysis of a number of university-community engagement literacy programs, including their own at Temple University in Philadelphia, Norton and Goldblatt derive the somewhat different, though not necessarily contradictory, lesson that sometimes traditional academic values, such as the valorizing of research, are called into question in ultimately productive ways when faculty become involved in community engagement. In their "Centering Community Literacy: The Art of Location within Institutions and Neighborhoods," Norton and Goldblatt explain how they've learned that "university-community literacy partnerships may be irritants to any and all involved, but this may be part of their appeal. By challenging business as usual, they bring a new attention to pedagogical practices and the relationship between a given institution—large or small—and its surrounding world" (xx). In their work in community literacy programs, university and college faculty confront evidence that the school literacies they've been accustomed to teaching may be not only unlike but irrelevant to literacies of non-academic settings. Norton and Goldblatt further note that the disruptions of familiar routines and practices that result when disparate institutions and agencies work together give rise to occasions for re-examination and reconsideration: "community literacy can help both universities and non-profit community organizations articulate their goals through lending perspective to each other in the context of shared work" (xx).

David Jolliffe's account of the development of the Arkansas Delta Oral History Project (ADOHP) is a story about how the University of Arkansas at Fayetteville learned what prospective students from the Delta already knew about community and what they needed to learn about academic literacy. The ADOHP is designed to help university students and faculty learn about the literacy practices and literacy events of Delta students' home communities, including "texts the students encounter in their home communities; the different realms and domains in which they experience literacy practices; the power relationships inherent in their literacy practices; the historical forces impinging on the practices; and the attitudes and actions they bring to developing new literacy practices." The project has not only helped prospective UAF students to prepare for college-level writing, it has also helped the university to prepare a curriculum that addresses these students' needs. The engagement program enabled university faculty to understand better what students coming from the Delta needed, and thus enabled them to understand that their writing program needed to change in order to meet the needs of these students, rather than trying to make the students ready for the university program. This understanding has come about because acknowledging these community practices as legitimate literacies made it possible to see academic literacy as only one variety of literacy, one shaped by its own particular power relationships, historical forces, and attitudes. Jolliffe notes that "Even with just two years of the ADOHP under our belts, we can see that, if we want these students to succeed at our university, we need to rethink our curriculum and pedagogy so that it does more to bridge the Delta students into the ideally open-minded, disinterested (in the best sense of that term) literacy practices that prevail in college life....We need to help the students see themselves as *bona fide* contributors to the production of knowledge, not simply passive consumers, just doing what they're told to do. We need to help our students see themselves as both the products of historical forces and the potential shapers of cultures to come" (xx-xx).

Jonikka and Colin Charlton work with students for whom the transition to college is not so clearly marked. In their "The Illusion of Transparency at an HSI: Rethinking Service and Public Identity in a South Texas Writing Program" they discuss how they've learned that an "engagement" emphasis on community involvement means something different for students like theirs at the University of Texas-Pan American, who bring with them to the university strong ties to community and a well-developed sense of community values. They explain, "One thing we have learned as WPAs working with students who have extended undergraduate educations is that it is extremely important to help them do writing projects that have real effects on a public audience, that create ripples, so that they can see their time and energy has effect in the moment" (xx). The importance of developing curricula significant in the here-and-now is a lesson we can apply to our work with any student population.

Timothy Henningsen, Diane Chin, Ann Feldman, Caroline Gottschalk-Druschke, Tom Moss, Nadya Pittendrigh, and Stephanie Turner Reich, co-participants in the Chicago Civic Leadership Certificate Program at the University of Illinois-Chicago and co-authors of the "A Hybrid Genre Supports Hybrid Roles in Community-University Collaboration," talk about what they have learned from their work with urban community agencies. In addition to developing a tool for genre analysis that can be used for a wide variety of rhetorical situations as well as with those involving community partners, they have also learned how to clarify expectations and limits for the instructor role to accommodate increased responsibilities presented by engagement activities. Lessons about students' learning apply to instructors and community partners as well: "learning takes place through social engagement and of course, through *doing*" (xx).

Susan Wolff Murphy's "Apprenticing Civic and Political Engagement in the First Year Writing Program" gives an account of how her work with colleagues involved in well-established service-learning and engagement programs across the curriculum at Texas A & M University Corpus Christi helped her understand principles of curriculum development. She explains how she learned that verticality of design incorporates more than cumulative content or development of skills, but also acknowledges and plans for ethical and moral development: "By initiating certain kinds of writing and exploring a shared value system, composition serves as an entry point in a student's legitimate peripheral participation in the community of practice that is an institution. As such, we are helping apprentice these students into the values of the community" (xx). Murphy's discussion reminds readers that engagement-focused writing curricula inculcate community values; engagement projects must be designed with a consciousness—indeed an embrace—of their contribution to students' ethical and moral development.

The role of engagement in a vertical writing curriculum is the focus of Jessie Moore and Michael Strickland's "Wearing Multiple Hats: How Campus WPA Roles Can Inform Program-Specific Writing" as well.

Moore and Strickland describe how the collaboration of Elon College's group of WPAs in coordinating students' work with community agencies across several curricular areas and levels helped them learn about relationships among the undergraduate writing programs and effective ways of working with one another. Their need to coordinate engagement-related activities provided the occasion for developing effective ways of working with one another in other aspects of their writing programs as well. Engagement projects require university and college faculty to articulate and coordinate efforts with one another as well as with community agencies and entities. Such projects challenge customary ways of doing things and require leadership in adapting to change.

In their "Students, Faculty and 'Sustainable' WPA Work," Thia Wolf, Jill Swiencicki, and Chris Fosen broaden the discussion of the context of writing programs' engagement projects to the local institution and its mission, arguing that effective engagement projects explicitly align writing program efforts with institutional missions and strategic plans. At California State University—Chico (Chico State) the first-year writing program participates in the university's focus on sustainability. The authors describe the role that their writing program's "Town Hall Meeting" has played in helping them connect student work on class projects with community needs. WPAs at Chico State learned that their writing program—their students, their curriculum, and their staff—benefits when they focus efforts on work that aligns with their university's mission and strategic plan, rather than insisting on protecting turf and maintaining the status quo.

In "The Writing Center as Site for Engagement," Linda Bergmann outlines four principles for effective engagement activities that she and other staff from the Purdue Writing Lab learned from their work with community agencies. These principles are: giving their work residual value by making it accessible for the long term; shaping materials produced for a more general audience than the immediate users; separating funding for special projects from the general operating budget; and listening to community collaborators' articulation of their needs. Each principle they adopted not only articulates how they learned to work more effectively with the university and community, but also explains how they gained new understandings of Writing Lab operations and practices they had taken for granted. These are design principles that can apply not only to the design of other engagement projects in other writing programs, but to other program initiatives as well.

Linda Shamoon and Eileen Medeiros offer a different perspective on a public writing focus in the context of the specific institution in their essay "Not Politics as Usual: Public Writing as Writing for Engagement." They share lessons about accommodating small scale changes, addressing ways to open up and explore possibilities for public writing in the context of an institution that is ambivalent about student and faculty involvement in civic action. Their response to their institutional context illustrates the rhetorical savvy engagement projects require of their faculty participants. Engagement projects evolve in a rhetorical context that constrains their design.

In his "Coming Down from the Ivory Tower: Writing Programs' Role in Advocating Public Scholarship," Dominic Delli-Carpini argues that his students' work on community issues helped them understand the purposes of their academic writing better. Their investigations of important local issues gave them insights that led them to appreciate the intellectual privileges and freedoms afforded by the academic context they participated in as students at York College of Pennsylvania. Delli-Carpini explains that attention to the middle-ground between academic writing and public genres can "provide students with both important tools for future academic research and an understanding of how that research can be reconfigured for the public good. And it can fulfill civic obligations to educate active citizens while at the same time suggesting to the wider public that the ivory tower is a space that is worth protecting for deliberations that serve the larger polis" (x). Engagement projects in writing programs need not preclude academic writing, but may view it in new ways or create new expectations and objectives for that academic writing.

Linda Adler-Kassner's "The WPA as Activist: Systematic Strategies for Framing, Action, and Representation" offers us language and concepts that help us recognize that engagement work transforms one's understanding of writing program administration and the role of a writing program administrator. Adler-Kassner's strategies constitute an applied rhetoric, a rhetoric of understanding contexts, adapting an appropriate persona or voice, and collaborating with others to form alliances that can bring about change. She argues that WPAs can and should be activists by working to change the frames, or assumptions, about what writing is and does and what writing programs do. Thus engagement becomes not only an activity and construct that can shape curriculum and pedagogy; it is also an activity that writing program administrators should embrace as public rhetors. Her essay emphasizes that the intellectual work of writing program administration should be understood to include efforts to change perceptions about the role of writing in society.

The volume closes with a short bibliographic essay in which Jaclyn Wells describes previous scholarship and research that has explored engagement issues that are of particular interest to WPAs. This brief review will help readers place our contributors' work in the context of other work at the intersection of issues in higher education engagement and writing program administration.

One final lesson we take from our contributors concerns the importance of WPAs to the continuity and success of this wide array of writing programs' engagement projects. Regardless of their varying scale and scope, all of these projects require attention, expertise, and dedication sustained over time. Often, given the nature of the projects, WPAs are among the few participants whose involvement continues over a number of academic years, across multiple agency funding cycles, and through the comings and goings of students and staff. This involvement demands dedication to an ideal of the educator as citizen. For our contributors, involvement in "engagement" is not simply a rhetorical strategy, but a rhetorical framework that names the civic action to which they have committed themselves and their work.

REFERENCES

Adler-Kassner, Linda. 2008. *The activist WPA: Changing stories about writing and writers.* Logan: Utah State University UP.

Boyer, Ernest L. 1990. *Scholarship reconsidered: Priorities of the professoriate.* Princeton, N.J.: Carnegie Foundation for the Advancement of Teaching.

Feldman, Ann M. 2008. *Making writing matter: redesigning first-year composition for the engaged university.* Albany, NY: SUNY Press.

Grabill, Jeffrey T. 2007. *Writing community change: Designing technologies for citizen action.* Cresskill, NJ: Hampton Press.

Goldblatt, Eli. 2007. *Because we live here: Sponsoring literacy beyond the college curriculum.* Cresskill, NJ: Hampton Press.

Flower, Linda. 2008. *Community literacy and the rhetoric of public engagement.* Carbondale: Southern Illinois University Press.

Long, Elinore. 2008. *Community literacy and the rhetoric of local publics.* West Lafayette, IN: Parlor Press and WAC Clearinghouse.

Michigan State University. 1993, rpt. 2009. University outreach at Michigan State University: Extending knowledge to serve society. *outreach.msu.edu/ProvostCommitteeReport_2009.pdf* (accessed 22 September 2009).

National Association of State Universities and Land-Grant Colleges. 2000. *Returning to our roots: executive summaries of the reports of the Kellogg Commission on the Future of State and Land-Grant Universities.* Washington, DC.

Syracuse University. 2007. Learning about scholarship in action in concept and practice: A white paper from the Academic Affairs Committee of the University Senate of Syracuse University. *universitysenate.syr.edu/academic/pdf/white-paper-nov-12-2007.pdf* (accessed 22 September 2009).

1

INFRASTRUCTURE OUTREACH AND THE ENGAGED WRITING PROGRAM

Jeff Grabill

This chapter is about writing programs, infrastructure, and the forms of work that can be supported by them. In particular, this chapter is about "engagement" as a form of intellectual work that writing programs are well-suited to support but that will, in turn, change the writing program that becomes engaged.

I argue here that a writing program constitutes a type of infrastructure that supports work. By "work," I am trying to name a category of activity that is broader than the commonplace activity of a writing program—teaching, learning, and administration. I mean that activity plus a range of activities associated with research and outreach in particular. Bounding or defining this activity is not important. What is more important is to understand a writing program as an infrastructure that "does work." That is, a writing program can be said to be the author of things such as a curriculum or a mission or an ethos. At the same time, a writing program enables the work of others—students, teachers, advisors, researchers—however that activity is understood. A writing program is both author and aggregator. As infrastructure, a program is a variable assemblage of people, technologies, missions, purposes, and other material and discursive things that is configurable. Because the meaning of infrastructure is emergent, I see the meaning of a writing program as something that is a function of the work of the writing program itself. In other words, infrastructure, as I will discuss below, is not stable, fixed—visible even—but rather emerges—becomes visible and meaningful—through use. What a writing program does, therefore, helps determine what it is. In many ways, this is an obvious statement, but the implications are potentially significant, as I hope to illustrate.

Given this understanding of institutional systems, I take up in this one recent challenge for writing programs: how various forms of outreach work (such as service learning) have required (or not) the support and resources of the writing program, and, therefore, have changed the very nature of programs themselves. Writing programs have become very complicated arrays of teaching, research, outreach, and service activity. I see tremendous potential in this situation for writing programs to become—much more explicitly—infrastructure that supports a range of intellectual activities of great value to the university. In particular, I take up the notion of "outreach" as a form of intellectual work that puts a particular kind of pressure on writing programs. I will then explore why I think writing programs constitute a powerful and potentially transformative infrastructure for outreach and engagement. Transformative for students and teachers, certainly, but—just as importantly—transformative for universities as a location for high impact experiences and not "merely" service.

OUTREACH AND THE WORK OF WRITING PROGRAMS

There is a distinction in this section that is important to keep in mind, and that is the difference among the work of faculty, the work of students, and the work of programs. This distinction is best understood as a tension, and it is a tension that I want to leave in place and just below the surface of the discussion here. In the interests of focus and space, I also set aside how we understand the work of students as part of the larger activity of a writing program. Student labor is often overlooked (see Horner 2000; DeJoy 2004 for examples to the contrary), and I believe this to be a significant mistake. I am mindful of making this mistake, but I need to do so largely because my concern here is for understanding "outreach" as a type of intellectual work and as a way of valuing intellectual work, and this is primarily a faculty and institutional issue. "Outreach" is not a common way to describe either faculty or programmatic work. The categories of research, teaching, and service are still the primary categories by which faculty work is understood and measured, despite many well-known attempts to displace or modify these categories.

Of these attempts to rethink the work of the university and establish new ways to understand and value intellectual work (e.g., Boyer 1997), one of the more interesting attempts is the 1996 report by the MLA Commission on Professional Service, which takes as one of its starting places the imbalance between research, teaching, and service. The commission notes that service in particular is almost completely ignored or seen as an activity lacking "substantive idea content and significance" (171). In response, the MLA Commission on Professional Service offers a rearticulation of research, teaching, and service into "intellectual work" and "academic and professional citizenship," with research, teaching, and service recast as sites of activity that can be found in both categories. I find this way of thinking compelling, but it doesn't seem to have caught on. There are at least three difficult issues here: one is the persistent problem with the category of "service" in terms of larger institutional value systems; a second (for my purposes here) is the fact that all of these conversations about work and value concern themselves exclusively with individuals and not groups; and a third (again for my purposes here) is the rather impoverished way that "off-campus" or "engaged" work is understood. Engaged or community work is often understood as "service," and "service" is no way to make a career or to build and maintain a program. I would like to cut across these categories by building on Michigan State University's (MSU) attempts to use "outreach" to name a form of intellectual work that may be particularly appropriate to describe the work of writing programs.

The MSU version of the story begins with a 1993 report to the provost entitled "University Outreach at Michigan State University: Enabling Knowledge to Serve Society." The committee that authored the report convened at the start of 1992 and was charged with "articulating an intellectual foundation for outreach and making recommendations for further strengthening university outreach at Michigan State University" (iii). Significantly for the report and for my purposes here, the committee argued for a notion of outreach that saw it as distinct from service, that was cross-cutting, and that was a mode of scholarship. While the authors recognize diversity and even disagreement regarding the concept of "scholarship," in this context, the committee understood scholarship as a research activity, a teaching activity, and even as a function of service: "Teaching, research, and service are simply different expressions of the scholar's central concern: knowledge and its generation, transmission, application, and preservation" (1). And so, consequently, "outreach has the same potential for scholarship as the other major academic functions of the University" (2).

In this respect, outreach serves two functions as the name for a category of work. It is a way of creating a new space within the typical trinity of university research, teaching, and service, and it is a way of calling attention to off-campus and engaged activity. Not surprisingly, the primary distinction in the 1993 report between outreach and non-out-reach activities is where the activity takes place. Roughly speaking, off-campus work qualifies as outreach, on-campus work does not. But out-reach as a category of work is not simply distinguished by location. It is meant as a value statement, and in particular, it is an argument for a type of work that should be integral to the mission of a university. The argu-ment is that a university that doesn't see, encourage, and value scholarly work across its research and teaching mission and with those outside the university is diminished. I am being provocative with my language because the claim that outreach be central to the mission of a university has a specific history. If I were to be more tempered here, I might more modestly assert that outreach is integral to the mission of land and sea grant institutions and of institutions with similar missions. Indeed, the use of "outreach" in the ways that I have presented it here enables it to be a driver for change. Therefore, outreach research is necessarily dif-ferent from "disciplinary" research. The same goes for teaching and ser-vice. Outreach transforms standard categories of work.

In Table 1, I attempt to capture the cross-cutting nature of outreach as a category of work and at the same time highlight gaps and problems in existing work categories. The shaded cells of the table are those cate-gories of work that are discussed in the MSU report and also the catego-ries that are relevant for promotion, tenure, and merit review for MSU faculty. Interestingly, this table calls into question the idea of "outreach" as a category of work parallel with research, teaching, or service. That is, it asks, is there such a thing as "pure" outreach? I don't think so, nor do I think that there should be. Instead, what MSU has in place—and what I am suggesting is appropriate—is a set of cross-cutting hybrids: outreach research that is research that takes place outside the normal on-campus spaces where research is thought to take place; outreach teaching, which is teaching that is said to take place in off-campus settings; and outreach service, which is the way to understand service to the broader commu-nity. This table illustrates, among other things, the basic spatial distinc-tion between on-campus and off-campus work.[1]

---

1. It also demonstrates the fundamental problem with service as a category that carries significant value. It has tested my imagination to think of work that might be consid-ered "research service," though examples for other common categories are relatively easy to find.

	Research	*Teaching*	*Service*	*Outreach*
Research	Disciplinary Research	Teacher Research		Outreach Research
Teaching	Teacher Research	"Normal" on-campus Teaching	On-campus, unpaid teaching work	Outreach Teaching
Service			"Normal" on-campus Service	Outreach Service
Outreach	Outreach Research	Outreach Teaching	Outreach Service	

Table 1. Outreach as a Cross-Cutting Concept

There are significant problems with this understanding of university work, however. For instance, one wonders if all research that takes place off-campus is "outreach research"? Of course not. In some disciplines, all inquiry takes place off-campus, and much off-campus research has no outreach component and no "engagement" ethic. The same sorts of questions can be asked of "outreach teaching." I have argued for community-based research as a particular methodological practice (see Grabill 2007), and I believe that outreach research (or teaching and service) should be similarly transformative for participants and therefore act as the driver for change that it was intended to be in the MSU context. There are, then, two components to the concept of "outreach." One is its concern with location and the other its focus on transformative engagement. The first value was clearly stated in the original 1993 report. The second value—engagement—was less visible, is less concrete, but nonetheless is part of the concept as currently understood.

Understanding and naming value is core to the project of establishing a concept like outreach. The authors of the 1993 report spend most of their time on issues of value, because they recognize that the institutional challenge is to make outreach work visible, rewarding, and rewarded. This is a similarly critical concern for any academic interested in outreach work as part of her own career trajectory or as a type of work to be valued by a writing program. If it is not visible and valuable to the institution, then it is risky work. For programs, it is probably then impossible work. Since that 1993 report, MSU has indeed created a category for outreach in reappointment, promotion, and tenure documents and forms. In 1996, another MSU faculty committee prepared an assessment tool called *Points of Distinction: A Guidebook for Planning and Evaluating Quality Outreach*, which is used as part of faculty review processes. MSU also collects regular data on outreach activity. Yet MSU is a research university, and so everyone at MSU understands that research activity is most valued and service least valued. What outreach as a category of work allows, however, is the ability to position community-based and other activity outside the university in a value system that avoids the label of service. This much is obvious, I know. What is more meaningful are the cross-cutting categories, particularly categories like outreach-research and outreach-teaching. Here it is possible not only to frame community-based teaching, for instance, differently and in a way that might more carefully capture its complexity, but it is also possible to use that teaching activity to drive change within a department, program, or college in terms of how that activity is understood and valued. Therefore, I don't see the use of outreach as a discrete category of work or the MSU model as an ideal system. Nor do I necessarily see it as a preferred model. Rather, I see this cross-cutting system as having heuristic value for making visible and intelligible the activity of a writing program that can easily be rendered invisible, making the writing program itself invisible. It is to this task that I turn next.

DISTRIBUTED WRITING PROGRAM, DISTRIBUTED WORK

I use the concept of "infrastructure" both conceptually and materially to describe chains of agencies that "get things done" (Grabill 2007; DeVoss, Cushman, and Grabill 2005; Star and Ruhleder 1996; Bowker and Star 1999). For Star and Ruhleder (1996) infrastructure is significantly but not completely material. It can be understood as stable at a given time and space, but its meaning and value cannot be said to be stable. It is a function of activity—that is, infrastructure emerges as infrastructural because of activity. This variability in the status of infrastructure *as infrastructure* is due in part to its invisibility. Infrastructure is often invisible, especially if it is working well. Star and Ruhleder describe infrastructure as having qualities like embeddedness, transparency, spatial and temporal scope, modularity, and standardization. Infrastructure is also learned as part of membership in groups or communities and linked deeply to conventional practices, and it is these elements of infrastructure that give the concept its human and cultural dimensions (113). In many ways, infrastructure is object-oriented in that any given infrastructure describes a relationship among objects—including humans— that by their interactions "do work." Infrastructure emerges, then, in a given time and place as both visible and meaningful, often because it breaks—or is broken—by use. The argument that I make with this concept of infrastructure is that if we want to understand the rhetorical work that people do together, we must render visible the infrastructure that remains (or wants to remain) invisible and that supports, locates— participates in—that rhetorical work. We must assemble it, and in doing so, we begin to render visible and available to us a set of agencies that are not exclusively human but that are essential to rhetorical work.

That is, admittedly, a quick overview of a difficult and slippery concept. I use it here, however, in a rather simple way. I want to call attention to the fact that infrastructures are required for work to happen, that they can be designed (to some degree), and that they are composed of an articulation of material and conceptual, human and non-human elements. Writing programs are infrastructure. They are assemblies of things—sometimes assembled by design, often not. I intend to use this concept as I turn to a particular writing program infrastructure (MSU's) as an example of a writing program as infrastructure for a kind of outreach-research work that I believe writing programs have the capacity to do better than most other university infrastructures. I focus on outreach-research because both terms are relevant here and perhaps unusual. To think of writing programs as infrastructure for outreach and for research is, in my view, to place writing programs in a new category within taxonomies of university programs.

What does the writing program at MSU look like? It consists of a number of degree programs, administrative entities, and institutional locations. There is a department (Writing, Rhetoric, and American Cultures—WRAC), a writing center, a graduate program that is a college-level program, and a research center (Writing in Digital Environments—WIDE). Faculty are commonly shared; most of the faculty in the graduate program have their tenure home in WRAC, for instance. And some physical space is shared—the graduate program and research center share some space and resources. However, each entity is independently administered. There are few shared students, however, as each of the degree programs serves a distinct group of students, the writing center serves the entire campus, and WIDE has no formal relationship with the teaching mission of any unit.

I call this collection of entities "the writing program" because this collection is responsible for the teaching and research of writing at Michigan State University. One of its virtues is its verticality (see Miles et. al. 2008 for more on vertical writing programs). That is, students are a part of the writing program in their first year, in a major (either as a writing major or engaged in writing in major classes or the writing center), or when learning to teach or research writing. There is intellectual "verticality" in that writing is taught in a conceptually coherent way, and then sometimes a given student is part of the writing program in more than one way at more than one point in her time on campus and so experiences that vertical movement through courses and programs.

I am most interested in the infrastructure that this writing program, like many writing programs, has at its disposal. Certainly included in any list of things that are infrastructural would be faculty, graduate students, undergraduate students, and support staff. Also included would be things like offices, phones, and computer networks, common to most university programs. But significantly, this writing program has its own servers and some unique software tools—largely a function of the research center—as well as access to shared display technologies (e.g., computer projection), meeting spaces (both physical and virtual), and (also largely through the research center) resources shared in common through projects with colleagues on and off-campus. This writing program has a diverse curriculum: first-year writing classes, writing classes in the major, and classes in graduate programs. Some of these curricular spaces are particularly important for the argument of this chapter. The concept of "outreach" is part of this infrastructure, as it names and enables a type of activity that can be found in the curriculum (e.g., service learning), in faculty work (e.g., outreach teaching and research), and in the work of organizations within the larger program (e.g., WIDE as community-based research center). Now, the concept of infrastructure as I am using it here only makes sense—both conceptually and pragmatically—if infrastructure has a sense of time and place. It must be kairotic. That is, infrastructure is never a dead list of things. It only exists at a given time and place in terms of how it is assembled by participants. In this respect, the writing program at Michigan State is a moving and fluid thing. I suspect that my colleagues who are primarily responsible for the care of first-year writing would understand the larger writing program differently than those who must care for the professional writing major. Given my work, I have some responsibility for outreach work, and so I understand this writing program as enabling outreach work. Indeed, a writing program may be unique among programmatic infrastructures for its ability to support outreach research. This makes the writing program a special and potentially transformative entity on campus.

Let me demonstrate the possibilities of writing programs and the productivity of outreach research through the example of one project. The project in question was called the Capital Area Community Information (CACI) project, and it was funded by an outreach research grant made available by Outreach and Engagement and MSU Extension. It was a project focused on collaborating with users to design information communication technologies to support their knowledge work in communities (for more, see Grabill, 2007). CACI was a study of an existing digital government effort called CACVoices (*www.cacvoices.org*), a resource that included the public website that hosts databases and other types of public information.

The goal of CACVoices was to increase the use of data and information in decision-making by residents. It was thought that the best way to do this was to create an open, collaborative system where users from various community groups could add and modify content themselves. The main component of CACVoices consists of vital records and statutory databases. Our study showed that while the CACVoices resource is valued by community-based organizations in the Lansing area, it has had less impact than both institutional sponsors and community organizations would like. For instance, available communication tools were not well known, understood, or utilized. Furthermore, we uncovered deep and pervasive usability problems with interfaces and database tools.

The usability problems by themselves were significant, we argued, because they literally prevented users from engaging in desired "citizen" activity because they made impossible the complex knowledge work required for that activity. Ultimately, we were interested in the collaborative functionality of CACVoices. That is, in the ability of people to design and use their own tools for supporting the knowledge work of citizenship.

This was an "outreach-research" project in the MSU context for a number of reasons: the project was located "out there" in the community (location still being a key driver of the concept); the project wove together key partners (one from Extension; one from the community); the partnership was intellectually and pragmatically substantive; and the project promised both research and outreach deliverables. We worked with individuals and organizations in the community to assist capacity building with respect to the changing CACI interfaces and tools. Significantly, the project also leveraged the resources of the professional writing program and the WIDE Center to assist the productive capacity of individuals and organizations to produce media and documents for CACI (e.g., websites, new media pieces, and other sorts of professional documentation). In other words, the project both added to and utilized the larger infrastructure of the writing program to support the CACI project. But here is the larger point: while the CACI project was ongoing, the writing program at MSU was literally a different program due to new forms of activity and a changed infrastructure.

Figure 1 is a representation of the activity—the energy—generated by one outreach research project within the writing program. There is a symbiosis here: outreach research drives change and alters the larger infrastructure; the writing program provides necessary infrastructure and benefits from the activity. Briefly, then, the project itself made possible a number of traditional scholarly practices: a book, a number of articles, and undergraduate research presentations. It made possible scholarly-programmatic activities, such as the thesis of one student that began as part of the CACI effort, and the support of one MA student's progress through the program (pay and tuition). But we also leveraged the project to generate internship opportunities for BA and MA students as well as class-based client and service learning projects. The CACI project also led to an effort to create a Community Media Center (described in Grabill, forthcoming).

The types of activity that I have described here are necessarily distributed, and this fact is important. Often when we write about research or teaching, we write in terms of "our" research or teaching and leave invisible the infrastructure required to support it and indeed its distributed nature. The distributed nature of work is almost impossible to keep invisible when we consider practices like service learning, community engagement, or the categories of outreach that I have presented in this chapter. We have, then, another programmatic relationship: distributed work requires infrastructure and infrastructure is created by distributed work. Fundamentally, therefore, the work that I have described here is the work of programs. Put more strongly, the work that I have described here can only be done by programs, and this fact makes the writing program a significant part of any institution of higher education.

The only other institutions within the university that have the type of capacity of a writing program are groups like labs and institutes in the natural, engineering, and social sciences and extension services. In those places, we will see work that is similarly and complexly distributed, a differentiated human and non-human infrastructure to support this

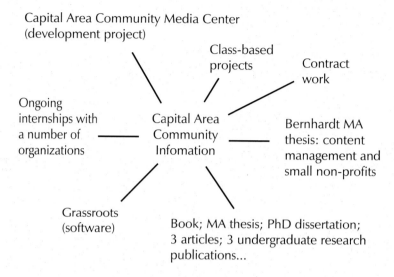

Figure 1. The Productivity of Outreach-Research

work, and even a mix of activities that would correspond to categories like research, teaching, and even outreach or service. But the image and identity of a writing program would not allow it to be placed within the same category of groups like labs, institutes, and extension services. When and where the writing program is understood only in terms of first-year writing, it is likely understood only in terms of teaching, and that teaching, perhaps, is understood only in terms of its service to the institution. The enterprise of writing on every campus is a more complex construction.

When we first launched the WIDE Research Center, we learned that the existence of the Center gave us—collectively as writing teachers and researchers—new status on campus. Our colleagues in other disciplines understood research as a category of valued work and understood research centers. We were suddenly recognizable to them. We developed a new identity that has cultural value within an institution of higher education. We also learned that our colleagues were surprised to discover that it was possible to research writing and that the course that most people knew—first-year writing—was rooted in a research context. The dynamic is similar with respect to the service learning, community engagement, and/or outreach work that may take place in any given writing program. We have been fortunate to have a service-learning writing project in place for many years, we have a writing center with an outreach profile, we have a research center with an outreach-research profile, and our degree programs have visible "slots" for the categories of outreach work. This is the work of a program, not the labor of individual faculty members, who cannot be infrastructure by themselves.

WRITING PROGRAM AS INFRASTRUCTURE

As I have said, writing programs are complex systems of activity and value. Most importantly for my purposes, writing programs are a type of infrastructure that make engaged intellectual work more likely and possible than other elements of university infrastructure. They are different from academic departments organized around faculty research and teaching. Think here about how the culture of the writing program and, say, the English department often differ. They are different from research labs and centers, as commonly understood and practiced. They are not extension services, technology transfer offices, or continuing education. Writing programs are already an odd assortment of teaching, research, service, and, increasingly, outreach activity in the form of service learning or other forms of community engagement. Indeed, it has been this move to more diverse forms of engagement in and through the writing class that prompts my essay. I have long struggled with how to engage and help my students engage in ways that are intellectually and ethically responsible and sustainable, and I have worked through this struggle using various aspects of the institution: departments, service learning offices, classes, majors, and research centers.

In this chapter, I have tried to make the case for writing programs as research centers, and I have tried to do so through the concept and value of outreach research. One reason for my focus on outreach and research has to do with the uniqueness of writing programs as an organization and because of the work that is already going on in many writing programs. The notion of a writing program as providing only teaching-related service isn't descriptively accurate. If writing programs are engaged in the forms of work that I have described in this chapter but are not understood to be centers engaged in these forms of work, then writing programs will remain invisible in many institutions if the work is not made visible. Key to making programs visible in new ways, I believe, is naming these activities using more accurate language. My use of MSU's outreach category is meant to provide a tool for naming that breaks with the more commonplace trinity of research, teaching, and service. More importantly, it provides a new category of research work that is suitable for the inquiry practices of writing programs. Furthermore, entities that do high-quality outreach research are rare because they lack the ethos, the personnel, the opportunity, or the disciplinary and methodological freedom to inquire in these ways. Writing programs can be the type of high impact research center that I am imagining here, but to do so, the infrastructure to support this work must be assembled. Some of it is already there—lying around on the floor like my son's clothing (if you will accept that metaphor). But other elements must be assembled, argued for, created. The key point is this: writing programs are already places where research happens and places for compelling engagement. The writing program of the future might more consciously and strategically "center" these activities.

Clearly, this potential can be realized only with consciousness and design. That is, with new ways to understanding a writing program (as infrastructure), with alternative ways to see the work of a writing program as distributed and in need of some coordination, and with an understanding of that work as crossing all categories of intellectual activity. In my experience, humanists are most likely to think of themselves as good collaborators and also most likely to be really bad at it. In humanistic disciplines in particular, work attaches to individuals: *my* research, *my* teaching, *my* service, and *my* outreach. This makes writing program work appear to be a liability because it distracts people from their individual work. However, any careful study of "my" work as a faculty member will reveal its thoroughly distributed and coordinated features (see figure 2). In this respect, the structure of writing programs is a tremendous asset, if understood as such, for a writing program can sweep together what is distributed and help to coordinate what is diffuse. Writing programs can be understood to be and can be made to perform as powerful infrastructure for a range of intellectual activities. So the forms of explicitness and coordination that I am suggesting as necessary for making/utilizing infrastructure are not easy and cut against the grain of many explicit and implicit value systems. And this is particularly true of outreach work. In taking up outreach in relation to writing programs, my goals have been to argue for a type of activity that I think is valuable and productive but also to pose the most challenging problem for a writing program interested in understanding itself differently: the problem of value. This is a serious and persistent problem for writing programs and for rhetoric and composition as a discipline. If a writing program understands itself as a cross-cutting institution capable of delivering value across the mission of the university, then, I am arguing, we stand the best chance of being transformative.

REFERENCES

Bowker, Geoffery, and Susan Leigh Star. 1999. *Sorting things out: Classification and its consequences.* Cambridge, MA: The MIT Press.

Boyer, Ernest L. 2007. *Scholarship reconsidered: Priorities of the professoriate.* Hoboken, NJ: John Wiley and Sons.

DeJoy, Nancy. 2004. *Process this: Undergraduate writing in composition studies.* Logan: Utah State University Press.

DeVoss, Danielle, Cushman, Ellen, and Grabill, Jeffrey T. 2005. Infrastructure and composing. The when of new-media writing. *College Composition and Communication, 57,* 14-44.

Grabill, Jeffrey T. (forthcoming). On being useful: Rhetoric and the work of engagement. In *The public work of rhetoric,* ed. John Ackerman and David Coogan, Columbia: The University of South Carolina Press.

Grabill, Jeffrey T. 2007. *Writing community change: Designing technologies for citizen action.* Cresskill, NJ: Hampton Press.

Horner, Bruce. 2000. *Terms of work for composition: A materialist critique.* Albany: State University of New York Press.

Michigan State University. 1993. University outreach at Michigan State University: Extending knowledge to serve society. Available: outreach.msu.edu/documents/ProvostCommitteeReport_2009ed.pdf (accessed 14 December 2009)

Michigan State University. 1996. Points of distinction: A guidebook for planning and evaluating quality outreach. *www.eric.ed.gov/ERICDocs/data/ericdocs2sql/content_storage_01/0000019b/80/16/14/b8.pdf* and *outreach.msu.edu/documents/pod_2009ed.pdf*

Miles, Libby, Michael Pennell, Kim Hensley Owens, Jeremiah Dyehouse, Helen O'Grady, Nedra Reynolds, Robert Schwegler, and Linda Shamoon. 2008. "Thinking Vertically." *College Composition and Communication, 59,* 503-511.

MLA Commission on Professional Service. 1996. Making faculty work visible: reinterpreting professional service, teaching, and research in the fields of language and literature. *Profession,* 161-216.

Star, Susan L., and Karen Ruhleder. 1996. Steps toward an ecology of infrastructure: Design and access for large information spaces. *Information Systems Research,* 7(1), 111-134.

2

CENTERING COMMUNITY LITERACY
The Art of Location within Institutions and Neighborhoods

Michael H. Norton
Eli Goldblatt

When university-based composition/rhetoric people engage in community-based projects, our tidy house goes up in flames. You remember the "tidy house"—the one David Bartholomae conjured up in 1993 when the field was becoming more comfortable with "basic writing" as a regular category in American postsecondary education. He warned us against what he called the "quintessential liberal reflex," the desire to embrace and act on the view that "beneath the surface we are all the same person" but also to control the "master text" that determines the definition of that sameness (323). As one who invented and supports a widely accepted approach to basic writers, Bartholomae articulates in that piece his reservations about an institutional arrangement in which "a provisional position has become fixed, naturalized" (325). The challenge non-traditional students make to the underlying assumptions of the college curriculum itself can be domesticated into a mere matter of sorting students by ability and ministering to their needs.

Seventeen years later, writing program administrators (WPAs) have become practiced at navigating the complex demands of first-year students, transfers, undergraduate majors, graduate students at various stages of training, and faculty across the curriculum. WPAs have learned how to represent to central administrators the peculiar alphabet of writing pedagogy—FYW, WC, WAC/WID—while accommodating demands for students to master speaking skills and develop media and information "literacies" in the context of writing program course work. Often WPAs design and execute some of the best assessment efforts on campus, both for individual student learning and for programmatic effectiveness. Just at the point when we have established broadly accepted program guidelines, textbooks for a range of pedagogical approaches, anthologies of reflection and theory, and a growing WPA national council with new local affiliates every year, writing programs must now adapt to a whole new dimension of their mandate, one that subjects all our hard-fought principles and procedures to critique and reframing. This essay considers the question of institutional placement: the location of community-based literacy projects in relation to campus writing programs so that "outside" and "inside" literacy practices meet and mix productively and the lessons from one environment can circulate to others.

Literacies beyond the college curriculum bring to campus waves of Bakhtinian heteroglossia with the roar of Whitman's famous cry in section 24 of *Song of Myself:* "Unscrew the locks from the doors!/ Unscrew the doors themselves from their jambs!" (41). Our first impulse might be to cordon off community literacy from other writing efforts on a campus, but this would be a mistake analogous to separating off basic writing instruction as a mere remedial chore performed outside the regular functioning of respectable college writing programs. We grow as a field when we address language practices that run counter to the norms and conventions of dominant culture, but locating university-community projects and partnerships within institutional boundaries remains a considerable practical challenge.

At the same time, universities and colleges are calling on non-profit organizations large and small to become partners in a newfound enthusiasm for the "community." Although this can be a great opportunity both for the community-based organizations and the people they serve, it can also become a burden for overworked and under-funded staffers. Schools, literacy centers, prisons, after school programs, recreation centers, or halfway houses all have their procedures and routines, and these don't typically involve mentoring students who, after all, won't even be around three months later. As Virginia Chappell notes in her aptly titled essay "Good Intentions Aren't Enough": "Busy people who don't have time to research potential funding sources or write newsletter articles are likely to have even *less* time to show someone else where to do the research or how to articulate an agency 'voice' in a newsletter" (46). For many agencies or centers the influx of academic types into their programs may be destabilizing, generating new tensions in an already fraught environment. They must find a way to accommodate outside partnerships into their institutional structure or refuse the partnerships altogether.

University-community literacy partnerships may be irritants to any and all involved, but this may be part of their appeal. By challenging business as usual, they bring a new attention to pedagogical practices and the relationship between a given institution—large or small—and its surrounding world. On the college side, normal classroom practice often prizes a brand of school literacy defined by teachers' assignments and evaluations. Once the door is open to literacies in different settings, A's and F's compete with communicative efficacy and human interaction as the measure of success. Hannah Ashley notes that in community literacy situations we need to be "teaching untidiness" (62) in the process of taking "into account conflict and civility" (63). Although she does not reference Bartholomae, Ashley's use of terms like tidiness and conflict recalls the way he contrasts the normalization of "basic writing" with Mary Louise Pratt's concept of the "contact zone," the site of contestation and conflict over language and culture in the classroom (318). Ashley calls for a "community based procedural rhetoric" (621) approach that she describes as arising out of local conditions in specific sites in response to the needs and abilities of participants in a given project. In short, such rhetoric would require speakers and writers to deal with differences, recognize available arguments, and inquire creatively in order to solve immediate problems they identify.

This is the approach that Higgens, Long, and Flower propose in much greater detail in their "rhetorical model for personal and public inquiry," an approach that evolved from years of experience connecting Carnegie Mellon undergraduates with teens and adults at the Community Literacy Center in Pittsburgh. Their approach builds upon the flexibility that comes from contact and conflict: "The texts and practices produced in these projects are not ends in themselves but only beginnings, and they work, as publics do, through multiple paths, circulating and re-circulating, evolving and changing—even if incrementally—the way we live and work together as a community" (34). This is a far cry from school discourse, in which plagiarized term papers and grade-grubbing attitudes serve as symptoms of the underlying conflict between developing new ideas and moving through the system. In school, students must accept the premise that original work produces learning, the good for which one strives. A student who does not accept such a premise is likely to see school assignments as tiresome tasks for which one is paid in grade points, and the temptation to find ways around the hard work is strong. Although the inquiry model proposed by Higgens et al. surely has its own pitfalls, a rhetoric based on school interactions does present an appealing alternative for teaching the exigencies of prose. Inquiry emphasizes the need to write and re-write because writing matters to others around you.

Non-profit organizations themselves may benefit from the disruptions college-based visitors can cause. All too often tutors or English faculty come into a neighborhood center or church ESL program only to find that the curriculum is basically old worksheets or grammar exercises based on outmoded views of language instruction. Adult learners who enroll in classes with tremendous motivation to learn the dominant language or pass their GED can become trapped in rote classes or fragmented lessons that have little to do with their lives or their dreams. Even in programs where the instructors want to present relevant material with libratory pedagogy, sometimes the approach can be too abstract or the assignments ill-designed. Negotiations between college-based tutors or supervisors and instructors or managers in neighborhood centers can sometimes get tense but, given enough sensitivity and good will, neighborhood programming can improve as a result of partnership with a post-secondary institution. In the end, the need is to challenge unexamined or deadening attitudes toward language and literacy wherever one might find them—in an insular college writing program or an under-resourced literacy project—recognizing that neither high-handed expertise nor reactive turf defense will win the day. Disruptions focus our attention on places where the accustomed patterns simply don't work, and we can use them as a chance to re-examine practices and reconsider accepted attitudes.

Perhaps the most crucial consideration, however, is the institutional positioning of a project in both its campus home and its community base. We share the view of Jeffrey Grabill "that those of us interested in changing the dominant meanings and values associated with literacy must focus on institutional systems" (xi). Sculptors will tell you that one of the central considerations for any three-dimensional art object is how it rests in space. Should the piece sit on the floor or on a pedestal, hang on the wall or from the ceiling? Should it float in space on a column of forced air? Whether statue, installation piece, or ritual artifact, sculpture must be mounted somehow with regard to the viewer. No matter how traditional or avant-garde, all sculptors must solve the design problem of setting their artwork down. A writing program has much in common with sculpture, although the space it must occupy is defined not only by three dimensions but also by institutional parameters that determine such considerations as flow of resources; student enrollment or participation; staff hiring, supervising, and training; and reputation within the community.

A program sits in a department, a college, or a central office just as it occupies office and classroom space on campus. WPAs often argue about whether first-year writing should stand alone or function as a component of an English department, whether a writing center is better off supported by a dean or a provost, whether writing in the disciplines should be centralized or scattered among curricular units. Location matters for program design in a college or university, but the factors multiply when the program in question is designed to serve not only students on a campus but learners in nonacademic settings or in K-12 schools. The more diverse the learner and instructor population for a program, the more complex are questions of ownership, accountability, and sponsorship. An outreach component of a writing program—or a community literacy project that happens to be sponsored in partnership with an academic institution—must have organic ways to connect with campus units teaching writing if the outside work is to challenge and broaden the college curriculum.

In either case external perspectives may contribute to a comprehensive picture of literacy for students, faculty, neighborhood instructors and learners alike. Researchers in other areas of university-community engagement have noted that the exciting possibilities in partnership also carry the potential for significant conflict within and outside the university setting (Bringle and Hatcher, Cone and Payne; Ferman and Hill). Recognizing the power of partnerships to disrupt or invigorate the routine functioning of local institutions, the art of location for community literacy projects can be crucial to the success and failure of even the best planned efforts.

EXPLORING COMMUNITY BASED LITERACY

We believe that university-community literacy partnerships benefit from a more conscious approach to the "art of location" within educational institutions. Thus, we investigated the institutional context for various established programs in community-based learning with an emphasis on literacy. We have been careful not to name institutions, and the four profiles below represent two composites of national literacy programs and two institutionally unique programs. This inquiry does not focus exclusively on composition/rhetoric initiatives but takes into account projects rooted in many different sectors of university life. Such a wide-angled perspective reveals possibilities, dangers, and principles involved in establishing literacy projects in particular structural configurations on campuses and in communities. Sometimes a "center" for community engagement is not particularly central to all parties on a campus interested in literacy. Other times a project may be heavily involved in a sector of the community but contribute relatively little to the post-secondary school in which it is housed. Indeed, no initiative can be all things to all groups on and off campus, and the term "center" may ultimately be misleading. In the conclusion we return to the perspective of writing program administration and composition/rhetoric, suggesting responses to disciplinary disruptions community literacy inevitably precipitates.

In an effort to understand the broad range of community based literacy programs operating around the country, we initially began identifying literacy programs on the web through related research into community based learning centers. We conducted more than a dozen interviews and conversations with university faculty and staff involved in community based literacy programs and engaged scholarship across the country. Relying on recommendations about specific literacy initiatives from individual informants, each other, and other colleagues we continued identifying other types of community based literacy programs. We intentionally sought out both national literacy programs that operate in post-secondary institutions, and institution-specific programs. By exploring both nationally sponsored and local community literacy programs we hoped to better understand the function and institutionalization of literacy programs on the basis of the program's origin. We tried to speak with individuals who were involved in different types of programs at different levels to get a sense of the broader scope of community based literacy at their institution. In nearly every conversation, we found that literacy was approached from a number of different perspectives and by a number of different entities within each institution. What follows are composite descriptions of two national literacy programs, followed by unique descriptions of two local programs. In our discussion of the national programs, our findings were broadly shared across institutions while the two particular cases provide a detailed window into these unique literacy programs. Within each program, we focus on three main areas: the institutional positioning and academic integration of each program, the way partnerships function in the program, and who the program serves. The distinctions between the national programs and the particular cases provide reference points for a more general discussion to follow.

Community Literacy Service Providers

National Writing Project

Roughly 200 universities across the country support literacy development in local school districts through membership in the National Writing Project (NWP). The NWP's focus on professional development through its 'teach the teachers' model and its reliance on state and federal dollars to privately contract out its services overshadow its connection to colleges and universities. All NWP sites must cultivate partnerships—primarily contractual relationships to provide professional development services—between host institutions and local school districts to be eligible for the federal dollars that support their services. As a federally funded program, colleges and universities match NWP funds with in-kind, monetary contributions, and private grants, and agree to house the programs at their institutions. Along with the contracted agreements with school districts—which leverage their own state and, sometimes, federal dollars as well—federal and state money essentially funnels through a variety of channels to support NWP programming and staffing. Typical NWP sites are collaboratively directed by a university faculty member and a local school district representative. The capacity of NWP sites is largely determined by the level of faculty involvement, their staffing structures, and other institutional supports which vary from institution to institution. NWP programs are housed within universities in a variety of sites, such as writing centers, graduate schools of education, English departments, among others.

A common thread through NWP programs is their external orientation. As primarily a contractual program, NWP services typically do not integrate diverse sectors of the university into their programming. Moreover, the instructors for their summer institutes are not necessarily university faculty and may be external consultants contracted through the NWP site. Due to this external orientation, while these programs may provide a great deal of benefit beyond the campus, their primary focus remains community literacy and not necessarily 'college student' or intra-campus program development. In this sense, NWP 'partnerships' are not reciprocal in the benefits they accrue: universities receive the honor of housing a program that delivers a service to school districts and teachers, while investing a significant amount of institutional resources in the process. While federal dollars are made available to the universities, the institutions must apply for the money, find a way to match those funds, develop a relationship with the local school district, administer the programming and the grants, and provide space without any expectation that university student involvement and learning will be a priority for the program. Certainly the work of NWP sites is beneficial to local school districts and these sites provide valuable services, but these sites don't represent 'partnerships' in the strict sense. These programs essentially provide a service to local educators, heavily subsidized by federal and state funding, and delivered by colleges and universities.

University involvement is certainly beneficial for the programs and clearly lends expertise and credibility to them, but the universities essentially deliver a service for the government. Universities may benefit should their faculty choose to participate in the professional development, as learners or educators (it was unclear from our research how common this was) and graduate students who become involved in their university's NWP may gain valuable experience in the process, but there is no intentionally designed avenue for post-secondary educational benefits in the NWP model. The university gains prestige and generally contributes to the common good of a region. Of course, prestige is not insignificant, nor is finding creative ways to fulfill an institution's civic mission through participation in the NWP. Moreover, participation in the NWP provides institutions opportunities to develop their relationships with local schools in ways that will provide additional avenues to engage the broader university community. This sort of integration was not explicitly articulated in any of our conversations with NWP informants, though the potential certainly exists within every NWP relationship to broaden the scope of the partnership to include diverse sectors of universities.

America Reads

Another ubiquitous literacy initiative housed at colleges and universities is also a federally funded program: America Reads. America Reads is a federal work-study program that places college tutors in K-12 educational settings to tutor under-served youth in reading and writing. In contrast to the National Writing Project, the America Reads program directly involves university students in the delivery of their services. In this sense, the spirit of reciprocity between the university and the partnership schools is apparent at first glance. Moreover, student involvement in America Reads presents opportunities to create intentional academic connections between students' literacy tutoring and their course work.

America Reads is a tutoring program that pays students to be reading and writing tutors in under-served schools, and is designed to teach college students to be tutors and educators. The students are supposed to develop leadership abilities, learn about the challenges of public education in America, develop empathy for children living in under-served areas, and cultivate a number of professional and self-reliance skills through their participation in these programs. In addition to these individual student benefits, in many instances college students may have opportunities simply to volunteer as tutors, and in some cases they can integrate their America Reads work-study into a community based learning course to receive academic credit for their work in the community. Reciprocally, partnership schools in America Reads reap significant benefits from their collaborations with local colleges and universities. America Reads tutors provide much needed capacity for underserved schools. They also provide one-to-one support for students and develop individualized learning plans and curriculum for each participant, in consultation with their primary teachers.

Typically, America Reads programs are housed in community service offices or centers for service learning and are primarily funded by federal work-study. In most instances, there is at least one full time staff person dedicated to America Reads and a host of student coordinators and organizers. The most dynamic America Reads programs make liberal use of student employees as site coordinators and liaisons with partnership schools. Having students involved in organizing and designing literacy curricula is a reciprocally beneficial arrangement that strengthens the learning of both the college and tutored students. However, the importance of professional staff dedicated to running the program and maintaining partnerships with participating schools cannot be understated.

While it is the case that the America Reads programs we researched were staffed with full time personnel, the degree to which these programs were academically integrated varied a great deal. In only one instance was there direct faculty involvement with the program in which courses were designed around student involvement in America Reads. In every other program, integration of America Reads tutoring with academic coursework as community based learning was done on a purely ad hoc basis. Much like the NWP, America Reads is first and foremost an externally focused program that delivers a service to the community. It is seldom, if ever, associated with a writing program or a composition/rhetoric department. On the other hand, America Reads explicitly enlists the services of university students who benefit from the partnership both monetarily and professionally, if not always academically.

Community Based Literacy and Academic Integration: Two Unique Cases

A significant sign that a community based literacy program will likely extend beyond a service orientation or intersect directly with academic programs on campus is the deliberate involvement of faculty as teachers and researchers. When faculty are involved in directing or sponsoring a community based literacy initiative, an array of opportunities emerges to integrate student experiences across various levels of the academic institution. These opportunities include teaching community based learning courses, mentoring graduate students who can integrate the literacy programs into their research, and publishing research of their own for academic and community dissemination. At a broader institutional level, having faculty involvement and/or sponsorship for community based literacy initiatives is an expression of value in the application of academic knowledge and expertise to social challenges.

An Illustrative Case

Here we use a particular example to illustrate how the confluence of faculty involvement and institutional support contributes to sustaining an ongoing partnership around literacy education. The foundation of this literacy program is a partnership between the university and a local elementary school that has existed in some form for nearly 20 years. The permanence of the relationship has created a mutually beneficial partnership, addressing the literacy needs of the local community's youth while providing students and faculty learning opportunities in the course of their contributions to the partnership. The literacy program is physically housed in the campus center that coordinates community service and service learning activities throughout the university. Students on campus are familiar with the center itself as the hub of community engagement opportunities, providing the literacy program with visibility on campus and the ability to recruit students who may be participating in other activities operating in the center.

The program is directed by a professional administrator and sponsored by two faculty, one from the school of education and the other the social sciences. While the professional administrator works to sort out the logistics of student participation and maintains connections with the school partner, both faculty sponsors are able to integrate their pedagogical and research agendas into the partnership. Freeing faculty members from the administrative and logistic details of engaged pedagogies is an essential support the university provides and greatly enhances the ability of faculty to pursue this pedagogical agenda. Participation in the literacy program initiates new tutors by mandating enrollment in a service learning course that focuses on literacy pedagogy and tutoring techniques. After this introduction, students can also continue to integrate course work into their tutoring in the literacy program, and can also take advantage of the position as a federally paid work-study if they qualify for financial aid.

Both faculty sponsors connect their research to the literacy program and disseminate their work and best practices in academic circles and increasingly with their partnership school teachers and administrators. The long standing relationship between the university and the public school has also provided opportunities for graduate students to both tutor and connect their research agendas concerning elementary education, literacy acquisition, and campus-community partnerships to the project. The history of the partnership, the strategic institutional position of the program, administrative support, faculty sponsorship, and varying levels of student involvement all combine to sustain this dynamic program. This example illustrates how a community literacy program has been integrated into a larger institutional structure. Overall, the program explicitly focuses on developing links between scholarship and service, a characteristic of community based learning that seems particularly successful in this case. Specifically, three key components stand out in this campus/community project.

The history of the partnership between the university and the partnership school is crucial. Long standing, institutional relationships take a great deal of effort to develop and sustain. Universities must recognize this reality and support the relationships with staffing structures that sustain partnerships in the community. Even if this work is done with significant contributions from student workers, the most sustainable literacy programs involve designated staff in addition to faculty sponsors and directors.

Strategically placing a community based literacy program alongside other engaged programming in a mutually reinforcing atmosphere presents a number of advantages. Civically inclined students gain exposure to other programs that can potentially enrich their experience at the university, and this context provides wider pools of potential participants. In addition, having a place on campus that coordinates and supports an array of engagement activities for students from community based learning and internships to public service and advocacy provides a codified space on campus where students can pursue their civic interests. At many colleges and universities, the disjunction between community based learning and public service has a tendency to create a dissonance in students who do not necessarily perceive the distinction between service as service, and service integrated into their academics. Finally, and perhaps most importantly, integrating the literacy program into the overarching structure of a community based learning center provides sustainable institutional funding for the project. This literacy program is sustained as part of the overall campus center's budget: 50% endowments, 35% gifts and grants, 15% university funds.

The unification of engagement activities in a dedicated institutional space points to a final crucial component in this example: students have multiple ways of being involved in the program. Initially, students are introduced to the program through the intentional integration of their participation in the community literacy program with their academic work. Later, students can become paid site supervisors and liaisons, develop more community based learning courses, or simply volunteer in the program; thus the program offers students choice in the way they participate. In the midst of the busy lives students lead these days, flexibility is important not only for student involvement, but for the partnering school as well. The more flexibility the university can afford students in the program, the more time elementary students get with their college tutors. The possibility of receiving credit for work they would pursue on their own time is a bonus for engaged students and an added perk that may bring marginally interested students into the program.

Writing Program Integration

Finally, we briefly review another individual case to illustrate how a writing program has integrated engaged pedagogy to their curriculum. Part of the College of Liberal Arts, this comprehensive writing program includes a first-year course, undergraduate writing majors and minors, as well as a graduate program in composition/rhetoric. The program also has a writing center, staffed by faculty and students, open to all members of the university community.

In the course of an undergraduate major or minor, students have a number of opportunities to take community based learning courses through the department should they choose to do so. The writing program faculty and staff maintain roughly seven core partnerships throughout the city to provide a variety of experiences for writing students. Moreover, the service learning courses are structured in a progressive sequence. First year students in introductory writing courses have service components that are relatively basic, and their writing is predominantly reflective. In more advanced courses, students are challenged to develop more professional and specialized writing done in concert with higher levels of engagement with partner organizations. The diverse range of partner organizations, from elementary schools to housing advocacy groups and senior centers, provide a variety of ways for writing students to be engaged in their communities while developing transferable writing skills.

The writing program also draws support from the university center for public service that coordinates what this institution calls service learning. The center provides logistical and administrative support for writing program faculty and students. In the first week of each service learning course, staff from the center for public service orient writing students to the expectations for students in the course of their participation in the class, and help writing program faculty coordinate with different organizations. Furthermore, students can be involved with community partners as semester-long interns, through 20 hour service learning commitments, or as volunteer tutors and mentors. Just as we saw in the previous case, this writing program also offers its students a wide range of engagement possibilities in the local community through literacy and intentionally integrates academic learning as a core component of community literacy. However, this writing program is firmly centered in, and predominately funded through, the College of Liberal Arts.

Interestingly, while there is collaboration between the writing program and the university center for public service, there was little mention of the writing program's service learning offerings on the center for public service website. While the only mention of the writing program's work was buried in a 'click-intensive' course listing guide, the center itself conspicuously touted four separate literacy initiatives run out of its office. In order to know what the writing program is offering students and community organizations, visitors have to browse the center for public service website or go directly to the writing program web-site and look for the 'service learning' link. In effect, the dynamic courses and programs offered through the writing program curriculum are essentially limited to writing program students and faculty.

In general, this was not an uncommon finding: writing programs involved in community based literacy initiatives were institutionally hard to find, not well known by other institutional informants, and typically not integrated into larger frameworks of engagement on campus in conspicuous ways. Yet the 'non-national' programs seen in both this and the previous example do an intentional job of integrating community literacy with the academic development of university students through credit bearing course work.

Challenges

Even with robust levels of support and dynamic curricula outlined in the previous examples, many community based literacy programs face a common set of challenges in the preservation and growth of their respective programs. First, the institutional location within the university itself can be a significant challenge. It is common knowledge in academia that most universities operate on a 'silo' based model of institutional integration, i.e. they are not very integrated. Therefore, when community based writing programs are located in particular departments and associated with particular faculty and their students, there is a tendency for the program to become isolated and to limit participation to departmental majors and minors. On the other hand, if they are not connected to academic units or sponsored by faculty they are not as likely to become intentionally integrated into students' academic course work. This is the dilemma of locating community based literacy programs: either be isolated within an academic department, be pigeonholed in student life, or be an 'externally' oriented program.

This challenge reflects the broader, cultural challenges of university-community partnerships that open the academy to charges of elitism. The higher education culture emphasizes discipline specific research agendas and pedagogies driven by "experts" in academic fields. Individual faculty often resist pursuing research and pedagogies beyond the scope of their particular disciplines, let alone collaborating with 'non-experts' in their local communities. Often faculty have the desire to protect their projects in the category of research, away from service projects that some perceive as "do-gooder charity." Unfortunately, these distinctions and prejudices increasingly reinforce old class-bound patterns and prevent students, faculty, staff, and community participants from challenging barriers that separate them from each other. Even among faculty who do develop community-based teaching and research partnerships, territorial protectionism exists at all levels within the partnerships: faculty protecting their community relationships and funding from university "interference", community partners protecting their relationships with their "clients", departments protecting their faculty, and the universities protecting their students and reputations. Within this prevailing environment, both institutional structures and individuals can be resistant to change, adaptation, and collaboration outside the institutions (Bringle and Hatcher; Walshok; Holland; Benson, Harkavey and Pucket).

Another challenge for community based literacy programs is the dynamics of partnering with underserved public school systems and community organizations. In many cases, the school teachers and staff are under significant pressure to meet state and federally mandated targets and to teach a particular curriculum in a particular way. It is often the case that the capacity of the partnership organization to supervise and coordinate student volunteers determines the scope of the partnership. Safety can also become a challenge, a concern more often articulated by university administration than actually felt by student participants. Regardless, actual or perceived safety concerns must be addressed and assuaged to ensure ongoing administrative support on both sides of the partnership.

External pressure on partnership schools presents another challenge for literacy programs in terms of information sharing. Judging from the programs included in our inquiry, the dialogue between university and community partners tends to focus on how best to manage volunteers and logistical coordination. While collaboration exists between student tutors and teachers in developing individualized curriculum and learning objectives for tutees, an ongoing dialogue around literacy acquisition and pedagogy between university and community partners seemed to be missing. Apart from the professional development services discussed above, there was little mention of direct collaboration between university faculty and/or graduate student researchers and partner school teachers and administrators with respect to literacy pedagogies. Admittedly, such collaboration between university-community partners would be extraordinary and may potentially present conflicts for district and state mandated curricula and pedagogy. On the other hand, such collaboration also carries the potential to bring leading academic research on literacy acquisition and pedagogies to bear in areas of significant need.

Finally, funding presents a significant challenge to the maintenance of community literacy programs. The most sustainable programs are those that have been institutionalized through department budgetary structures, are government supported like the NWP, or are integrated into campus wide centers for community based learning or the like. Even within these structures, community based literacy programs rely heavily on external grant funding or endowments for their continued viability. Faculty and staff operating community based literacy programs would be well served to collaborate with their colleagues involved in other engaged pedagogies throughout their institutions to find a way to articulate the value of engaged pedagogies to university decision makers. Institutional support is crucial because no matter how well faculty and staff write grants and run programs, many programs are sustained by the dedicated work of a small cadre of individuals, any of whose sudden absence could lead to the demise of a program.

A WRITING PROGRAM PERSPECTIVE

Our inquiry suggests much about locating community literacy projects within institutions. A wider perspective on the National Writing Project alone is revelatory, setting aside the long history of the NWP and the high regard it has among scholars and teachers in our field. Writing Projects are often extremely influential in local schools but may be relatively unknown within the college that houses them. Our findings highlight the fact that NWP isn't conceived as a means to improve university teaching or learning practices, and it is seldom located in such a way that the circulation of knowledge and attitudes toward writing could have a significant impact on the college community. That is probably appropriate in many places, because a Project may be better off doing its work without much scrutiny from post-secondary faculty colleagues as long as it functions well and pays its bills. Yet writing or English or even education students and faculty may never be confronted or enlightened by NWP work *outside* campus life unless they make significant efforts to become involved. From a more distant perspective, NWP is a service a university provides for a fee, a contribution to instructional and curricular quality in regional school districts, but local Projects may have little influence on the educational lives of their university communities. This may not be bad, but it is a choice we have made by the way we "center" it in institutional space, i.e. how we staff, locate, and fund the programs.

We want to focus on four areas for growth of community literacy programming that seem to us most notable for WPA's. None of these is entirely surprising, but all four suggest that institutional location can maximize benefits from these features in the overall design for such programs:

- Equilibrium between centralized support and decentralized programming
- Group dynamics among faculty, designated staff, students and community participants
- Partnership across institutional lines respecting the integrity of each institution
- Leadership role for composition/rhetoric in interdisciplinary literacy-related projects

Few projects achieve full flowering in each of these areas because political considerations, time, money, and staff capacity often prevent them from reaching the potential for which they aim, but these indicate exciting possibilities in the work.

Centralized support/Decentralized programming

Like writing centers in basements and WAC programs held hostage by hostile deans, community literacy projects can survive under almost any circumstance. However, they are most likely to thrive if they have both unequivocal support from central administration and considerable investment from the units most involved with their staffing and use. A president cannot successfully order community engagement from the top, but individuals struggle to establish projects over the long term without administrative and collegial support. Central administration can help by providing even a modicum of institutional funding and also assisting in the search for grants and donors; involvement by the university or college development office indicates to funders that the effort really does reflect a priority for the larger institution. On the other hand, exciting and creative programs may arise as a result of an individual faculty member's interest or the enthusiasm of a few entrepreneurial undergraduates. Projects must be close enough to the pressing interests of faculty and students to be energized and fed by their constant attention. Any program is likely to be a source of tension and misunderstanding within a school unless the sponsor puts effort into developing a relationship with the institution and convincing others above and below of the project's consonance with the institutional mission. In other words, serious rhetorical work must go into centering a project or program, the sort of work we recognize well in writing program administration. As we have seen in the WAC movement, the rightness (or righteousness, if you like) of the work cannot simply speak for itself.

As we have seen, writing programs often find themselves operating apart from other community based collaborations operating within their university. Even logical connections between writing programs and literacy tutoring programs throughout higher education tend to go undeveloped. In fact, sometimes competing or parallel projects come out of writing centers or composition/rhetoric programs that have little connection to the literacy tutoring sponsored by student organizations. In response to this challenge a university-wide central office for engaged learning and community partnerships may provide a concrete place where intentional connections, within the university and beyond the campus, can begin to develop. These centers support projects of all types and sizes along a spectrum of commitment levels for students and instructors, even if projects themselves are not based in the center. Not only do university participants learn about innovative opportunities through the center, but community partners are also likely to contact a center to initiate new partnerships or find volunteers.

We should encourage diversity of programming, and specialized projects with more sophisticated training and reflective methods that are better fitted to particular purposes. Connections to the university-wide centers can be advantageous for recruiting students and gaining attention in a crowded public marketplace of extracurricular activities.

Group Dynamic among Participants

The dynamic among those involved with university-community partnerships is another crucial issue our inquiry raises. Good programs have strong participation of faculty with active research agendas and a significant commitment to teaching as well as community development. At the same time, dedicated staff can make the difference between a program that thrives and grows and one that cannot remain stable from year to year. Students and community partners have to have someone they can contact throughout the day, someone who knows about schedules and procedures and alternative plans. Again, in this respect community literacy is no different from first-year writing; both need professional leadership and stable administrative staff. One difference is the potential to tap undergraduate and graduate students as leaders and mentors in community-based work. Distinctions in status, so strictly enforced by academic rank and privilege, can become less pronounced in situations where the needs of marginalized people and the goal of social justice become the driving force. And as the dynamic on the university's side becomes more egalitarian and focused on the job at hand, the relationship with community center managers, instructors, and learners can evolve beyond the old-fashioned town/gown divisions into genuine partnership. Bartholomae's warning against the "liberal reflex," with which we began this essay, should not be taken as a rejection of the notion that we should navigate difference with integrity and sensitivity. Indeed, we must treat all people with respect and honor, but this must not blind us to the many and persistent gaps and hierarchies that make working relationships difficult across institutional boundaries. Consistent efforts to be explicit about every participant's self-interests and historical assumptions, as well as a common purpose for individual projects, can help us overcome the difficulties for dialogue.

Respecting Partners' Integrity

Partnerships across institutional lines are extremely tricky. The executive director of a large social service organization may feel silenced by the strange procedures of an academic bureaucracy, while a full professor may feel unranked and unprepared in the midst of a community meeting where he is simply one participant among many. Humility is a word with great resonance for successful partnerships. One common approach to building partnerships is to develop community advisory boards for university-based centers that carry on literacy or other development projects. These boards can be helpful or disastrous, depending upon the clarity of definition for the board's role and the care taken to compose a balanced and representative group. Less often, faculty and students are asked to join boards of partner non-profit organizations. This can be a valuable experience, and a great help to the organization, but it does require that those who engage with communities to which they do not belong come to the task with a certain humility—a willingness to listen to institutional lives that are quite different from one's own and offer responses based as much on empathetic imagination as a rigid idea of what is right.

Again, experience and training in composition/rhetoric can give us some guidance here. We learn that social context shapes language use and that positions are held through common and often unexamined tropes. We also learn that writing and speaking can be a matter of discovery as much as presentation. We can be open to what people say and how they say it, and we have a high value for learning as a way of being. The experience of the WAC/WID movement is that teaching writing has actually helped disciplines articulate the desired outcomes in their major sequences and graduate training. In the same way, community literacy can help both universities and non-profit community organizations articulate their goals through lending perspective to each other in the context of shared work.

Composition/Rhetoric Leadership

This leads us to a final point about composition/rhetoric in particular. Well-meaning activists and researchers in our field have sometimes developed literacy projects without adequately reaching out to allies inside the same university to develop programs together. Writing program directors and instructors should be leaders in the field of service learning and community engagement, but in fact few in groups like Campus Compact or Habitat for Humanity know that the field of composition/rhetoric even exists. A few years ago Goldblatt led a workshop for people who directed local chapters of a national program connecting undergraduate tutors with older immigrants to help in preparation for their US citizenship exam. Nearly every program used "reflection" as a part of service learning courses that trained the tutors. However, practically none of the teachers had thought about what "reflection" entailed, how to teach it, or what other sorts of writing they could use to get students to consider and critique their experience. This lack of interaction between composition/rhetoric and the service learning community suggested that our profession has let the movement down. We have not adequately invited the conversations that would challenge our tidy campus houses, and we have not facilitated the messy conversations with our outside partners. We must turn toward what Linda Flower calls "the *local, inter*cultural publics of community literacy by circulating new models of dialogue across difference" (6). Her compelling vision of the rhetoric of public engagement will shake our neat institutional arrangements but ultimately give us a richer conception of speaking and writing in all environments. It is time for WPA's and other students of composition/rhetoric to apply their experience and knowledge to endeavors outside of the writing classroom in collaboration with scholars from other disciplines and people who do not earn their living in schools.

REFERENCES

Ashley, Hannah. 2006. Between civility and conflict: Toward a community engaged procedural rhetoric. *Reflections* 5(1-2): 49-66.

Bartholomae, David. 2005. The tidy house: Basic writing in the American curriculum. *Writing on the margins: Essays on composition and teaching,* 312-326. Boston MA: Bedford/St. Martin.

Benson, Lee, Ira Harkavy, and John Puckett. 2000. An implementation revolution as a strategy for fulfilling the democratic promise of university-community partnerships: Penn-West Philadelphia as an experiment in progress. *Nonprofit and Voluntary Sector Quarterly* 29: 24-45.

Bringle, Robert G., and Julie A. Hatcher. 2002. Campus-Community partnerships: The terms of engagement. *Journal of Social Issues* 58: 503-516.

Cone, Dick, and Paul Payne. 2002. When campus and community collide: Campus-Community partnerships from a community perspective." *Journal of Public Affairs* 6: 203-218.

Chappell, Virginia. 2005. Good intentions aren't enough: Insights from activity theory for linking service and learning. *Reflections* 4 (2): 34-53.

Ferman, Barbara and T. L. Hill. 2004. The challenges of agenda conflict in higher-education-community research partnerships: Views from the community side. *Journal of Urban Affairs* 26(2): 241-257.

Flower, Linda. 2008. *Community literacy and the rhetoric of public engagement.* Carbondale, IL: Southern Illinois UP.

Grabill, Jeffrey T. 2001. *Community literacy programs and the politics of change.* Albany, NY: SUNY P.

Higgens, Lorraine, Elenore Long, and Linda Flower. 2006. Community literacy: A rhetorical approach for personal and public inquiry. *Community Literacy Journal* 1(1): 9-44.

Holland, Barbara A. 1999. From murky to meaningful: The role of mission in institutional change. In *Colleges and Universities as Citizens,* ed. R.G. Bringle, R. Games, and E.A. Malloy, 48-73. Boston: Allyn & Bacon.

Walshok, Mary L. 1999. Strategies for building the infrastructure that supports the engaged campus. In *Colleges and Universities as Citizens,* ed. R.G. Bringle, R. Games, and E.A. Malloy, 74-95. Boston: Allyn & Bacon.

Whitman, Walt. 1959. *Complete poetry and selected prose by Walt Whitman.* Ed. James E. Miller. Boston: Houghton Mifflin.

3

THE ARKANSAS DELTA ORAL HISTORY PROJECT
A Hands-On, Experiential Course on School-College Articulation

David A. Jolliffe

I am not now a writing program administrator. I have, however, spent a substantial portion of my career as a director of composition, director of a writing center, and director of a writing-in-the-disciplines program. So I have a clear sense of how the work I'm currently engaged in as holder of the Brown Chair in English Literacy at the University of Arkansas, developing a high school-university literacy articulation program in Arkansas, could support the efforts of a WPA to shape programs that productively build on the literacy experiences of incoming students and that especially open the institution's doors to populations that might otherwise believe a college education is out of the question for them. In what follows, I first take a brief look at high school-college articulation programs, speculate about why they seem to have had such a small impact on college composition, and offer what I hope is a broad, useful perspective on articulation and transition from local literacy to college-level literacy. I then describe a literacy outreach program that my office has developed, suggesting how such projects offer an alternative, but potentially promising, institutional approach for helping students, particularly from under-served populations, make the transition from high school to college writing—and, more generally, academic success. Finally, I maintain that WPAs could either sponsor such programs themselves or simply make use of their insights in planning curriculums and preparing their teaching staffs.

ARTICULATION PROGRAMS: WHERE ARE THEY? DO THEY WORK?

I can't imagine any WPA actually admitting that he or she would oppose efforts that would enable students to make a smooth transition from high school to college literacy experiences. I know that in my nearly three decades of working in college composition programs, hallway conversations have regularly coalesced around a familiar set of topics related to articulation: incoming students' adherence to rigid formulae, particularly the five-paragraph theme; their general lack of familiarity with genres of serious, argumentative non-fiction prose, either from academic or popular-press sources; their hesitancy to go beyond the literal and superficial in their reading of texts; their belief in certain "thou shalt nots" about academic writing—incantations about never using the first person or second person, not beginning a sentence with a conjunction, avoiding contractions; and so on. But rarely do administrators and instructors in a first-year composition program take the opportunity to find out precisely *why* incoming students adhere to these beliefs and practices—*who* taught them to think this way about writing in college and *why*—and then to act on their discoveries with curricular innovations or changes in instructors' training.

A cursory review of scholarship on high school-college composition articulation turns up a relatively brief bibliography. Articulation has been a blip, albeit a very small one, on the English/composition radar screen for the past 80 years. I have no data on which to base a claim that high school-college articulation programs have not succeeded or even have had any discernible effect on how composition is taught on either side of the "divide." But in addition to citing the relative paucity of attention to articulation in the literature, I can offer two related propositions, one an anecdotal observation and the other a bit of conjecture, that might explain the low profile of articulation efforts. To begin with, in my experiences with articulation, the conversation is invariably unidirectional: high school teachers want to know how *they* need to change so that their students will be better prepared for college composition. This power dynamic reminds me of some institutional discussions of diversity: a university, a corporation, a not-for-profit organization says it wants to include more under-represented populations, but the university, corporation, or not-for-profit doesn't acknowledge that *it* needs to change in any way. Can articulation (or diversity, for that matter) really work if change is only moving in one direction? Moreover, I wonder if high school-college articulation efforts seem to have little impact on the field because the scope of their view of literacy is too limited. The underlying argument of articulation programs seems to be this: high school courses foster a certain type of literacy and college courses demand a different type of literacy, so the transitioning high school students need to change their literacy beliefs and practices.

Contemporary new-literacy theorists would offer two related responses to these points. First, they would argue that all literacies are, to some extent, local and that the literacy a student brings to college is affected by so many more contextual forces than simply the teaching about reading and writing he or she has received in high school. Second, they would propose, as do Sylvia Scribner and Michael Cole, that studies of populations learning to write have suffered from "a near-exclusive preoccupation with school-based writing" (127); they would urge scholars, as Anne Ruggles Gere puts it, "to uncouple composition and schooling, to consider the situatedness of composition practices, to focus on the experiences of writers not always visible to us inside the walls of the academy" (279). One of the principal goals of the literacy outreach efforts my office is sponsoring is to take a broader, more inclusive look at the literacy of high school students in an effort to help bridge these students from their home and community literacy beliefs and practices to those embraced by the university, and to help the University of Arkansas understand how it must change if it proposes to welcome students from diverse, under-represented populations and help them succeed.

A FRAMEWORK FOR UNDERSTANDING LITERACY AS LOCAL

What does it mean to examine the literacy of high school students in a broad contextual perspective? David Barton and Mary Hamilton, in their 1998 book, *Local Literacies: Reading and Writing in One Community*, offer six points—touchstones that can be used to frame such a perspective:

- Literacy is best understood as a set of social practices; these can be inferred from events which are mediated by written texts.

- There are different literacies associated with different domains of life.

- Literacy practices are patterned by social institutions and power relationships, and some literacies become more dominant, visible, and influential than others.

- Literacy practices are purposeful and embedded in broader social goals and cultural practices.

- Literacy is historically situated.

- Literacy practices change, and new ones are frequently acquired through processes of informal learning and sense making. (7)

The first point lays the foundation for the other five. All people engage in "literacy practices," which Barton and Hamilton define as "the general cultural ways of utilizing written language which people draw upon in their lives" (6); these general practices are played out in "literacy events," or "activities where literacy plays a role" and which usually involve a written text (7). Moving, then, from this foundation to the other five points:

- A typical student might have a set of literacy practices related to his or her activities in school, but a different set of literacy practices related to his or her life in church, his or her job, and so on.

- These literacy practices are affected by the power relationships inherent in the different social institutions. For example, in school the student is generally engaged as a reader or writer in lots of knowledge comprehension and production activities—reading textbooks to "acquire" content and taking tests and writing papers to demonstrate this acquisition to the teacher, who will determine how successfully the knowledge has been demonstrated. At church, on the other hand, the student might be engaged as a reader of scripture or lessons, but generally not as a writer—except on those occasions where the youth of the church run the service and are expected to write the prayers and the message. Typically, the pastor is in the "power" position, writing sermons and directing the reading of the congregation. At his or her job, to consider yet another literacy site, the student might be required to read product and service manuals and to fill in various report forms, but the reading and writing rarely puts the student in any kind of independent, powerful position. He or she is generally reading and writing to meet demands posed by the supervisor or the corporate structure.

- All of these literacy practices are embedded in the culture's implicit purposes for each of these institutions: School is expected to equip the student with "book learning"; the purpose of church is to instill in the young person a set of religious, spiritual, and moral principles that will guide his or her life choices; the job is there not only to provide the student with some disposable income but also to teach him or her principles of responsibility, industriousness, and economy.

- All of these literacy practices are historically situated. There are historical precedents in every community for how students read and write in school, who reads and writes and how in church, and what kinds of reading and writing students do on the job. And, of course, all of the literacy practices are affected strongly by the histories of race, gender, and class in a community, histories that invariably influence who is expected to do what kind of reading and writing in different contexts and institutions.

- The historical precedents and forces do not set the literacy practices in stone. Students can and do acquire new ways of reading and writing, but generally they do so only when they can perceive a personal, social, or economic reason for doing so.

Ideally, to develop articulation programs that would try to help students effect a transition to university-level literacy practices, a WPA could attempt to gain some insight into each of these dimensions of the incoming students' home and community literacies: their practices and events, power relationships, purposes, histories, and methods for change.

STUDYING LOCAL LITERACIES IN THE ARKANSAS DELTA

For the past two years, my office has been developing a literacy outreach project that was not at the outset designed to be a source for generating such insights but which has serendipitously produced substantial food for thought about how local literacy practices in Arkansas match up with those at the flagship state university, and what we at the university might do to accommodate any mismatch.

A prefatory word about the institutional impetus for this program is in order: I am honored to be the initial occupant of the Brown Chair in English Literacy, an endowed chair supported by the Brown Family Foundation and the Walton Family Charitable Gift to the University of Arkansas. In coming to the University of Arkansas, I was given *carte blanche* to define *literacy* in any way I saw fit and then begin engaging undergraduate and graduate students in courses and programs to address issues related to literacy. Arkansas is a geographically large state with a relatively small population, around 2.8 million. It has only two concentrated metropolitan areas, Little Rock and Northwest Arkansas, the latter comprising a string of four cities—Fayetteville, Springdale, Rogers, and Bentonville. The remainder of the state is rural and agricultural. Nearly 16% of all families live under the federal poverty level. About 10% of all adults have eighth grade as their highest level of educational achievement. According to Stephen Reder's synthetic estimates of literacy, 21% of all adults in Arkansas read at the "below basic" level, and an additional 35% read at the "basic" level; only 44% operate at the "proficient" and "advanced" levels. Arkansas now ranks 50th among the states in the percentage of adults who hold a bachelor's degree.

To help address the inequities and social ills that invariably accompany poverty, the University of Arkansas has given its highest priority to diversifying the student body. In 2006, the African-American population of the state was 15.6% of the total population, with the great majority residing in Little Rock and eastern Arkansas; at the beginning of the 2008-2009 academic year, the African-American population in the student body at the University of Arkansas was 5.3% of the total enrollment. Any effort my office could make to reach out to the students in poor, rural regions of the state and help them to think about going to college in general and the University of Arkansas in particular would be a welcome contribution to the university's goal to diversify and the state's efforts to grow economically.

One of the first projects my office generated, therefore, was the Arkansas Delta Oral History Project (ADOHP), which, as of January 2009, is heading into its third year, having involved 40 University of Arkansas students and nearly 150 students from eight high schools in its first two years. The ADOHP aims to accomplish three goals: to engage young people (and by extension their parents, grandparents, aunts, uncles, neighbors, and so on) in a set of activities that bring education to life and life to education in their communities; to teach these young people (and those with whom they are in contact) something about the nature and power of literacy; and to contribute to efforts to revitalize a region in Arkansas that many folks appear to have written off as unsalvageable.

What is the Arkansas Delta? While the unofficial boundaries of the region are fluid, most Arkansans define the Delta as the 15 counties that either have a Mississippi River shoreline or sit between the river and an odd geological feature, Crowley's Ridge. This crescent-moon-shaped bump stretches from just south of Cape Girardeau, Missouri, to Helena, Arkansas, and is the only high ground in the otherwise flat alluvial plane of the region.

The most influential geological feature of the Delta, however, is not so much the flat plane as it is the rivers: the Arkansas, the White, the Cache, the St. Francis, and, of course, the Mississippi. These rivers flood regularly, and with receding flood waters comes a superabundance of rich soil, so the Delta economy has always been agricultural. Cotton has consistently been a strong crop in the Delta, and the region has also provided a fertile home for rice, soybean, and sorghum grain crops. An old saying seems true about the Delta: The soil is so rich that you could toss out a pound of nails and harvest a bucket of crowbars.

There is nothing resembling a big city in the Delta. One might claim that Jonesboro, with a population of 53,515 represents something like a population center in the north end of the region, while Helena, with a current population of 6,333 in the recently-combined metropolises of Helena and West Helena, anchors the southern end. Most of the rest of the burghs are small farming, river, or railroad towns. There was a time, according to Arkansas Historian Willard Gatewood, when many of these towns were bustling: They had main streets—often two of them, one for Whites and one for Blacks. They had shops and businesses. They had restaurants, movie theatres, even opera houses.

But a true triple whammy hit the Delta. First, like many other sites in small-town America, the Interstate came in the late 1960s and whizzed past the small towns, moving commerce either to larger cities or to malls on a bypass outside of the downtown. Second, the agricultural economy that dominated the region was victimized by the twin forces of mechanization and globalization. The cotton plantation that used to take 100 people to operate now employs three or four people. The Delta cotton that once upon a time was sold directly to the textile mills in the Carolinas now must compete with cotton grown in South America and Asia. Third, the economy essentially converted from family agriculture to big agribusiness. As a result, despite some rare bright spots in the Delta economy, the region is clearly in a decline: businesses go under, industries shut down, populations dwindle, and schools suffer. As Gatewood puts it, one clearly notices "the deterioration of the human condition in the Delta. Virtually all the usual indices, from per capita income, unemployment, and housing to health, teenage pregnancies, and school dropouts, provide a statistical portrait of a people in distress" (23).

And yet the Delta keeps on trying. Communities institute civic improvement projects; school systems bring in new curricular programs; economic development commissions try to entice new businesses and industries to locate there. The Delta residents, and those who care about them, realize that here is a region with a storied past of oral legend and lore. They know the Delta as home to a rich ethnic mix of populations, both those who came to the region willingly to make a home and those who were brought there in servitude. They know the Delta as a place where the religious roots of southern American culture, particularly the Protestant ones, run deep and wide. They know the Delta as a region where the family traditions of cooking, putting up vegetables, sewing, hunting, and fishing get passed on from generation to generation. They know the Delta as the locale where, as Gatewood puts it, "people are likely to emphasize manners and exhibit 'the small courtesies'" (25). Given the richness of its legend and lore, therefore, my colleagues and I saw the Delta as a region where an oral history project could bring local literacies to life.

The ADOHP works this way: A public high school in the Arkansas Delta that wants to participate agrees that in *one class,* the teacher will not alter *what* he or she is planning to teach for a semester, but instead will agree to use oral history as a *teaching method.* That is, no matter what the content of the course, the students will do the following:

- Identify a topic that in some way involves local history, legend, or lore;

- Do some background research on the topic;

- Identify someone with a unique perspective on the topic whom they can interview;

- Plan, practice, conduct, and transcribe the interview verbatim;

- Write a final project of their own design—an essay, a story, a series of poems, a play or video script, a brochure, and so on— that grows out of the interview.

At the same time that the high school students have embarked on their oral history projects, the English and History departments at the University of Arkansas at Fayetteville offer a cross-listed, writing-intensive undergraduate course in which students do three things:

- They read, write, and learn about the history of the Arkansas Delta;
- They plan and complete oral history projects of their own on some aspect of Delta life;
- They act as mentors and role models to the high school students participating in the project.

Both the University of Arkansas course and the selected courses in the participating high schools consult two texts about creating oral history projects: Glenn Whitman's *Dialogue with the Past: Engaging Students and Meeting Standards through Oral History* and Pamela Dean, Toby Daspit and Petra Munro's *Talking Gumbo: A Teacher's Guide to Using Oral History in the Classroom.*

The project begins with a day-long meeting in Helena, Arkansas, involving all the University of Arkansas students and the high school students participating in the project. At this meeting, four hour-long workshops introduce the participants to the defining characteristics of an oral history project, to best practices of planning and conducting an oral history interview, to options for converting an interview transcript into a creative final project, and to the logistics of participating in on-line discussions about one's on-going project. At this initial meeting, all the participating students are organized into four- or five-person working groups. Chairing each group is a University of Arkansas student; the other members are students from the different participating high schools. Each group is given an agenda for the project, detailing when members should have selected a topic, finished their background research, selected an interviewee, drafted interview questions, practiced the interview, conducted it, transcribed it, and started working on their final projects. At the end of the initial meeting the students go back to their respective institutions with the agreement that each student will, at least once a week, log on to the University of Arkansas' electronic discussion platform, WebCT, and share drafts, ask questions, participate in discussions—in general, work together on the project.

After about six weeks of this kind of group activity on the project, everyone participating in the project comes to Fayetteville for a weekend of face-to-face group work and campus activities. The visiting high school students tour campus facilities and meet with university admissions and academic officers. The writing groups convene to work on the emerging project. A local playwright, Bob Ford, runs an afternoon-long work called "From Page to Stage," which involves the students in various activities designed to help them bring their interviews to life in their final projects. They take advantage of some aspect of the cultural scene in Fayetteville: a play in year one, a poetry slam and drumming workshop in year two.

At the end of this weekend, everyone returns to his or her home school invigorated and ready to bring the project to a stunning conclusion. Working in their on-line writing groups again, the students move from interview transcripts to stories, essays, poems, plays, and so on. About four weeks later, the whole group reassembles at the University of Arkansas Community College of Phillips County in Helena for a day of celebration and performance of the final projects.

LEARNING FROM ADOHP: ENGAGED WORK, PLUS A WINDOW INTO LOCAL LITERACIES

I believe it is the consensus among the instructors who have worked with the ADOHP—in addition to me, the team includes a tutorial learning specialist, graduate students in creative writing, history, and anthropology, and the participating teachers from the high schools—that the project has generated outstanding student work. Even a sample of topics and genres for the final projects hints at the energy and engagement students have experienced. The junior English class from Forrest City High School, for example, produced videos based on interviews about the tensions generated when a farmer sold a portion of his land to African-American buyers in the 1970s. The junior English students from Lee County High School produced a live play about the boycott of Marianna, Arkansas, businesses in 1972 when the high schools desegregated—the black students came to the white school—and didn't change the name of the sport teams' mascot. Junior and senior students in a consumer science class from Marvell High School produced two wonderful skits about what family meals were like in the 1950s—normal, everyday ones and special ones when the preacher came to dinner—and then fed the special meal to the audience. Junior and senior English and history students from McGehee High School produced a public television-quality documentary on the history of the great flood of 1927. The final projects created by the University of Arkansas students were equally impressive—for example, a documentary on Lily Peter, the first woman ever to run a substantial farming operation in the Delta; a radio essay on the rise of private academies in the Delta in the wake of Brown versus Board of Education; a narrative history of medical care in small Delta communities; a substantial essay on whether "big box" retail outlets killed small businesses in Delta towns.

The ADOHP has also elicited strong, positive reviews from students and teachers alike. Mallory Day, who participated as a high school senior at McGehee High School in year one of the project, wrote, "When I started this project, I thought it was just another assignment that I would get a grade for, but I was completely wrong. I did get a grade and do all of the work, but I was very surprised when I actually made the project a part of my daily life at school and at home." Jean Jones, who was a senior English major and African-American Studies minor at the University of Arkansas when she participated, offered this perspective:

> Throughout school, we are often called on to research and make arguments about issues and ideas with which we have no direct experience. Participation in the ADOHP made our work directly relevant to our lives. The best thing about the project was that it was student-centered—we were able to choose topics of concern to us and therefore had an immediate sense of motivation.

The student-centered nature of the project was also cited as a major benefit by one of the teachers, Brenda Doucey from Pine Bluff High School: "My first step in the project was to allow the students to brainstorm and come up with ideas that they wanted to work on, not what I wanted, because I felt that if it was their choice, they could be more interested in completing the project." And while the ADOHP gave students the opportunity to find a mirror reflecting their own lives and interests, it also gave them a window to the world beyond their own. As Yogi Denton, the teacher from McGehee High School put it, the collaborative work with the University of Arkansas students provided

> more than just a working relationship. It allowed students to share more than their writing and research. It gave them the opportunity to share ideas and culture with people they might never have known otherwise. The Fayetteville students, usually a much more culturally diverse group than my high school students, have been a constant reminder to my students that there is a world outside of the Delta. The Fayetteville students' interest in the stories and culture of the Delta has made my students realize that there is a rich heritage in their hometowns that must not go untold.

While we have yet to assess formally the impact on students and teachers of the ADOHP, we feel as though we're doing something right.

But enough tooting our own horn. What are we learning from the ADOHP that might help us build programs at the University of Arkansas that would invite and welcome students from the Delta? What are we learning about these students' local literacies that could assist in their transition from high school to college? Let me draw on some retrospective accounts of the project from three University of Arkansas student mentors, Kelly Riley, Hillary Swanton, and Laine Gates, as well as on some personal observations, to flesh out a perspective using the six touchstones provided by Barton and Hamilton.

From the outset we sensed that, because this was such a novel literacy event for them, the high school students were both a bit anxious and somewhat at a loss for words when they discussed their work with their university mentors. Probably because the university participants cast it as such, the high school students perceived the project very much as a college-level literacy event, calling on them to define, plan, and carry out their own project, rather fulfilling an assignment provided by the teacher. Some of the students, those "from more fortunate families," as Hillary put it in her account, seemed to know more about what going to college might require of them as readers and writers, while those "who seemed like they came from families that were not as well-off" posed such questions as "Are there parties?" and "Are all the parties really crazy?" and "What is the basketball team like?" and one that actually impinged on literacy practices, "Do you have a lot of homework?"

For some of the Delta students, their material circumstances seemed to conflict with the literacy practices the project was asking them to engage in. In other words, what we were asking the students to write about sometimes ran counter to what Barton and Hamilton would call the participants' "broader social goals and cultural practices" (7). Consider this story that Laine tells about one of her group members' experiences during the "page-to-stage" writing workshop during the "Fayetteville weekend" in year one:

> One of the students in my group, a fifteen-year-old tenth-grader, ran into some trouble with creating an antagonist to provide the conflict for her narrative. Her interviewee was her grandfather, and she was planning to interview him about a tornado that hit their hometown. For her, there was no clear good and bad around which she could create her story. After some discussion about the idea of conflict in narrative, my student thought for a little while, then began to write intently. She wrote a monologue for her grandfather in

which he weighed the potential costs of going to work, despite the danger of a tornado, against the potential costs of missing that day of work. This might seem like a dilemma with an obvious answer, but for many, the danger of losing a job or even a day's wages can seem just as perilous as a random, disastrous act of nature.

Considered from the abstracted distance of a college writing program, the student is simply being invited to participate in the common college-level literacy practice of considering alternatives and arguing for what might be considered the most reasonable option. Her initial hesitancy to do so, however, suggests that, for her, the reality of economics can outweigh rationality of academic literacy.

We discovered that the WebCT platform as a site for their literacy practice was not uniformly comfortable for all the Delta students and actually intimidated some of them. Hillary reported that, in her group, "some students were more comfortable using the Internet, frequently using 'online language,' like abbreviations or emoticons. Another student was more formal in her approach and less frequent in her postings, which made me think that the Internet was more associated with schoolwork and academics and than with recreation and communication"— which is what the student apparently perceived the writing group work on WebCT to be. An anecdote related by Kelly reveals the same ambivalence toward the electronic communication:

At our first face-to-face encounter in Helena, we attended a meeting that served as a brief introduction to WebCT. After the meeting, I gave each student a slip of paper on which was written their username and password. Both Vanessa and Katelyn accepted their paper with a quick nod and a knowing smile. However, I noticed that Lauren, Monique, and Tanisha took the paper from my hand reluctantly. As soon as these three girls took possession of their paper, they looked down at the writing with furrowed brows. Because the meeting was over, we immediately broke for lunch and joined the buffet line. Fortunately, my group decided to sit together. When I came back to our table, I found Tanisha waiting for me. She held a plate of catfish in one hand and her username and password in the other. As I sat down, I asked her if she had ever used a discussion board before. "Kind of," she said. I asked if she wanted me to explain WebCT to her again. She nodded enthusiastically. As I started to explain, Lauren sat down next to Tanisha and asked me to start over. Instead, I waited for everyone to return to the table before explaining WebCT again. Both Vanessa and Katelyn added their computer experiences to our conversation. We explored the idea of using Facebook as an alternative means of communication, but the students stated that their high schools had filters to block the use of the social networking site. Once everyone felt better about WebCT, Tanisha told me that she was worried about being able to get online regularly. She explained that she had limited computer access at school. Monique and Vanessa expressed the same concern. I helped to relieve their fears by telling them that they just needed to do the best that they could in keeping up with their online correspondence. By the time we had finished our catfish, everyone seemed to feel more at ease.

It can be easy to assume blithely that high school students, having grown up with computers and living in a mediated world, automatically take to programs that involve technology. We discovered that, in the Arkansas Delta at least, there are many students with great academic potential for whom electronic, mediated communication is completely *terra nova*.

The project did not offer us much opportunity to learn about the literacy practices in other domains of the Delta students' lives, but it did give us the chance to consider the power relationships that are generally involved in academic literacy projects in many high schools. While we thought that the structure of the WebCT groups—a University of Arkansas student as the convener and three or four members from different high schools in each group—would be conducive to open, participatory conversation, we were surprised and a bit disappointed that many of the Delta students saw the university student not as a peer mentor but instead as a power figure—a stand-in for the teacher. For the first several weeks of the project, the Delta students would post material to their WebCT group only if the university mentor would pose a direct question to them. They were initially very hesitant to report on their own work to the group as a whole or to offer comments and suggestions to other members of the group. After about a month of this frustrating practice—the Delta students' essentially saying to their university mentors, "Tell me what you want me to do and I'll do it," and the university mentors' essentially responding, "Let's just all share our work and see how we can help one another with this project"—one of the project's co-directors, Anne Raines, actually brought in tutorial material from a supplemental instruction program that taught students explicitly how to ask questions of, and offer constructive suggestions about, one another's work.

While the ADOHP did not give us the chance to learn about the history of specific literacy practices, we were struck by the number of student projects that dealt in some way with what is perhaps the thorni-est issue in the history of the Delta, race relations. In a project that essentially allowed students a free choice of topics, notice the regular surfacing of the issue: Forrest City students wrote about racial tensions resulting from real-estate transactions; Lee County students wrote about the desegregation-related boycott; Pine Bluff students also wrote about the desegregation of high schools; Augusta High School students wrote about the history of a rural neighborhood that old-time residents refer to using a demeaning racial epithet. We got the sense that these were simmering topics that the high school students had had relatively little opportunity to write about and that the ADOHP gave them some license to work out their thinking on the sensitive issues.

Finally, we learned that for many Delta students the physical, material concept of home and community was very important to them and the prospect of going away to school seemed pretty daunting to them. Here is a story from Kelly's group:

> At our first meeting in Helena, a member of my group, Vanessa, introduced herself to me and then immediately stated "I get my schooling in McGehee, but I live in Arkansas City." When I asked what she meant by this declara-tion, she just shrugged her shoulders and looked up at me with eyes that seemed to say "you figure it out." After prodding her again, she responded by saying "I guess it's supposed to be a better education or some such thing. I don't know," and she shrugged her shoulders again. There was something in the way she shrugged her shoulders that has remained with me ever since. With this simple gesture, Vanessa seemed to convey a profound sadness and a sense of defeat. A month later during one of our small-group meetings, Vanessa mentioned to the group how much she wished she could have gone to school in Arkansas City. She stated, "I could have walked to school, but there's nothing in Arkansas City now. Nothing to do. Just nothing." I ques-tioned her about this, but she shrugged her shoulders again in the same fashion. Vanessa's haunting gesture prompted me to do some reading about Arkansas City's high school. Because of consolidations mandated by the state legislature, Arkansas City's schools were closed in July of 2004. Students from these schools were forced to attend McGehee schools. Losing a school also means losing an important sense of community; and to a rural area and par-ticularly to the Delta region, community is a highly valued and indispensable resource. The community acts as a safety net for Delta people. When I asked my students if they wanted to come to the University of Arkansas, all five told me they couldn't because they wanted to go to college close to home; they

wanted to have their family and friends nearby. None of them could fathom the idea of moving far from home. As one of my students put it, "What would I do if my car broke down?" Community is a resource these students have come to depend on.

New-literacy theorists like Barton and Hamilton would argue that novel educational locations nearly always carry with them new literacy practices. But for many very promising students in the Delta, the "new" and the "distant" can seem so exotic and unreachable that they hesitate even to approach the literacy practices inherent in the new settings.

RETHINKING ARTICULATION: LEARNING ON BOTH SIDES OF THE DIVIDE

In his wonderful book, *Because We Live Here: Sponsoring Literacy Beyond the College Curriculum*, Eli Goldblatt poses two instructive rhetorical questions as he prepares to tell his readers about his own experiences with visiting English courses at several high schools in the Philadelphia area that send substantial numbers of students to Temple University, where he is the WPA:

> What if our program were designed to take into account the types and varieties of instruction students received in the high schools from which they graduated and the neighborhoods out of which they grew? Would a more textured understanding of literacy education in the region help us improve our program or refine it in productive ways? (46)

I, of course, have taken the opportunity to talk regularly with the WPA at my own institution about what I hope is a more "textured understanding of literacy education" that incoming students bring to the University of Arkansas. As the ADOHP grows in each succeeding year (we are now entering year three and bringing three new Delta high schools into the fold), we hope to learn more and more about the nature of literacy practices, events, and texts the students encounter in their home communities; the different realms and domains in which they experience literacy practices; the power relationships inherent in their literacy practices; the historical forces impinging on the practices; and the attitudes and actions they bring to developing new literacy practices.

Even with just two years of the ADOHP under our belts, we can see that, if we want these students to succeed at our university, we need to rethink our curriculum and pedagogy so that it does more to bridge the Delta students into the ideally open-minded, disinterested (in the best sense of that term) literacy practices that prevail in college life. We need to teach incoming students to understand more fully the interactivity of argumentative writing in college, helping them to see that thesis statements are the beginnings of conversations with readers, not the ends of them. We need to show students more clearly how to use narratives, such as the ones they develop for their ADOHP projects, in support of complex, nuanced arguments. We need to give incoming students the opportunity to see how writers' views on various topics are connected to, but not necessarily determined by, the writers' material circumstances, and we need to set students to work on projects that will call on them to synthesize an array of different points of view on their topics. We need to assess what incoming students need in terms of an introduction to mediated, electronic communication and do something to meet those needs. We need to help the students see themselves as *bona fide* contributors to the production of knowledge, not simply passive consumers just doing what they're told to do. We need to help our students see themselves as both the products of historical forces and the potential shapers of cultures to come.

And we realize, of course, that the college and university writing curriculum is not the only site where change is necessary. At both the college and the high school level, but particularly at the latter, curricula and pedagogies need to change so that students will have more opportunities to engage in literacy practices in service of projects that they design, carry out, and present to public audiences. The ADOHP has demonstrated to all of its participants—high school and university students and instructors at both levels—that literacy work can become more meaningful and engaging when it transcends the requirement of solely reading and writing in response to a given prompt, no matter when that prompt has been "canned" by an instructor or a textbook.

Certainly, a WPA interested in forging productive articulations between high schools and his or her college or university could learn many of the things he or she needs to know by visiting schools, consulting with teachers and administrators, and examining curricula and methods used in high school courses. Working with the ADOHP has convinced me, however, of the great efficacy, the great learning power, of having university students *write with* high school students whom we're attempting to welcome to the university and ultimately to the world of university alumni.

REFERENCES

American Fact Finder. n.d. *factfinder.census.gov* (accessed 17 Sept. 2008).

Barton, David, and Mary Hamilton. 1998. *Local literacies: Reading and writing in one community.* London: Routledge.

Dean, Pamela, Toby Daspit, and Petra Munro. 1998. *Talking gumbo: A teacher's guide to using oral history in the classroom.* Baton Rouge, LA: Williams Center for Oral History.

Fortune, Ron. 1996. *School-College collaborative programs in English.* New York: Modern Language Association.

Foster, David, and David R. Russell. 2002. *Writing and learning in a cross-national perspective: transitions from secondary to higher education.* Mahwah, NJ: Erlbaum; Urbana, IL: National Council of Teachers of English.

Gatewood, Willard B. 1993. The Arkansas delta: The deepest of the deep south. In *The Arkansas Delta: Land of paradox,* eds. Jeannie Whayne and Willard B. Gatewood, 3-29. Fayetteville, AR: U of Arkansas P.

Gere, Anne Ruggles. 2001. Kitchen tables and rented rooms: The extracurriculum of composition. In *Literacy: A critical sourcebook,* ed. Ellen Cushman, Eugene R. Kintgen, Barry M. Kroll, and Mike Rose, 275-289. Boston: Bedford St. Martin's.

Goldblatt, Eli. 2007. *Because we live here: sponsoring literacy beyond the college curriculum.* Cresskill, NJ: Hampton P.

Kwalick, Barry, Marcia Silver, and Virginia Slaughter. 1982. *Selected papers from the 1982 conference "'New York writes: Kindergarten through college."* New York: City University of New York Instructional Resource Center.

National Council of Teachers of English. 1963. A Blueprint for Articulation. *College English* 24(5): 400-403.

Reder, Stephen. 1997. Synthetic estimates of literacy. *www.casas.org/lit/litdata/reder.pdf.* (accessed 17 September 2008).

Scribner, Sylvia, and Michael Cole. 2001. Unpackaging literacy. In *Literacy: A Critical Sourcebook,* ed. Ellen Cushman, Eugene R. Kintgen, Barry M. Kroll, and Mike Rose, 123-137. Boston: Bedford St. Martin's.

Thorpe, Clarence D. 1939. Articulation. *English Journal* 30(1): 23-24.

Tremmel, Robert, and William Broz. 2002. *Teaching writing teachers of high school English and first-year composition.* Portsmouth, NH: Boynton/Cook.

University of Arkansas. 2008. Enrollment at University of Arkansas sets records for freshmen, minorities, and total Students. September 12, 2008. *dailyheadlines.uark.edu/13476.htm* (accessed 17 September 2008).

Whitman, Glenn. 2004. *Dialogue with the past: Engaging students and meeting standards through oral history.* Lanham, MD: AltaMira.

4

THE ILLUSION OF TRANSPARENCY AT AN HSI
Rethinking Service and Public Identity in a South Texas Writing Program

Jonikka Charlton
Colin Charlton

> [The engaged institution] must be organized to respond to the needs of today's students and tomorrow's, not yesterday's.
> Kellogg Commission on the Future of State and Land-Grant Universities, *Returning to Our Roots*

> At the new border, the obstacles are in what you can't see.
> Héctor Tobar, *Translation Nation*

To teach at an Hispanic Serving Institution (HSI) is to work and live in a place that is both defined and ambiguous. By definition, an HSI "serves" a student population that is at least 25% Hispanic, and to be eligible for federal Title V funding, at least 50% or more of that group has to be low income (Hispanic Association 1999-2005). That's where the clarity ends. Unlike Historically Black Colleges & Universities (HBCUs), HSIs do not share a common mission (Kirklighter, Murphy, and Cárdenas 2007; Santiago 2006), but that doesn't mean there aren't some common (mis)conceptions about work at an HSI. We've spent our first four years as faculty at an HSI in Texas' Rio Grande Valley with an 86% Hispanic enrollment (Office of Institutional Research and Effectiveness 2007), and we're still trying to make sense of the language used to describe our university, our students, and our work. While university administrators, local politicians, and happy transplants speak of the community's untiring work-ethic and artisanship, we also hear students, teachers, administrators, and public documents giving voice to a rhetoric of student deficiency. While we struggle to engage students in meaningful writing projects driven by their personal intellectual interests, some faculty prioritize students' adoption of more "academic" ways of understanding. Still others pursue, and support students in their engagement with, border-related projects of cultural reinforcement and reclamation. And in the relevant scholarship we read, we see a promotion of HSI diversity—an understanding that "lived realities are shaded and distinct" (Mendoza & Herrera 2007, 15)—in an uneasy tension with a desire for knowledge of a student body that is ethnically constructed in its identity, preparation, and perspective.

The care, energy, and people that underlie these realities are not our targets; they are reacting in the most productive ways they can to the university they see, to the students they imagine populating it. As writing program administrators, we do the same. At best, we all know that our students, by their very presence on campus, represent a hope of transforming their community through their success at the university, but you don't have to attend too many faculty meetings or read too many reports on Hispanic education before it's clear that a dominant vision of Hispanic students sees them as at risk and under prepared. But the students *we* see every day don't seem particularly "at risk" or "under prepared." That vision of our student body is not one we recognize. We can't say we know *that* student body.

Of course, we do come to know our students to various degrees each semester through their development as writers, through conversations both in and out of class—even through their absences and silences. As we live and work with these individuals who may assume multiple roles and authorities during their time in higher education, the appeal of the "type" is understandable, especially when we're mentoring new teachers who need to see a pattern in, and effective responses to, what they're experiencing. For better or worse, types don't work for us. With almost thirty years' collective teaching experience, we think that the rhetorical choices and the inventiveness of writing that we foreground in our philosophies of writing and teaching have probably kept us from becoming too comfortable—with people, forms, situations, or potentials. And the tensions we feel all too often occur between local specifics and global generalities, though we theorize and practice through both. Narratives of lack, cultural singularity, or even the intractable tales of overcoming adversity demarcate an *assumed transparency of institutional purpose* that we want to challenge here the way we challenge it in committee meetings, classrooms, and hallways. First, we need to unpack that unwieldy phrase.

ENGAGING TRANSPARENCY

A university and its faculty depend a great deal on how they meet their students. If students come to the university believing it will make them whole, or they think that the university offers the only worthwhile type of "success," or if they assume that just being in college will do the trick, they are assuming that higher education is good, fulfilling, better than.... It has a *transparent* good. But the purpose of higher education, in terms of mission statements, strategic plans, and public relations, is anything but transparent. The various mission statements we craft at every institutional level, regardless of how well they dovetail, are only representations, not enactments, of desire. What teachers do as they try to work in these environments of missions, goals, and outcomes, and what students do with the institutional language that defines their lacks, even when that language is rarely written *on their terms*, are acts that require systematic reflection so that students and teachers can learn from each other in writing classrooms. In other words, the tensions among various student, teacher, and university narratives of success should be foregrounded in our teaching and programmatic decisions so that we have opportunities to challenge and revise a language of service that collapses difference.

The disconnection between what we say we will do and what happens in our doing is an unavoidable educational and organizational phenomenon not unique to HSIs, but the context of an HSI puts it in sharp relief because of the increased number and power of the narratives by which *we try to know our students*. When people who define themselves as outsiders—say a new faculty member who believes in and practices a Marxist critique of the university he's traveled from New York City to work in or a Chicago-born Latina sociology professor who is discovering how "terrible" her Valley undergraduate students are—they will eventually come into contact with a group of naturalized narratives about these students: "We all know why people go to this school—to save themselves from poverty, to escape the migrant past of their parents," etc. The just-arrived individual confronts an imagined collective of already-heres. Meanwhile, we're faced with students in our classes every day who don't necessarily fit into the narratives that the university, and the university with the community, have created for them—through brochures and advertising campaigns, through Presidential convocation speeches, at faculty parties, and throughout the network of secondary schools that tell students who they are (and are not) before we at colleges and universities even get a chance.

When we think we know why people enroll in a university, then we start to act as if the college, its goals, and the faculty's goals are *transparent*—they aim to save students or provide them with what they lack. In the midst of this, there are many stories we cannot imagine, comprehend, or readily categorize. There are rich students from Monterrey who have apartments in town and estates to return to in Mexico; there are women with large families and inattentive husbands who are hoping that a degree will help them find a way to self-sufficiency; there are future teachers who only speak English and have a strong desire to help Spanish-only speaking students; there are very articulate and ambitious students who follow their significant others to the local college; and, as always, there are people who don't know why they're at a university, what such a place even exists for. If we can't know or predict all these reasons for being at the university, it suggests that we can't know or predict all the ways that students are already engaged with different parts of the community.

Think, for example, of the differences between how students and teachers think and talk about the "real" world. Considering the massive amount of physical, textual, financial, and commercial structures that separate a university from the people that move around and through it and the places that surround it, it's tempting to re-inscribe a separation between what we do on campus as teachers and what students will do in the "real" world. Faculty can use the "real" world as a fear tactic to scare students into performing now in hopes that the work will pay off in a deferred place more "real" with success and personal autonomy. Students often talk about the "real" world in order to draw attention to how useless some of the required activities in college are when juxtaposed with a future of specialization and perceived arrival. Both perspectives are suspect because they depend on a future we don't know, a future we can't know, because we will never approach it together as teachers and students. This is the "real" world as the eternally retreating horizon that we call on when we're unhappy with our lack of control (over what we study as students or what we want students to accomplish as their teachers).

These powerful "real" worlds are especially important for us, as WPAs, to de-familiarize so we can better work with a diversity of student and teacher experiences. The more we let them go unchallenged, the more distance our teachers and students assume between public and university lives. Our desire, then, is to build a writing program that reminds us, project by project, how meaningful writing integrates the public and the university without depending on HSI service narratives.

Our job, however, is not necessarily about creating a network by going out into the community and finding people who want to engage with our students. Because we work at an HSI in which most of our students live, work, and study in close proximity to their home communities, our job as public-minded WPAs, in this respect, is simpler than it might be at other schools where students are far from home. All we have to do is learn to tap the networks that are already in place, networks that are already so familiar to the students, many of them don't even imagine that they're intellectually relevant or appropriate for a college classroom.

ENGAGING WRITING STUDENTS

We cannot promote a complex understanding of writing and create innovative pedagogies if we couch our WPA work in the simplicity of a common Hispanic identity or set of experiences, needs, and desires. Instead, we must foreground the contradictions of "service" in our public acts as teachers, WPAs, and sponsors of our students' public discourses. In complicating the illusion of transparency at an HSI, we hope to push ourselves, our students, and writing programs developing in similar contexts to re-consider the ways we deploy heritage-based stories and identities in the rhetorical contexts of first-year writing.

Despite the commonplaces about HSI students, Michelle Hall Kells rightly argues that "What [the HSI] label disguises is the tremendous heterogeneity within these educational contexts [...]. What this label risks is essentializing students who share a few historical traits: a linguistic connection to Spanish (past or present), a sociocultural link to Spain (recent or from generations long ago), and the legacy of colonization (as colonizer or colonized)" (Kells 2007, *xii*). The students we teach are poor, rich, middle class; activist, apathetic; philosophers and wrestlers; Catholic, Lutheran, Mormon, atheist; fluent or marginally bilingual in Spanish/Tex-Mex/Spanglish, English only. But there are some statistics we know about our students at University of Texas-Pan American (UTPA). 86.3% of them are Hispanic, 5.4% White, 5.7% International, .6% African-American, .1% Native American, 1.1% Asian, and .8% Other. In 2007, we had a 13.7% 4-year graduation rate, a

28.3% 5-year graduation rate, and a 32.8% 6-year graduation rate. Most go to school full-time (67.9%), though a large number go part-time (32.1%) because of extra-institutional responsibilities, and 92.7% of our students come from the Rio Grande Valley (Office of Institutional Research and Effectiveness 2007). These facts bear on our work as teachers and administrators.

We want more of our students to graduate faster. In spring 2008, 14.6% of our students dropped (or, due to absences, were dropped from) English 1302, the second of the required first year writing courses. Another 12.1% earned "D" or "F," and, because of a general education requirement, students must pass the course with a "C" or better. Researchers at the University of Texas San Antonio Educational Leadership and Policy Studies reviewed hundreds of studies about Latina/o students and wrote a "PoliMemo" called "What We Know About Latina/o Student Access and Success in Postsecondary Education" (Padilla 2008). They found two important things about Latina/o success that are directly relevant to engaged writing program work: 1) "Framing educational pursuits as methods by which students can fight discrimination, enhance ethnic pride, and assist their communities when they return with college degrees can make college going more attractive to Latino students," and 2) "Latina/o student college success can be driven by the student's ability to create new networks and maintain old ones, and by relying heavily on old networks. Students who go at it alone and are unable to create new networks or keep old ones, do less well" (Padilla 2008). If we're interested in keeping our students, mostly Hispanic students, in school, then the writing classroom that encourages, even requires engagement with their communities and networks, can go a long way towards keeping students in school and showing them how they can use those networks to their advantage. The key, as Jody Millward, Sandra Starkey, and David Starkey note in "Teaching English in a California Two-Year Hispanic-Serving Institution" (2007), is "to show students how to negotiate between their different communities—their different linguistic, familial, class, and cultural identities. [They] use assignments that allow them to see that the skills or talents they develop in one arena can support their success in another" (50).

We feel relatively comfortable with the generalization that students at our HSI are very committed to the Valley and to their families. One of the first things a colleague of ours told us when we moved to the Valley was that one of the local valedictorians of a magnet high school had been admitted with a full scholarship to several Ivy League schools, but would be attending UTPA in the fall because her father wouldn't let her, as a young Hispanic woman, leave the family and go to school. Several of our best undergraduate students have been very hesitant about leaving the Valley for graduate school despite our assurances that they would fit in and fair well in graduate programs anywhere in the country. For many, the thought of leaving can only be made better by the thought of coming back. Some see the Valley as very isolated; though there are millions living here, geographically, we are cut off from the rest of the state. The closest mega-city is San Antonio, and it is four hours away. Though far too many Hispanic students face overt racism here, there isn't a sense that being Hispanic makes you significantly different than those around you. Leaving the Valley means feeling like a minority for the first time for some of our students.

Family, especially, is a significant part of our students' lives. As Beatrice Mendez Newman (2007) notes, "the pull of family cannot be outdone by the pull of educational responsibilities" (22). It is common to have students miss 20% or more of a semester because they're taking and picking up their younger siblings from school; the student's brother, who works full-time, needs the family car and there's no other transportation; mom got sick and can't watch the student's young children; grandmothers and aunts are sick, and the student is the only family member to take care of them. "Family expectations," as Newman (2007) writes, "constantly conflict and compete with academic expectations, a conflict ... [some teachers see] ... as an apparent inability or unwillingness to attend class regularly, to complete assignments on time," etc. (19-20).

Though connection to home and family can create conflicts between the academic and the personal and can sometimes hinder our HSI students' abilities to move through their education in a timely manner, those connections are also a blessing both for the students and for us as administrators. When we taught at a large research university in the Midwest, Jonikka was involved in a syllabus approach that was predicated on writing as social action. The curriculum asked students to investigate their new university communities, find groups or issues that were important to them, and engage in the creation of public documents. As the Assistant Director of that writing program, Jonikka worked with the WPA to create a network of contacts on campus so students would know who to contact to learn about relevant campus issues and programs for their projects. Most of these students had left their home communities behind to go to school there, and the sheer size of the university and its networks of people meant it could take years to develop those networks on their own. Asking students to do engaged writing at that university meant the WPA had to be more actively involved in the creation of those networks.

At UTPA, we can rely on our students' already established networks and the openness and ease with which they share their networks with others. A student in one of our classes was interested in shadowing an engineer, but didn't know any engineers and was nervous about making a connection out of the blue. Another student sitting nearby immediately offered her brother, an engineer, as an interview subject for her classmate, and a project was realized. While it is sometimes difficult to get students to avoid falling back on using their family members and friends as a comfortable default, we have found that our students are able to use their networks to their advantage.

Another dimension of engagement we need to address, especially when projects are public and the variables get increasingly complicated, is time. At our HSI, one could choose to see conceptions of time as defined by such familiar cultural norms as *mariachi* time, or to pay attention to faculty disdain for absenteeism, or you could emphasize the language of "progress" and draw from the statistics on the average time-to-degree for Hispanic students (a 4-year 13.7% graduation rate compared to 6-year rate of 32.8% in 2007). We suggest, however, that the issue really deserving our attention is how to better conceptualize time and contributions to knowledge for undergraduates who are progressing at different, non-traditional rates. The idea of a university as a "threshold" loses capital when a four-year degree plan takes place over six to ten years but is still accomplished, as is the case with many urban universities which serve their local communities as well. Students at these types of universities often remain engaged in learning, even when it's punctuated with non-university involvement because of finances, family obligations, etc., because the curriculum and the writing program we're trying to build doesn't differentiate between time spent in school and time spent out of school.

Having relationships with students that are not bound by conventional university time standards requires that faculty re-think notions of vacuum-sealed apprenticeship, and that we build our pedagogies and writing projects out of the complexity of students' lives as learners who are trying to "do" higher education, as future employees who might benefit from knowing the history of jobs and labor-value across the globe, as people who may know they are Hispanic but have not always used that identifying characteristic to define their interests, their questions, and their direction. One thing we have learned as WPAs working with students who have extended undergraduate educations is that it is extremely important to help them do writing projects that have real effects on a public audience, that create ripples, so that they can see their time and energy has effect in the moment.

That means our jobs as writing teachers and WPAs become much more complicated and much more simple. When a student in our program was investigating teen pregnancy in Texas, she became lost in the maze of state government statistics and websites designed for a user we have yet to meet. Yet she was partly interested in the topic because her cousin was a social-worker in Austin who was stressed about his lack of effect on the "system." Her teacher asked the simple question: "Why is your cousin stressed?" With a little wariness about her cousin's appropriateness as a source, the student spent thirteen weeks interviewing him and learning about an insider's view of parental irresponsibility and government red-tape. Her design of a workshop project for Valley parents with pre-teen daughters was a learning experience for her teacher who knew nothing about social work, for her as a concerned student unaware of the relevance of her network, and for the social-worker cousin who thought no one cared about his concerns.

Students like this respond well to writing projects which ask them to engage in meaningful ways with "public" issues because they see their value both in and out of our classrooms, because they see those projects as an opportunity to integrate their lives outside of school with the intellectual work the university asks of them. They have a genuine desire to make the lives of people around them better and a genuine desire to find a foothold in the university, and they do those things by rhetorically theorizing issues that matter to them, often in an effort to advocate for their families and their communities.

As WPAs, we are excited by our students' engagement both inside and outside the university's walls. We knew, as Michelle Hall Kells writes in the Foreword to *Teaching Writing with Latino/a Students: Lessons Learned at Hispanic-Serving Institutions* (2007), that "[a]gency in language does not begin and should not end in the college classroom" (*ix*). Reading and writing texts in traditionally *academic* ways is important to our students' futures, but "[l]iteracy education is [about] more than reading and writing a set of texts. It is [also] a process of cultivating authority within and across social worlds" (*xi*). Asking students to work on projects that engage them "within and across social worlds" enables them to use what they know *and* shows them that the intellectual work of the university can be meaningful, that their school lives do not have to be separate from their other lives, and that what they do academically can have direct impact on the lives of those they care about.

ENGAGING THE WRITING PROGRAM

We are still relatively new to our WPA positions here, and over the past four years as faculty, we have listened and learned from those around us. As WPAs, we are still trying to figure out how to work with the different, and sometimes competing, needs we all have to serve our students, and we are trying to figure out how we can all engage in the kind of rhetorical, pedagogical work we'd like to build the program on.

Competing (?) Visions

Our university's "vision" is to be "the premier learner-centered research institution in the State of Texas ... actively engag[ing] businesses, communities, cultural organizations, educational organizations, health providers and industry to find solutions to civic, economic, environmental and social challenges through inquiry and innovation" (Office of the President, 2008). The first-year writing program that we envision calls for just this kind of inquiry-based engagement. The difficulty we face as WPAs is in selling such a vision to our faculty.

Like most universities, we have a range of faculty, most with MAs, a growing number of Ph.D.s, and a handful of TAs. Most were educated to be literature specialists with some creative writing experts. Some have taught at UTPA for more than twenty-five years; a considerable number are new each year. Some grew up in or have become part of the Valley community; others will quickly decide their home is elsewhere. With rare exception, our writing instructors are well-meaning and dedicated, working long hours and sacrificing much of their own quality of life to help our students become better writers, more successful students. But our program represents the gamut of ideas about who our students are, how to achieve our purposes, and even what our purposes should be. The range of faculty perceptions we talked about in the beginning of this chapter emerge sometimes subtly, sometimes overtly, in faculty meetings, professional development workshops, and hallway conversations. The trick for us is to figure out how to negotiate our colleagues' diverse narratives of student success, draw out the best of everyone's intentions, and suggest ways we can capitalize on our students' strengths in order to build a program that fosters student engagement, supports our university's vision, *and* helps our students use writing to good effect in their communities.

There are a significant number of faculty at our HSI who believe that, in order to reach our (mostly) Hispanic students, we should have them read culturally relevant (i.e., Hispanic) texts. They argue that doing so helps students connect to academic life in more meaningful ways. Students can see themselves mirrored in those Hispanic texts, and they can see what's possible for them if they, too, become educated and respected as a professional. And, no doubt, for some students, this is powerful. If you've been told all your life, overtly or implicitly, that you cannot amount to anything because you're Hispanic, then evidence to the contrary can have life-changing effects. Araiza, Cárdenas, and Garza (2007) engaged in a survey of faculty at their institution, Texas A&M-Corpus Christi, designed to elicit their ideas about what it means to work at an HSI. They argue that

> Faculty at HSIs, as well as faculty at any university serving a large percentage of minority students, need to develop a "culturally responsive pedagogy" that is "structured to connect what is being learned with students' funds of knowledge of cultural backgrounds" [Scribner and Reyes 1999, 203], but these pedagogical decisions must be based on the reality of students' lived experiences. (Araiza, Cárdenas, and Garza 2007, 93)

The reality of our students' experiences is that they may and *may not* see themselves reflected in "culturally relevant" texts. But, at the heart of these faculty members' intentions, we think, is the desire to give their students confidence, a way to see themselves acting with agency in their communities. We also think there's a desire, however conscious it is, to have students be able to use their own experiences, traditions, and cultural values as a way to connect life outside of school to the academic world, which, for better or worse, will change them. This means "[w]e must think of [our students] not as objects of instruction," Araiza, Cárdenas and Garza (2007) argue, "but as subjects of their own local situations, and we must construct classroom environments where they can create agency for their own purposes" (93). We think that projects that ask students to choose their own purposes, their own audiences and genres, and to engage with their communities accomplish both our goals as writing program administrators who wish to promote meaning-ful writing instruction and the culturally sensitive goals of some of our best faculty.

We also have faculty who want very much to teach our students "aca-demic writing." Some are more (current) traditional than others, and some are more sensitive to what it means to teach academic writing than others. But all want to give our students the tools to succeed in their other college classes and the academic literacy that would mark them as educated in the eyes of the larger public, including future employers. As anyone who's tried to make the argument for rhetorically diverse, mul-timodal pedagogies knows, it's often hard to sell the value of "writing" a T-shirt or a YouTube video or even a brochure or letter to the editor. As WPAs, we are sensitive to these faculty's concerns and are trying to find ways to match their specific goals with ours. Since we don't believe in a single, monolithic thing called "academic writing," it is hard for us to imagine devoting ourselves to a pedagogy or a curriculum with teaching "academic writing" as its main focus. We think it's important that students become rhetorically adept, aware of the kinds of questions writers have to ask in any given writing situation, and aware of the value of feedback, revision and continued inquiry about writing for each new situation. And we think having students work on meaningful writing projects, with a mix of (academic and other) genres, can help students learn when and of whom to ask these kinds of questions.

Collective Vision

For several years (before and since we came on as faculty here), the WPAs and Writing Program Committee have been trying to revise course goals and create student learning outcomes for our program that are more in line with composition theory and pedagogy. We struggled with the wording and perennially got bogged down in the process, so, our first year as WPAs (our third as faculty), we listened and watched as we began teaching observations and monthly professional development on assignment design and response strategies. The next year, we decided it was time to finally make the changes we had been hoping to make, and we were determined to make the process move more quickly and give every instructor a chance to shape the direction and purpose of the pro-gram. We were nervous what might emerge in those program conversa-tions because we thought, with so many disparate ideas about teaching and our students floating around in our department, that we would never find common ground. We were, thankfully, not as right about that as we thought.

During our first "Soup's On!" professional development workshop of the year (the value of cooking for your colleagues cannot be underestimated), we asked our colleagues to generate a list of program goals and course goals for each of the two required writing courses. We told them not to get lost in wording full statements, just to list ideas. They grouped themselves mostly as we had thought they might—the TAs got together, the long-term lecturers grouped up—but, as each group offered their suggestions to the whole room, a few key ideas were repeated. Each group, no matter what language they used to describe the feeling, longed for their students to feel "engaged" with their work. And so, we had a perfect place to begin.

The next workshop, we asked everyone to say what they hoped students would be able to do, know, and value by the end of the first course; then we asked the same for the second course, focusing, as well, on how the second course builds on the first. Jonikka was able to make connections, as she facilitated the conversation, between the group's desires and ways to design more meaningful projects that ask students to engage in the kind of work we hoped to build into the program. She turned those notes into new course descriptions, goals, means, and outcomes statements for each course. The most notable change is a new means statement that asks all instructors to require at least one project in the first course in which students choose their own purpose, audience, and genre to compose in. This represents, we hope, an initial phase in the emergence of our engaged writing program.

We recognize that this change, the requirement of at least one "alternative" writing project, will make some of our instructors understandably nervous. The textbooks they have become comfortable with don't have assignments like these in them; they're not likely to know yet how to design them. But our plan is to offer examples, not only from our own teaching, but from their other colleagues who are beginning to try this kind of thing, and we stress the importance of a reflective cover letter/essay in which students write about their rhetorical choices. We hope this "meta" work will make teachers who want to teach "academic" writing feel at least a little better about the kind of engagement work we want to ask them to include in their curricula. No one, after all, would think it's bad for students to work closely with their community, but the argument for how this work helps them become better writers does have to be made explicit, especially for those who aren't familiar with recent scholarship in rhetoric and composition which theorizes and calls for engaged writing programs.

ENGAGING OPACITY

With experiences at a small regional university, a Research One university, and now an HSI that is growing rapidly, we've witnessed the public vs. private dichotomy played out in a variety of educational contexts, and that dichotomy has been fruitless in all of them when it comes to engaging students and asking them to engage our imaginations as teachers. To foster a culture of inventiveness, we have to actively deconstruct the insularity that a writing teacher might use as a form of defense (against large course loads and packed classes), a means of intellectual survival (to pursue personal research interests), or to make room for one's "personal" life. Interestingly enough, the more we have opened our lives and time to our students, the easier our jobs have become and the more time we have had to reflect on our jobs as teachers, our lives as parents, and our potential as WPAs trying to build a program that means something to students and teachers beyond the language of core requirements or college-preparedness.

Plain and simple, the public is private and the private is public. The dichotomy is false, and we need to neutralize it with a healthy dose of listening to what we want out of our influence and what our students want in terms of their lives as "public" intellectuals. There are unlimited service-learning opportunities that, to some extent, address what we might call a desirable collapse of the public and private. There is a small world of examples and theories that can consume a secondary area of interest or a primary desire. As WPAs, we know we can't force service-learning projects on students and guarantee civic engagement, and we certainly can't force service-learning pedagogies on teachers. But that doesn't mean we can't make the university an object of study for the newest student. And we can craft writing projects that make room for public opportunities that can have real-time (meaning within a semester) effects.

At least for us and the teachers we work with, we are negotiating a new pedagogical scene where we stop thinking of our HSI context and start thinking about what any writer can accomplish in a sixteen-week chunk of life divided by family, work, friends, and other classes. The trick is to highlight the complexity of what we're doing (like studying how a university works) while simplifying or localizing the goals of our rhetorical creations:

- a t-shirt for a younger brother that speaks to parents about what he wants to do with his life;

- a video orientation made for a mother who wants to go back to school to learn computers but is too nervous to take the first step;

- an interactive website for potential employers to learn about the social and financial benefits of hiring ex-cons through a state-sponsored program;

- a comic-strip addressing the personal fear and administrative difficulties with approaching a financial aid office;

- a University Chutes & Ladders game, by students for students, designed to determine if you're college material or not.

Our part as WPAs is making the space for writing projects like these, which will challenge at-risk warnings—space where students' public concerns could de-privatize learning and re-invigorate public networks humming with potential.

Our university is very serious about its mission to serve what it determines to be the unique needs of its "host" community, a place where many young people don't think of themselves as college material, where the label of "first-generation" is a descriptor for many more experiences, exposures, and positions than just that of being a college student. Many of our colleagues engage in service-learning pedagogies in attempts to connect student life, university study, and community engagement. The university supports these activities, in part, because retention rates are so low and our average time-to-degree so long. We've participated in a reading group interested in the rhetorical formations of Hispanic identities, though we were there to challenge what we saw as assumptions more than as truths. We've seen new teachers, good teachers, time and again whip out an Hispanic anthology for their first first-year writing class because students will relate to the "stories." We, like Araiza, Cárdenas, and Garza (2007), just haven't seen evidence that the problem of engagement has to be framed in the language of lack that pervades the discussions of ethnic identity we have heard and read:

Faculty teaching at HSIs may rely on the prominent discourse surrounding these institutions and Latino/a students for an understanding of the students with whom they work, but that discourse may not accurately represent the reality of the students who choose to enroll at the institution. Most of that discourse employs an "at-risk" tone, so faculty may have nothing to shape their perceptions but this negative discourse.

Araiza, Cárdenas, and Garza (2007) refer to an example of this kind of negative discourse from the 2004 Pew Hispanic Center report, "Federal Policy and Latinos in Higher Education," which says that "most Latinos/as are first-generation college students, are low income, and have less academic preparation than their peers" and are "less likely to complete college through the traditional path compared to whites and Asians" (88). The negative discourse is compounded by some faculty's "limited knowledge of the population at the HSI where they teach," where some "may have even less knowledge of the institution as a whole and how being an HSI shapes the mission of the institution" (Araiza, Cárdenas, and Garza 2007, 88).

People are working hard on solving the "problem" of engagement, but the commonplaces of student identity and cultural value cannot hold. As WPAs, we need to invent ways to make unfamiliarity workable for writing teachers so that designing and implementing meaningful writing projects have more gravity in their first year writing classes. We've begun to do this by having monthly meetings that deal in the particulars of assignment design and hold commonplaces like plagiarism and errors at a distance. We're circulating the projects that our students do that engage public audiences with appealing rhetorical strategies. We're providing syllabi to new teachers that are built on fewer readings with more discussions and fewer projects with more revision so that both teachers and students have more built-in time to reflect on the work they are doing. We're writing arguments that offer alternatives to the language of student lack and teacher expertise. We're trying every day to not "know" our students but to ask them how they want to be "known." There is no bulleted list of "deliverables," no theoretical application of *this* idea to *that* system. Just a simple question we return to again and again.

How do we, as WPAs, best serve our writing students and teaching colleagues at an Hispanic Serving Institution?

This is the question we need to ask as WPAs at an HSI to begin a new discussion of the publics that students already navigate through. We have to talk more and theorize more about how to understand a border-centric language that promotes a *diversity* of Hispanic experiences and simultaneously calls for pedagogies adapted to Hispanic places and students. We don't dismiss this language as inauthentic, but the diversity of our students suggests that, in a nutshell, their lives are not *just* border lives. Their identities are both known and unknowable.

REFERENCES

Araiza, Isabel, Humberto Cárdenas Jr., and Susan Loudermilke Garza. 2007. Literate practices/language practices: What do we really know about our students? In *Teaching writing with Latino/a students: Lessons learned at Hispanic-serving institutions,* ed. Cristina Kirklighter, Diana Cárdenas, and Susan Wolff Murphy, 87-97. Albany, NY: SUNY Press.

Cárdenas, Diana and Susan Loudermilk Garza. 2007. Building on the richness of a south Texas community: Revisioning a technical and professional writing program through service learning, *Teaching writing with Latino/a students: Lessons learned at Hispanic-serving institutions,* ed. Cristina Kirklighter, Diana Cárdenas, and Susan Wolff Murphy, 135-144. Albany, NY: SUNY Press.

Hispanic Association of Colleges and Universities. 1999-2005. *Hispanic-Serving Institution Definitions. www.hacu.net/hacu/HSI_Definition_EN.asp?SnID=2* (accessed 13 August 2008).

Kellogg Commission on the Future of State and Land-Grant Universities. 1999. *Returning to our roots: The engaged institution.* Washington DC: National Association of State Universities and Land Grant Colleges, Office of Public Affairs.

Kells, M. Hall. 2007. Foreword: Lessons learned at hispanic-serving institutions. In *Teaching writing with Latino/a students: Lessons learned at hispanic-serving institutions,* ed. Cristina Kirklighter, Diana Cárdenas, and Susan Wolff Murphy, *vii-xiii.* Albany, NY: SUNY Press.

Kirklighter, C., Murphy, S. W., and Cárdenas, D. 2007. "Introduction." In *Teaching writing with Latino/a students: Lessons learned at hispanic-serving institutions,* ed. Cristina Kirklighter, Diana Cárdenas, and Susan Wolff Murphy, 1-13. Albany, NY: SUNY Press.

Mendoza, Louis G., and Toni Nelson Herrera. 2007. *Telling tongues: A latin anthology on language experience.* National City, CA: Calaca Press.

Millward, Jody, Sandra Starkey, and David Starkey. 2007. Teaching English in a California two-year Hispanic-serving institution: Complexities, challenges, programs, and practices. In *Teaching writing with Latino/a students: Lessons learned at hispanic-serving institutions,* ed. Cristina Kirklighter, Diana Cárdenas, and Susan Wolff Murphy, 37-59. Albany, NY: SUNY

Mendez, Newman, B. 2007. Teaching writing at Hispanic-serving institutions. In *Teaching writing with Latino/a students: Lessons learned at Hispanic-serving institutions,* ed. Cristina Kirklighter, Diana Cárdenas, and Susan Wolff Murphy,17-35. Albany, NY: SUNY Press.

Office of Institutional Research and Effectiveness. 2007. *Stats at a glance.* Edinburg, TX: University of Texas-Pan American.

Office of the President 2008. *UTPA Mission. portal.utpa.edu/utpa_main/pres_home/pres_mission* (accessed 13 August 2008)

Padilla, Raymond. 2008. *What we know about Latino/Latina student access and success in Postsecondary education: A report to the Lumina Foundation. /utsa.edu/polimemos/whatweknow.htm* (accessed 13 August 2008).

Santiago, Deborah 2006. *Inventing Hispanic-serving institutions (HSIs): The basics.* Washington DC: Excelencia in Education.

5

A HYBRID GENRE SUPPORTS HYBRID ROLES IN COMMUNITY-UNIVERSITY COLLABORATION

Timothy Henningsen
Diane Chin
Ann Feldman
Caroline Gottschalk-Druschke
Tom Moss
Nadya Pittendrigh
Stephanie Turner Reich

This chapter describes how community-university collaboration is created by the Chicago Civic Leadership Certificate Program (CCLCP), an undergraduate program offered at the University of Illinois at Chicago (UIC). In CCLCP, partners from community-based, not-for-profit organizations mentor first- and second-year students who complete writing and research projects that their partner organizations need. In effect, then, CCLCP's community partners function as co-teachers, collaborating with university instructors to direct, monitor, and evaluate student work; this teaching relationship builds on a deeper and more interesting collaboration: the bilateral development of students' community-based projects.

Bilateral project planning engages community partners and classroom instructors in hybrid roles. When community partners come to see that research and writing intended to do public work can also fill the bill as an academic assignment, they begin to envision themselves as civic leaders who also are teachers. As classroom teachers re-imagine their students' academic work as forwarding the civic missions of our partner organizations, they begin to re-imagine themselves as teachers who also are civic actors. This rare "double vision" arises from CCLCP's collaborative planning process, and the center of gravity of our reciprocal planning process is a document we call the "partner project planner." The planner, we think, is an instance of a hybrid genre born from the fortunate conjugation of a traditional, syllabus-borne description of a class writing assignment and a project management tool commonly used to coordinate work in the professional and business worlds. Our planning document, we argue, provides a vehicle for pursuing the collaborative knowledge-making that creates valuable opportunities for student learning. We further argue that genre—defined as the dynamic nexus of individual agency, social structure, historical imagination, and everyday practice—plays a vital role in our enactment of community-university collaboration.

SOME NECESSARY BACKGROUND

CCLCP is a four-course civic engagement program that selected students enter as incoming freshmen. High-school seniors who have been admitted to UIC hear about CCLCP in postal and electronic mailings soliciting applications for the program. Successful applicants are selected, not on the basis of their ACT scores or writing skill, but for their interest—a "spark," we call it—in exploring and addressing major social and civic issues and their willingness to work collaboratively. Over their first two years at UIC, our students take one CCLCP course each semester, earning four credit-hours for each course: the three credits normally attached to the course and an additional field research credit that recognizes the 30 hours each semester each student spends working on-site with his or her community partner organization.

During their first year, our students take CCLCP versions of UIC's two required writing courses. (Students who "test out" of the first writing course take the CCLCP version of a General Education rhetoric course in its place.) During their second year, CCLCP students take a specially designed version of a non-English department General Education course such as "Community Psychology" or "The Sociology of Youth." In the fourth and final CCLCP course, "English 375: Rhetoric and Public Life," students independently initiate community-based partnerships and complete projects with and for their partners; they also compile portfolios of their CCLCP work and produce résumés and cover letters aimed at securing internships. After receiving their civic leadership certificates, students may return to CCLCP as juniors and seniors to take part in our community-based, for-credit internship program.

We must pause in our discussion a little longer to explain a few basics about our university, our program, our writing philosophy and ourselves. The first task is to clarify the "we" who are writing this. No writing program administrator can "go public" on his or her own: it takes a team to extend the core principles of UIC's First-Year Writing Program into a community, or civic, context. The 2007-08 CCLCP team included the WPA and Director of CCLCP (Ann Feldman), the Assistant Director of CCLCP (Diane Chin), CCLCP Assessment Coordinator (Tom Moss), and the four Ph.D. students who that year designed CCLCP's first-year courses and initiated our collaborations with community partners: Timothy Henningsen, who took the lead on this essay; along with Caroline Gottschalk-Druschke; Nadya Pittendrigh; and Stephanie Turner Reich.

As mentioned at the outset, this essay chronicles the development of a document we call our "partner project planner"; we tweak the planner every year, but this essay will focus on the version used to prepare for the second CCLCP cohort of 39 students that entered UIC in fall 2007. During the previous spring and summer, we sought and initiated partnerships that would involve these incoming CCLCP students in the "communities of practice" (Wenger) of thirteen local, not-for-profit organizations. These partnerships would allow our students to become familiar with the inner workings of local organizations while learning about writing strategies and tactics. Each student's ultimate goal was to complete a written project—informed by both classroom lessons and community-based experience—that was needed by his or her community partner organization. We hoped that by moving from not-for-profit organizations to the classroom and back again, our students would see how rhetorically infused situations give rise to carefully crafted writing— that writing is not a random act driven only by creative genius. These community partnerships were designed to give our students valuable insights into the consequences of various genres of public writing as it occurs in and for Chicago not-for-profits. At the same time, the partnerships would enable non-profit organizations to meet some of their needs for written projects, to make connections with other non-profits and with UIC, and to receive a modest stipend for their efforts to mentor our students and teach them the ways of the not-for-profit world. Our program's emphasis on reciprocal partnership underscores our interest in the well-being and success of both students and partners, and demonstrates how the work of a writing program can, as the title of this book suggests, "go public."

CCLCP's attempt to build partnerships among teachers, community partner organizations, and students is rooted in the belief that all parties can and should collaborate to make knowledge. Indeed, we view collaborative partnership as an effective method of teaching writing (Feldman, et al.) In connecting the classroom with the community, we've learned much and our fundamental assumptions about teaching have been rigorously challenged, even changed. We would argue that teaching writing through community collaboration calls for a redirection of the ingrained impulses of both teacher and student, even as we negotiate, re-negotiate, and hybridize the shifting roles of our community partners and ourselves.

LEAVING THE IVORY TOWER

This book's title—*Going Public*—signals a turn from the vision of the university as an ivory tower, splendidly isolated from the larger community. This turn is especially relevant to UIC. The university was born in the wake of World War II, filling the educational needs of a burgeoning urban population, many of whom were returning GIs. When the U.S. Navy stopped training pilots on Chicago's Navy Pier, a new campus of the University of Illinois moved into the location that, jutting out more than half a mile into Lake Michigan, was connected to, but distinctly separate from, the city. Because, until then, there had been no public university in downtown Chicago, demand was incredibly high; after running out of room on the pier, Mayor Richard J. Daley in the early 1960s pushed for a new campus to be built on Chicago's historic Near West Side.

The reaction of those displaced by construction of the new campus was vigorous and widespread. Neighborhood residents felt the university was out to destroy their community; stories still swirl on campus of angry neighborhood business owners refusing to serve anyone associated with the new campus. The university did little to quell this anger, failing, in those early years, to develop a partnership with the community. Back when highways and railroad tracks served as distinct and well-recognized boundaries among races, ethnicities, and social classes, the brick walls built to surround the U of I's new Chicago campus only exacerbated these divisions, leading to the campus's disparaging nickname, "Fortress Illini."

UIC has worked to change this perception, as best exemplified by the UIC Neighborhoods Initiative, which builds partnerships between the university and its surrounding communities as a means of strengthening both. The Neighborhoods Initiatives program is one actualization of the UIC's Great Cities Commitment to broadening and deepening the university's research agenda. The broader infrastructure offered by UIC's

Great Cities Institute (GCI) includes a seed grant program for research built on community-university partnerships, a year-long faculty fellowship program, several urban policy research centers linked in various ways to UIC's College of Urban Planning and Public Affairs, support for invited researchers who take up residence at the Great Cities Institute, and a professional education initiative that offers on-line courses such as non-profit management. UIC's commitment to its urban context also has influenced the First-Year Writing Program and, subsequently, CCLCP. From its earliest years, UIC Neighborhoods Initiative offered support to the First-Year Writing Program by awarding the WPA, Ann M. Feldman, a seed grant to develop an individual partnership with a community organization (Feldman 2003) and, later, a year-long faculty fellowship to develop the theoretical and pragmatic underpinnings of the situated writing pedagogy of UIC's writing program. The director of the Great Cities Institute, David Perry, was centrally involved in the development of CCLCP and was a co-principal investigator on the grant from the federal Corporation for National and Community Service that allowed us to initiate CCLCP in 2004.

SITUATED WRITING

CCLCP's pedagogy grows from UIC's First-Year Writing Program, although "mainstream" writing classes do not depend on community-based partnerships as CCLCP classes do. Those who teach first-year writing here talk about the "situated writing triad": a framework created by welding together genre theory, rhetoric, and social learning theory. We argue that all writing is situated in the social conditions that prompt it, and we believe that students take this axiom more seriously when an actual audience and a "real-life," complex social context are elements of the writing situation. We see genre awareness as shaping our students' writing, giving us the opportunity to connect our emphasis on social context and local situation to important concepts in genre theory. Not merely a taxonomy of "types" of writing, genre theory asks students to redirect the trajectory of their written inquiry from self to situation and/ or to the rhetorical conditions that constitute that situation (Bawarshi 153). Examples can be found in many of our genre-based writing assignments, especially those designed collaboratively by instructors and community partners, to which we'll return later.

Genre theory obviously relies heavily on rhetoric and rhetorical theory, which constitute the second element of our triad. As Michael

Bernard-Donals and Richard R. Glejzer argue, rhetoric is best described as "the use of language to produce material effects in particular social conjunctures" (3). If social situations materialize through rhetoric—which we feel they do—then we must direct our students to aim for awareness and understanding of the conditions that enable their own participation in, and influence on, social situations. Once they see and understand, students begin to think about their own possible participation in creating social change. When they consider the unique rhetoric employed in the genres of political speeches, manifestos, academic essays, and annual reports—to list a few examples of our in-class work—students gain access to the powerful histories that often go hand-in-hand with certain words or phrases; knowing these histories helps our would-be writers realize the motives and consequences of language when it is wielded as an agent of change.

And finally, given the "public" nature of both genre theory and rhetoric, our pedagogy requires an emphasis on social learning theory. Our notion of social learning is based on the work of Etienne Wenger, who argues that practice, which he defines as the interaction of social entities, is both "a process by which we can experience the world and our engagement with it as meaningful" (51) and a "shared history of learning that requires some catching up for joining" (102). Quite simply, learning takes place through social engagement and of course, through *doing*. And so, in CCLCP, we ask our students to engage in the social situations of our partners, which emerge from life in urban Chicago. Pedagogically speaking, we echo Wenger when he argues that "*learning cannot be designed*; it can only be designed *for*" (229; italics in original), which helps explain our insistence that collaborative knowledge-making requires the ability not only to design well-informed plans, but also to roll with the punches when those plans are disrupted and must change, as they so often do . In other words, student learning is often beyond our control; the more we, as CCLCP instructors, recognize this, the better the collaborative experience for all involved. In sum, because our pedagogy thrives upon social situations, both within and beyond classroom walls, we seek to make those walls as porous as possible.

INITIATING PARTNERSHIPS

Partnerships aren't born: they are made. In spring and summer 2007, we began recruiting partners by inviting the return to CCLCP of some of the organizations with which we had partnered while working with our first cohort of students, from fall 2004 through spring 2007. (In its original incarnation, CCLCP was a three-year program.) A larger and more diverse range of partnerships was needed to satisfy the second cohort's larger number of students and various interests, so we looked for prospective partners whose missions addressed urban challenges or offered programs intended to improve the quality of urban life. Of course, we considered organizations that the CCLCP instructors had connections to or interests in, given our team's variety of civic, activist, and rhetorical engagements. And, as we had in 2004, we drew on our ongoing relationship with UIC Neighborhoods Initiatives.

After we'd created a list of potential partner organizations, the assistant director of CCLCP, Diane Chin, sent a Request for Proposal (RFP) to the community-based, not-for-profit organizations that had not previously partnered with us. (Partners who had worked with the previous cohort and with whom we wished to continue a relationship were simply invited back.) Our RFP explains not only the nature of CCLCP, but also the benefits and responsibilities of a CCLCP partnership. Because we differ very significantly from volunteer and/or internship programs (programs with which most partners already are quite familiar), the RFP is the crucial first step in acquainting new partners with the structural and philosophical features of CCLCP. The RFP encourages potential partners to "identify student projects that serve *both* learning goals and our partners' missions" in order to emphasize the program's dual interest in academics and community engagement. After an appropriate interval, Diane contacted potential partners by phone for a series of very important conversations. These calls gave prospective partners not only an opportunity to ask questions, but also a platform for discussing writing projects that might help fill their organizations' needs. These conversations also gave us the chance to see if the organization's staff was receptive to—and could make time for—engaging with our students as co-teachers and mentors.

Responses to the RFPs were reviewed by CCLCP's teaching staff, director, and assistant director. Organizations accepted into partnerships were invited to a mid-summer orientation and project planning event that launched both the new and continuing partnerships for the school year ahead. This event included a dinner followed by a planning workshop, at which CCLCP administrators and instructors and representatives of our partner organizations got to know each other and began to brainstorm student projects. After this session, instructors, armed with our partner project planner, then visited the partners' community sites to work individually with partners on developing the projects students would complete during the coming semester. (We'll say more about this process in a moment.) The project development process was completed a few weeks into the fall semester. Then, after students and partners were matched, the assistant director prepared and sent to each partner a formal UIC Memorandum of Understanding (MOU) or, in some cases, a formal Board of Trustees-approved contract, that officially acknowledged the collaborative effort and set out the terms of the $450 per-student stipend to be paid to each partner at the end of each semester "for services rendered to CCLCP students."

HOW A HYBRID GENRE CREATES A SITE FOR ACTION

On the most obvious level, the partner project planner, which we include below, is an instance of a hybrid genre derived from mating UIC's First-Year Writing Program assignment prompts with professional project management documents. What is much more interesting, though, is the living source of this hybridity: the diverse, even incongruous, communities that come together through this genre to collaborate on writing projects and, what is more important, to participate in social change. The notion of the hybrid genre emerges from the work of Mikhail Bakhtin and, in particular, his famous essay on speech genres (1986). In this essay, he argues for the situatedness of genre and how every speech act occurs with a sense of the consequences that will emerge. This work on speech genres evolved, carrying with it earlier themes of answerability, in which all subjects must become authors who participate in the forceful energy that genres emit (1993). This rich sense of genre as a "form of life" and as a frame for social action (Bazerman 1997, 19) has informed contemporary composition studies as evidenced in such edited volumes as Schroeder, Fox and Bizzell's *Alt Dis* (2002) and John Trimbur's *Popular Literacy* (2000) that examine the varied and situated roles of discourse.

CCLCP's partner project planner emerged to solve a very real problem and to respond to something of a role reversal. (The partner planner is Figure 1 in the appendix.) Our instructors, who were accustomed to setting up classroom-based writing projects, needed to coordinate with our community partners to envision the nature of students' community-based projects. And, on the other hand, the community partners, who knew exactly what sort of projects their organizations needed, had no easy way of communicating this need to students or their instructors.

Things grew even more complicated with the cohort starting in fall 2007 because two new structural features of our program required that we develop our partnership relationships differently than we had in the past. First, in fall semester, we offered the incoming cohort two CCLCP classes: English 160, the first required writing course, and English 122, a rhetoric course that carries General Education credit for students who had "tested out" of English 160. Second, to give students more and more varied choices, we had recruited twice the number of partners as in previous years. But how could we give all CCLCP students a choice of partners and projects if certain partners were "attached" only to a certain class? Our administrative solution was to uncouple the role of instructor and the role of partner liaison. Until the advent of our second cohort, instructors taught a single group of students and worked with a single group of partners to develop projects for those same students. Now, each of our instructors would play two distinct roles: each would co-teach a section of either English 160 or English 122 and, in that role, be responsible for the students enrolled in that particular class. But, besides being a "classroom teacher," each instructor also would act as a "partner liaison" by developing, collaboratively, a project or set of projects with three or four of the community partners who had come on board with CCLCP. These partner relationships—at the insistence of the instructors—crossed classroom boundaries. That is, students could choose from the full range of civic missions represented by the thirteen partners, and partners would find themselves working with some students enrolled in English 160 and others enrolled in English 122. With this important structural change, instructors' role identities began to depend on shifting situations——they flexed between serving as classroom instructors and partner liaisons. This is where the collaboration begat hybridity; suddenly Timothy, Caroline, Nadya, and Stephanie were not "just" teachers of writing.

In their role as liaisons between partners and students, the "CCLCP Four" needed a tool to facilitate their collaborative work with partners by clearly defining the projects their students would produce. This tool, born of necessity, is the "partner project planner." And, as we look back at our creation of this worksheet-like document, we realize the extent to which current work in genre theory, rhetoric, and social learning theory contributed to its development. The partner project planner illustrates how situated writing stems from and responds to the demands of collaboration. Instructors, on the one hand, had planned a course curriculum that they hoped would bring students into their partners' communities of practice and prepare them to undertake the projects needed by their partner organizations. (We describe this curriculum briefly below.) Each partner, on the other hand, needed a particular project but didn't have time to extensively tutor each student on how that project should be imagined, designed, completed, and delivered.

The partner project planner turned out to be an example of a "hybrid genre," as it had to be if it were to meet the needs of both community partner organizations and students in unique ways. For students, the partner project was the culminating work of their course. All previous course projects, which incrementally prepared students for the final one, had been assigned using a version of the assignment template that is routinely used in the First-Year Writing Program at UIC. This information-packed template reflects our commitment to situated writing as expressed in four key terms: situation, genre, language, and consequences (see Feldman, Downs, and McManus 2005). The standard classroom writing project template consists of eight sections, each elaborated with the appropriate information: the title of the writing project; a list of resources students may choose to use; due dates and length; detailed descriptions of the writing situation, the specific task, the genre, and the potential consequences of the piece of writing; and evaluation criteria. This classroom document can speak through a shorthand of sorts because, from their first days in the English 160 classroom, students learn the meaning of situation, genre, language, and consequences, or more commonly, SGLC. These terms were familiar to our instructors, of course, but entirely unfamiliar to our community partners and so not very useful.

Our partners had an entirely different orientation to the much-needed projects that were to be completed by our students. Their role in CCLCP was not to teach writing, but the context from which writing would emerge; their job was to integrate students into the community of practice of their organizations so that student projects could succeed. To create effective projects, students needed to know how knowledge was made in their partner organizations and how the culture of their partner organizations defined and governed daily work. (Of course, working with CCLCP students was a minute portion of the community partner's monumental daily responsibility.) Our assistant director, Diane

Chin, knew from her previous work with not-for-profits that the partner project planner must function as a two-way bridge, connecting students and teachers with the specific and unique context and culture of the not-for-profit organization and connecting community partners with the concepts to which writing teachers expose their students. In earlier years of her career, Diane had created similar documents as a way of communicating to her staff what the C.E.O. of her organization wanted a specific project to accomplish. In more recent times, Diane had taught first-year writing at UIC. These experiences gave her a grasp of both worlds' vocabularies and concerns that enabled her to create a *lingua franca* for our project planner. Once intensive, individualized planning had taken place on the bridge between instructor and partner, the students needed to enter this collaborative terrain: the partner project planner would become their road map. Here is another example—or perhaps a consequence—of hybridity: the planner is not only the offspring of two genres, but also fills the roles of both bridge and map.

And more hybridity: once completed, the planner served as a communication tool between instructors and partners, the basis for a contract between the community organization and the university, and a guide for students.

The fall 2007 planners explicate an arresting variety of projects. One partner organization, whose partner planner we include at the end of this chapter, focuses on collecting and sharing oral histories of immigrants; this partner wanted to compile the "success stories" of their service consumers in a booklet and needed a CCLCP student to write promotional material for the book's launch. Another partner needed CCLCP students to write articles for a bilingual newsletter to be distributed to parents of elementary-age students at a community school. An activist organization that works with the majority Latino/a population of a neighborhood near UIC wanted ideas for drawing residents into involvement with community causes, ideas which would be presented in a student-written report to its advisory board. Other planners call for sections of annual reports, marketing materials, and museum display text. Despite this variety, every project depended upon ongoing conversations between instructor-as-liaison and the community partner, and each was an attempt to create, as the RFP explained, "projects that serve *both* learning goals and our partners' missions."

Although, in all cases, the most intense bursts of teacher/partner collaboration occurred while completing the project planners, it's safe to say that the process was different with each of our thirteen partners. Some partners made it easy by responding to the prompts included in the planners with such clarity and detail that their project planners were virtually ready to hand over to students with little instructor input. Others needed a good deal of prodding just to return phone calls, which is not surprising, given the hectic environment of most not-for-profits. Some partners, because of changing organizational needs and resources, modified their project planners mid-semester, presenting another challenge—one familiar to those working outside the classroom—to both instructor/liaisons and students. The creation of the project planner often became easier when our instructor/liaisons asked partners to identify an example of the genre in which they wanted students to work; for some organizations, however, this was impossible, as they wanted students to create a document that they badly needed primarily because nothing like it existed.

CLASSROOM PREPARATION FOR PARTNER PROJECTS

Instructor/liaisons began meeting with community partners over the project planners in late summer 2007, just after an orientation dinner at which partners learned about CCLCP and the crucial importance of their roles as mentors and co-teachers. The dinner meeting launched collaborative knowledge-making by enabling partners and CCLCP staff to bounce around ideas for approaching their partnerships. Using the partner project planners as a basis for brainstorming and discussion, partners described projects they needed and considered whether they were feasible. Instructors explained how the academic curriculum helped prepare students for engagement with partner organizations' communities of practice. Figure 2, included in the appendix, offers an outline of the five assignments required for English 160 and English 122, and the CCLCP "calendar" illustrates the integration of classroom and community activities.

Students began fall semester by writing a manifesto. This writing project prompted students to identify the social or civic issues that mattered most to them. Besides fostering student thinking about current issues, the manifesto has several virtues as a writing assignment. To create this document—a very public declaration of the writer's stand on a particular issue or cluster of issues—a student must rely on a keen awareness of audience, social context, and language. Instructors hoped this assignment would prepare students to identify partners with similar interests and agendas at the "Partnership Fair" set for the second week of the semester. Also before the fair, students were assigned to independently research several of the thirteen partner organizations that most attracted them. The fair was an exciting event, full of buzz: partners set up booths in the Residents Dining Hall of Jane Addams Hull-House, which graces the east border of UIC's campus, and students circulated among them, asking questions about the work of their organizations, and learning about projects partners needed. We had hoped to have the partner project planners complete by the Partnership Fair but not all were; even so, the fair was a great success. An unexpected but most welcome synergy had occurred, and both students and partners were charged up for the semester ahead. Two days after the Partnership Fair, the classes met jointly, so students could match themselves to community partners through a process fondly referred to as "the land grab." Poster-size sheets, each listing a partner organization and the number of student positions available there, were displayed around the room; students were instructed to stand ("walk, don't run" was the mantra) in front of the poster naming the partner with which they most wanted to work. The students were responsible for resolving disputes among themselves through the use of their budding powers of persuasion. We realized this student-driven process bore some risk, but thought it was the best way to encourage students to "own" their new partnerships. (We are pleased to report all student competition for partnerships was peacefully and cheerfully resolved, albeit, in a few cases, through the device of "rock-paper-scissors.")

Next, students were assigned to introduce themselves to their new partners in a professional e-mail describing their skills, interests, and experience. This was the first step toward "handing students the keys to the car"—a metaphor for the self-responsibility and leadership so important to CCLCP. The next project—due some time after students became generally familiar with their partners—was a community strengths profile. Creating this assignment had been tricky; only one of our instructors had experience writing a community strengths profile, and so the project was included with some hesitation. The community strengths profile required students to immerse themselves in the communities that their partners served and develop their skills at writing a complete profile from field notes. The focus on community strengths, rather than deficits, was intended to help students see how their partner communities could springboard from existing strengths to positive change. We also wanted students to resist the news media's clichéd focus on poverty, helplessness, and hopelessness. The students were required to read a model of the genre, but had to rely on their own observations and analyses when crafting their strength assessments. The fourth genre-based assignment leading up to the final project—the much-planned-for community partner project—was an interview and written summary; students interviewed their contact person at their community partner organization to garner information that would enhance their understandings of their partner projects. The interview and focused summary assignment gave students an important opportunity to craft questions and discuss with their partners what they needed to do to make their projects successful. When our students turned in their interview assignments, we were pleased to discover that this activity really did help them understand their community partner organizations' missions and the role of their final writing project in advancing those missions.

By mid-term, collaboration took on a new form and came to include a new partner: the student. Although intensive planning between instructor/liaisons and partner/teachers had initiated the collaboration, the CCLCP student soon became the key player. Aside from occasional check-ins, the instructor-partner relationship moved to the back burner unless difficulties arose. Most of the instructor-partner conversations that occurred after students began working with their community partner organizations were sparked by student or partner scheduling problems and occasional misunderstandings. In an end-of-semester focus group, one partner lamented that there was no mechanism for sustaining the collaborative nature of the early brainstorming sessions that began at the July dinner and continued during the individual partner-instructor meetings that followed. In response, CCLCP has begun to consider sponsoring end-of-semester partner-student colloquia for our second-year classes so partners can continue to participate in conversations about the issues that drive their organizations.

WHAT IT MEANS WHEN WRITING INSTRUCTION GOES PUBLIC

The result of our particular instance of a hybrid genre, the partner planning document is, of course, a student project, which we hope the community partner can use. We include in Figure 3 (see appendix) an example of a project planner created collaboratively in fall 2007 by Margot Nikitas of the Jane Addams Hull-House Museum and Caroline

Gottschalk-Druschke of CCLCP. This document provided a road map for Carla Navoa, then a CCLCP first-year student, who would develop a promotional flyer for a forthcoming book called *Chicago: An Immigrant City.*

What did Carla have to learn in the writing classroom and at the Hull-House Museum to complete this project? How did these diverse understandings come together in Carla's mind and work successfully to achieve the project's purpose? Richard Lanham argues in his recent book, *The Economics of Attention: Style and Substance in the Age of Information,* that the answers to these questions largely depend on where we focus our attention. The arts and letters, as well as rhetoric, he claims, are "wholly occupied with creating attention structures" (21), which simply means directing awareness (26). Lanham reminds us, though, that Kenneth Burke was fond of saying that "Every way of seeing is a way of not seeing" (164): paying attention over *here* means you cannot pay attention over *there*. And each new element that we focus on is in some way changed by our attentive gaze.

Framing our classrooms and our partner organizations as "communities of practice" redirects our attention and so changes the way we understand them. Our student, Carla, had to learn that producing a flyer was not simply a translational activity. She was, as we said earlier, "using language to produce material effects" in a very particular situation (Bernard-Donals and Glejzer, 3). She was taking action, not simply producing sequences of words. Carla was surrounded by genre: manifestos, e-mails, partner project planners, promotional flyers. All of these she needed to understand materially because they were connected to actions, to steps taken, to visions imagined and realized, and to missions hoped for and accomplished. The partner project planner, which Carla received soon after choosing to work with Margot Nikitas at the Jane Addams Hull-House Museum, targeted the creation of an effective promotional document. To hit the bull's-eye, Carla needed to reconsider classroom lessons in *ethos, pathos, logos,* and *kairos,* as well as lessons in situation, genre, language, and consequences. In thinking about her partner organization as a community of practice, she had to use her on-the-ground knowledge of the Hull-House Museum and what makes it tick every day. In conversations with Margot, Carla learned why the planned book is important and what problems and issues the Hull-House staff were hoping the book would address. She learned through engagement and connection, rather than through the reified practices that so often pass for education. And most important of all, Carla had to imagine what work this book would do, what conditions it would change, what narrative about Chicago's immigrant population—a population that Hull-House has served throughout its history and will serve in the future—it could rewrite.

The project planner, a small and seemingly insignificant tool of both writing assignment-making and project management, functioned as a dynamic point of contact for the knowledge-making activities that contributed to CCLCP's partnership with the Hull-House Museum and with the many other organizations we worked with during one memorable semester. Working with the planning document taught us that genre, rhetoric, collaboration, and reciprocity constitute the glue that holds CCLCP together. It also taught us that collaboration doesn't always proceed as planned. Collaboration is typically more complicated than one might expect simply because of differences in the co-planners' objectives. Partners' goals for students naturally center on producing work that benefits the partner organizations, while instructors' goals for students naturally center on enhancing the teaching and learning of course matter. While all this is as it should be, the difference in perspective produces tensions that sometimes show up—albeit very politely— in planning sessions and in periodic check-in conversations involving instructors and partners. We've learned that this tension is a good thing because it sparks creativity in planning and executing projects. In this sense, partner-instructor differences can become highly productive once they're accepted as a natural part of the process; so all the lessons about genre, rhetoric, collaboration, and reciprocity learned by students in our program are institutional lessons as well. Going public and engaging with community partners in ways that benefit everyone concerned can present challenges, but we make significant new knowledge when we find ways to understand and overcome those challenges.

While WPAs typically concern themselves with the writing that students do, our work with CCLCP has challenged us to coordinate engagement and reciprocity on many levels, administrative and contractual as well as cultural and linguistic. We carried our genre-based work with the partner project planner in 2007-08 forward into the second year of our two-year program and onto entirely new terrain as we coached two faculty members, both new to CCLCP, who were to teach specially designed CCLCP sections of community psychology and the sociology of youth. Here we saw once again the challenge of hybrid roles as discipline-based faculty attempted to integrate their particular approaches to the social sciences into the unique projects needed by community partners. In their final course, English 375, CCLCP students will identify their own partners and develop proposals for their own projects; they will assume the hybrid role of student-project manager. And finally, as juniors and seniors, these students will have an opportunity to receive credit for writing and research internships with community partners of their choice. Our goal in CCLCP is nothing less than changing our institution's culture. One proper goal of an urban public research university such as UIC, is to make knowledge in partnership with others in its metropolitan area. CCLCP's aim is for our colleagues—both faculty and administrators—to see writing instruction not only as preparation for upper-level classes but also as a way to contribute to our university's knowledge-making activities. By doing precisely that, the writing activities of CCLCP students parallel the writing activities of faculty, and these public efforts focus our attention on writing's situatedness and, most important, its consequences.

REFERENCES

Bakhtin, M. M. 1993. *Toward a philosophy of the act.* Trans. Vadim Liapunov. ed. Vadim Liapunov and Michael Holquist. Austin: U of Texas P.

Bakhtin, M. M. 1986. The problem of speech genres. *Speech genres and other late essays.* Trans. Vern W. McGee. ed. Caryl Emerson and Michael Holquist, 60-102. Austin: U of Texas P.

Bawarshi, Anis. 2003. *Genre & the invention of the writer: Reconsidering the place of invention in composition.* Logan: Utah State UP.

Bazerman, Charles. 1997. The life of genre, the life in the classroom. In *Genre and writing: issues, arguments, alternatives,* ed. Wendy Bishop and Hans Ostrom, 19-26. Portsmouth, NH: Boynton/Cook.

Bernard-Donals, Michael, and Richard R. Glejzer. 1998. Introduction. *Rhetoric in an anti-foundational world: language, culture, and pedagogy.* ed. Michael Bernard-Donals and Richard R. Glejzer,1-30. New Haven: Yale UP.

Bringle, Robert G., Richard Games and Edward A. Malloy. 1999. *Colleges and universities as citizens.* Needham Heights, MA: Allyn and Bacon.

Brukardt, Mary Jane, et al. 2004. *Calling the question: Is higher education ready to commit to community engagement?* Wingspread Conference, Institutionalizing University Engagement, 18-19 Apr. 2004. Milwaukee: Milwaukee Idea Office, University of Wisconsin-Milwaukee.

Burke, Kenneth. 1950, 1962. *A rhetoric of motives.* Berkeley, CA: University of California Press.

Chin, Diane, et al. 2006. Strong at the seams: Joining academic and civic interests. In *Quick hints for educating citizens,* ed. James L. Perry and Steven G. Jones, 5-6. Bloomington: Indiana UP.

Feldman, Ann M. 2008. *Making writing matter: Composition in the engaged university.* Albany: State U of New York P.

Feldman, Ann M. 2003. Teaching writing in a context of partnership. In *City Comp: Identities, Spaces, Practices,* ed. Bruce McComiskey and Cynthia Ryan, 203-215. Albany: State U of New York P.

Feldman, Ann M., Ellen McManus and Nancy Downs. 2005. *In Context: Reading and Writing in Cultural Conversations.* 2nd ed. New York: Pearson/Longman.

Feldman, Ann M., et al. 2006. The impact of partnership-centered, community-based learning on first-year students' academic research papers. *Michigan Journal of Community Service Learning* 13(1): 16-29.

Gibbons, Michael, et al. 1994. The new production of knowledge: The dynamics of science and research in contemporary societies. London: Sage.

Holland, Barbara A. 2000. Institutional impacts and organizational issues related to service learning. *Michigan Journal of Community Service Learning* Fall: 52-60.

Lanham, Richard A. 2006. *The economics of attention: Style and substance in the age of information.* Chicago: U of Chicago P.

Maurrasse, David J. 2001. *Beyond the campus: How colleges and universities form partnerships with their communities.* New York: Routledge.

Schroeder, Christopher, Helen Fox and Patricia Bizzell. 2002. *Alt dis: Alternative discourses and the academy.* Portsmouth, NH: Boynton/Cook Heinemann.

Trimbur, John. 2001. *Popular literacy: Studies in cultural practices and poetics.* Pittsburgh: U of Pittsburgh P.

Walshok, Mary Lindenstein. 1995. *Knowledge without boundaries: What America's research universities can do for the economy, the workplace, and the community.* San Francisco: Jossey-Bass.

Wenger, Etienne. 1998. *Communities of practice: Learning, meaning, and identity.* Cambridge: Cambridge UP.

APPENDIX 1

CCLCP Partner Project Planner, Fall 2007

CONTENT AND SUPPORTING DETAILS

Describe the content (what is this project "about"?) and other pertinent project details not discussed below.

GENRE/FORMAT

Describe the form (NOT the content) of the document you want students to produce. (Do you envision a brochure, a report, a map with accompanying narrative, a Web page, or ...?) Why have you chosen this format for this project? Where might students see useful examples of this kind of document? How do you want the finished project to "look"? That is, what kind of impression do you want to create (slick, accessible, scholarly, etc.)? How many pages or what size should the finished product be?

SITUATION

Explain how this project supports your organization's goals and research efforts. Describe the project's consequences for the broader mission it supports.

Define and describe the audience for which this document is intended. What is the document's purpose? That is, what response is it intended to elicit from its audience? (What do you want the audience to think or do after encountering this writing?)

USEFUL TIPS

Offer advice on gathering data, conducting an analysis, developing, framing, designing, and/or shaping the product.

SUGGESTED TEMPLATE OR SAMPLE DOCUMENTS

Please identify a particularly good example of a similar project you can share with your students. The example should illustrate the standard you expect this project to meet.

READINGS/RESOURCES

What material (articles, book s, Web sites, videos, etc.) can your organization provide or recommend to prepare students to work on this project?

EVALUATION CRITERIA

What elements do you think should contribute to assessing this project? Please list the criteria you think the instructor should apply to evaluation. If this project were done by a staff member, on what basis would you evaluate its worth to your organization?

APPENDIX 2

CCLCP Writing Projects for English 160 and English 122, Fall 2007

	Manifesto	Professional Email	Strengths Assessment	Agency Interview	Final Product
	Students compose statements on the CCLCP program or important issues in Chicago.	Students introduce themselves to their partner agencies.	Students investigate and write about their agencies and communities.	Students conduct interviews to develop understanding of final products.	(differs for each agency)
	AUGUST	**SEPTEMBER**	**OCTOBER**	**NOVEMBER**	**DECEMBER**
	28th: first day of class	11th: Partner Fair @ UIC; Manifesto project due 13th: Students choose partners; begin writing field notes 18th: Professional emails due (sent out to agencies)	11th: Strengths Assessment due *interviews to take place between October 16th and 25th*	1st: Interview due *throughout November, agency works with student on drafting final project*	6th: last day of class; Final Project due

beginning Sept. 25th, students to spend ~3 hours per week at agency

APPENDIX 3

CCLCP Partner Project Planner

*Jane Addams Hull-House Museum (JAHHM) Immigrants'
Guide to Chicago Project*

Margot Nikitas, Hull-House
Caroline Gottschalk-Druschke, CCLCP
Carla Navoa, Student

CONTENT AND SUPPORTING DETAILS

*Describe the content (what is this project "about"?) and other pertinent project
details not discussed below.*

The final project will promote JAHHM's immigrants' guide to
Chicago project, fully described below:

The Jane Addams Hull-House Museum is creating a comprehensive
immigrants' resource guide to Chicago. Written by and for immigrants,
Chicago: An Immigrant City will compile critical information for both doc-
umented and undocumented immigrants on how to obtain basic goods
and services. The book will also emphasize solidarity building, social
entrepreneurship, and how new immigrants can develop and build cultural capital in our diverse city by accessing arts and culture in Chicago's
many public spaces. These include community centers, galleries,
schools, public events, and all of Chicago's major cultural institutions.

Since its founding by Jane Addams and Ellen Gates Starr in 1889,
Hull-House served as a vital community center for its immigrant neighbors. Hull-House offered citizenship and English classes, developed
innovative programs in the visual and performing arts, provided space
for social gatherings and celebrations, and advocated for the rights of
immigrants, workers, and women. Drawing on Hull-House's tradition
of emphasizing arts programming to promote a more participatory
democracy, the book will feature an in-depth guide to arts and culture
in Chicago. Here immigrants will learn about Chicago's wealth of muse-
ums, historic sites, ethnic fairs and festivals, music venues, public gar-
dens and parks, theaters, and more.

One of the most unique aspects of *Chicago: An Immigrant City* will be a chapter on Chicago's immigrant youth culture, written by young people from immigrant communities across the city. These young writers will incorporate different creative media such as spoken word, poetry, and visual artwork to reflect on and grapple with the immigrant experience. The writing process will also provide an opportunity for intergenerational dialogue in immigrant families.

In addition to a convenient directory of service organizations and information about basic needs such as housing, childcare, employment, legal aid, and medical care, *Chicago: An Immigrant City* will also include sections on legal rights and the justice system—featuring a detachable "Know Your Rights" card; Chicago's diverse media; educational institutions; and how immigrants can get locally involved in the struggle for a more just society.

Chicago: An Immigrant City is currently slated to be published in one volume in English, Spanish, Polish, and Chinese in order to serve Chicago's fastest-growing immigrant communities. Chicago-based immigrant organizations including Heartland Alliance's National Immigrant Justice Center—the direct legacy organization of Hull-House's Immigrants' Protective League—Korean American Resource and Cultural Center, Chinese Mutual Aid Association, United African Organization, El Zócalo Urbano, and Polish American Association have already joined on as partners and consultants.

GENRE/FORMAT

Describe the form (NOT the content) of the document you want students to produce. (Do you envision a brochure, a report, a map with accompanying narrative, a Web page, or ... ?) Why have you chosen this format for this project? Where might students see useful examples of this kind of document? How do you want the finished project to "look"? That is, what kind of impression do you want to create (slick, accessible, scholarly, etc.)? How many pages or what size should the finished product be?

The form of this document will be a flyer/program—or text within a flyer/program—about the immigrants' guide project for the Jane Addams Day promotional materials. This flyer will be designed to look consistent with other Museum publicity materials. Carla will be responsible for the text, NOT the design that will be on the flyer/program. Carla will have access to examples of the Museum's previous/existing promotional flyers/programs to get an idea of the form, style, and tone the text should have. The size of the finished text will be approximately 250-500 words. Carla will also assist with choosing appropriate images for the flyer/program.

SITUATION

Explain how this project supports your organization's goals and research efforts. Describe the project's consequences for the broader mission it supports.

Define and describe the audience for which this document is intended. What is the document's purpose? That is, what response is it intended to elicit from its audience? (What do you want the audience to think or do after encountering this writing?)

This project will be promotional materials for *Chicago: An Immigrant City*, which is a project of JAHHM to create a comprehensive immigrants' resource guide to Chicago. This resource guide will continue the legacy of the Hull-House Settlement's commitment to supporting immigrants' rights and aiding their transition to American, urban society. Specifically, this promotional text will appear on a flyer/program for the Museum's Jane Addams Day celebrations on December 9-10, 2007. Officially, Jane Addams Day is December 10, the day on which she received the Nobel Peace Prize in 1931.

The audience for which this document is intended is the general public, JAHHM visitors, and visitors who attend the Jane Addams Day celebrations on December 9-10, 2007. The text on the flyer/program will connect the immigrants' guide project to Hull-House history and Jane Addams's vision of peace as not merely an international concern but as actively fostering the conditions for peace to flourish in local neighborhoods and communities.

USEFUL TIPS

Offer advice on gathering data, conducting an analysis, developing, framing, designing, and/or shaping the product.

Carla should look at previous examples of JAHHM promotional materials to get an idea of the tone and style of the text. Carla will also need to be familiar with existing publicity text on the immigrants' guide project. In order to make a successful and accurate link to Hull-House history, Carla will need to read articles/books to which I will direct her.

SUGGESTED TEMPLATE OR SAMPLE DOCUMENTS

Please identify a particularly good example of a similar project you can share with your students. The example should illustrate the standard you expect this project to meet.
See above.

READINGS/RESOURCES

What material (articles, books, Web sites, videos, etc.) can your organization provide or recommend to prepare students to work on this project?

News about current immigration debate: Chicago immigrant/ethnic history and Chicago's current demographics; Books by and about Jane Addams and Hull-House (available at JAHHM's resource library and the Richard J. Daley Library); www.hullhousemuseum.org and www.uic.edu/jaddams/hull/urbanexp/; New York Times Guide for Immigrants to New York City (as an example of an immigrants' guide but NOT as a direct model for the guide JAHHM will create); Existing text about the immigrants' guide used for promotional materials.

EVALUATION CRITERIA

What elements do you think should contribute to assessing this project? Please list the criteria you think the instructor should apply to evaluation. If this project were done by a staff member, on what basis would you evaluate its worth to your organization?

This project will be evaluated for: grammar, usage, choice of language, style, tone, accuracy of content, creativity, etc.

6

APPRENTICING CIVIC AND POLITICAL ENGAGEMENT IN THE FIRST YEAR WRITING PROGRAM

Susan Wolff Murphy

JOINING A CAMPUS CULTURE OF ENGAGEMENT

When I joined the faculty at Texas A&M University-Corpus Christi (TAMU-CC) in 2001, I quickly learned that the culture was infused with the values of giving back, community service, enabling and mentoring students, and equity in educational access, going back to the lawsuit that forced Texas to build the campus in the first place. As Bringle, Games and Malloy (1999, 202) explain, "The engaged campus will promote a culture of service." For any engagement or service learning initiative to work, a campus has to have a culture that welcomes it. At TAMU-CC, this culture is both "official" and also "underground." While mission statements and public information announcements may proclaim the value of community connections in the official media, it is in the minds and practices of faculty and students where the culture of the university resides. These thoughts and practices may be underground in the sense that they are communicated from faculty to students via lectures, discussions, and/or assignments, within closed classrooms. Connections to community might occur between students and teachers or business leaders on their own time, driven not by official policy, but by deep-seated beliefs. Common practice can be modeled in casual conversations in the hallway or communicated via personal email, rather than an official newsletter or press release.

TAMU-CC is a regional, Hispanic-serving institution, serving about 9,100 students, many of whom are first generation in college. TAMU-CC is a very young campus. In 1994, it first opened its doors to freshman and sophomore students; previous to that, Corpus Christi State University taught only juniors and seniors. TAMU-CC admits competitively, generally from the top 50% of a high school class. Located in the Coastal Bend region, on the Gulf of Mexico between Houston and Brownsville, TAMU-CC was built on an island at the end of expensive Ocean Drive, which runs along the Corpus Christi bay. It is close to home for many of our students who do not want to venture far to attend college.

We enroll 38.5% Latino/a students, compared to the community's 58% Latino/a population overall (TAMU-CC Planning and Institutional Effectiveness; DemographicsNow 2008). 56% of our Latino/a students speak only English, and 27% who use Spanish or code-switch report doing so less than 10% of the time. Out of the 180 Latino/a students surveyed in fall of 2003, only 1 reported using Spanish half the time, and none reported using Spanish more than that (Araiza, Cárdenas, and Loudermilk Garza 2007). In looking at all our first year students, they are traditional in age only: in many ways, they resemble non-traditional commuter students. They have families, often children at a very young age; they have jobs, and many work more than 20 hours per week; and some care for elderly parents or grandparents.

Early in my time at TAMU-CC, I was introduced to "founding faculty," those who were here for the design of our general education and learning communities programs for the 1994 introduction of freshman and sophomore students. These faculty members wrote our mission: to educate, provide access, and serve our community in South Texas. As new faculty are hired, they encounter this passion for service that extends beyond the level demanded by the institution's policies for promotion and tenure. As a result of this culture, many faculty members' teaching is shaped by the desire to connect their new learning with the lived experience of students, to do community service and service-learning projects, and to try to make the Coastal Bend region a better place for everyone to live.

Shortly after I arrived on campus I was given a syllabus for an English education course that incorporated interviews with teachers. This assignment demonstrated the respect and value placed upon community engagement. Hearing teachers' voices through our students' interviews has allowed the faculty teaching English education courses to see the wide range of philosophies in local schools, as well as the need for the Coastal Bend Writing Project site we are initiating in 2009. Also soon after I arrived, Edward Zlotkowski was brought to campus to support service learning. I was asked to join a grant project and run our summer writing camp for children in elementary and middle schools, which was 10 years old by the time I led it. The camp focuses primarily on creative writing; it is an attempt to encourage children to use writing for their own purposes. Each summer camp finishes with a publication/performance party to which family members are invited. Over the course of a few years, I came to recognize that the community of practice was heavily invested in improving the community, making connections, and finding ways to serve. This was the process of my acculturation: not a designed, planned initiation, but a gradual coming to knowledge through activities, responsibilities, and practices engaged in over time; rubbing shoulders, eating lunch, and most of all, attending meetings with faculty colleagues, some of whom were founding faculty. Through these means, I received lore about previous outreach efforts and invitations to join current efforts.

Another way I was acculturated in this expectation of service was by observing and hearing about the practices of faculty teaching in the majors in various colleges, and how they included service learning into those courses. These discussions surfaced primarily during and after the visit by Edward Zlotkowski; however, they are still active today because they arise from faculty's beliefs, not a top-down campus initiative. In the following paragraphs, I provide some examples of the ongoing service-learning activities my colleagues engage in.

One of the largest majors at TAMU-CC is communication. In that discipline, several faculty incorporate civic engagement and community-service activities in their courses. In her public relations class, for example, communications professor Kelly Quintanilla asks student groups to construct public relations plans for a campus-based organization she has chosen (Quintanilla 2008). Leadership from that organization comes to the class to hear oral/multimedia presentations of the various student proposals and are given the developed materials for use and/or further development. In the past, these presentations have focused on the campus's American Democracy Project effort (about which more later) and the honors program. In each case, Dr. Quintanilla's choice of nonprofit, campus-based clients defined the kinds of values, audiences, and purposes of the campaigns.

In the college of business, faculty have encouraged community service in their courses. For example, Dr. Karen Middleton received the Distinguished Educator Award from the Texas Recreation and Parks Society for projects she and her students conducted for the Corpus Christi Parks & Recreation Department. Dr. Middleton's students completed projects at the Lindale Senior and Community Centers and the Joe Garza Recreational and Teen Center (Paschal 2006). In addition to the physical labor involved in these service projects, students were asked to communicate with business leaders to solicit funds for the projects. Upon receiving the honor, Dr. Middleton said that "to succeed in the business world you must give back to the community, know business leaders, be able to present yourself to businesses and be willing to work hard" (2005 Corpus Christi Daily, Inc., corpuschristidaily.com).

In the college of education, majors work intensively in the community before graduation. In education, students spend two days a week with a mentor teacher the semester before they teach full time as student teachers. A full year in the classroom gives students a clearer idea of the demands of the field before graduation. In addition, it provides faculty and students many connections in the community and opportunities for service learning, community-based projects. For example, Dr. Sue Elwood has her education technology students observe classrooms and propose software-based solutions to teaching challenges.

Our technical writing program requires a service-learning component in every class (Cárdenas and Garza 2007). Students in criminal justice, computer science, and the professional writing minor take this course as a requirement, and others take it as an elective. The faculty and coordinator have spent years developing relationships with community nonprofit leaders, business contacts, and civic leaders to facilitate paid and unpaid internships and projects for these technical writing students.

These initiatives, though supportive of the service-focused mission of TAMU-CC, are "underground" because they are initiatives of individual faculty members and program directors, not part of a campus-wide or centrally administered engagement program. In conjunction with our campus's participation in the American Democracy Project, our Community Outreach office conducted a survey of civic engagement activities on our campus. One of the interesting responses from faculty was that they did mentor students in various forms of service learning activities related to their courses and majors, but they did not want the university as a whole to attempt to coordinate service learning because they believed that the bureaucracy involved could only harm the activities currently being done. In other words, faculty wanted to be left alone to run their projects in peace. Part of this sentiment arises from the sense that the hard work of faculty might be exploited for purposes not pertaining to their goals, and part arises from the red tape that seems to appear whenever we attempt to engage students in the community through official channels. In general, there is the sense that with monetary or other kinds of support for engagement and/or service-learning projects will come strings that would be unacceptable to faculty.

BECOMING THE WPA

In 2004, I agreed to take on an administrative role with two main parts: co-directing the university's First Year Learning Communities Program (FYLCP) and coordinating the First Year Writing Program. These go hand-in-hand because all first year students are enrolled in learning communities and, therefore, almost all of our composition courses are offered as part of a learning community structure. The teachers and administrators of these programs are one unit with common learning goals, physical office space, meetings, students, and staff. I came into this role with a great deal of mentoring and guidance, and gradually I came to recognize how this "official" structure provides a means to introduce students to the campus's culture of engagement and some of the more "underground" engagement activities they are likely to encounter in later courses. It made sense to me that the structure and curriculum of the first-year writing program should preview the values of the surrounding institution—acting like a welcome mat, giving some indication of what is to come; beginning to help students acquire and practice the values and literacies they will encounter later in their careers.

One of the key choices the founding faculty made was to enroll all first-year students in learning communities comprised of a large lecture, a seminar class, and a composition course. These courses are required for graduation. The small classes of composition and seminar allow teachers to form relationships with their students, facilitating the acculturation process. The incorporation of writing courses within this interdisciplinary structure facilitates writing connections with political science, sociology, and history; courses that include various factors of civic awareness within their learning goals.

I inherited this interdisciplinary structure for writing courses and have come to recognize how it can begin a vertical experience of engagement that runs from composition through to senior year, apprenticing students not only in the practices of research-based writing, documentation, and visual rhetorics, but also in the value of engagement and service. First-year composition, especially courses that are embedded or linked with other disciplines in learning communities, can be a site for the development of the civic and political awareness that is necessary for full democratic citizenship. This can be helpful if many faculty espouse these values and under-gird their assignments with them.

The interdisciplinary connections formed in learning communities integrate several disciplinary ways of knowing in the process of engaging with social and community issues. In addition, the first-year composition course is guided by activity and genre theories, and Anne Beaufort's *College Writing and Beyond* (2007). These theories provide an awareness of writing as an act that is performed within a discourse community to achieve particular aims. Beaufort's longitudinal study of the writing of an undergraduate student from composition through his first job in engineering helps composition faculty and writing program administrators see how writing tasks can build vertically throughout the curriculum. Beaufort argues that departments within universities should deliberately construct assignments that increase in challenge and complexity over the years so that students build writing skills in deliberate and planned ways.

As Beaufort and others explain, a "vertical" curriculum is one that is aligned from year to year, sometimes within a major or across the core/general education program. Beaufort's schema of the five knowledge areas used in writing also provides an analogy to political engagement. Beaufort argues that writers use four areas of knowledge: subject matter, writing process, genre, and rhetorical, all of which operate within and are defined by the fifth area, the discourse community. Similarly, a program to teach the values and skills of political and civic engagement could build vertically through the curriculum. An articulation between a first-year program of civic and political engagement and later, upper-division service-learning projects or internships can lead to a gradual, deliberate development of sophistication and commitment. A curricular verticality of engagement can develop through efforts coordinated in ways similar to WAC programs and coordinated writing development in majors, something that is faculty-driven and also serves the needs of a public institution.

As the previous examples of engagement in communication, business, education, and technical writing demonstrate, as WPA, I can trust that in students' experiences at TAMU-CC, they will be asked to engage with the community at some point. So in our first-year courses, I attempt to initiate them into these values, this community. Writing assignments must engage students in critical reading and questions, preferably of political processes and issues, connect those issues to individual and community concerns, and ask students to reflect meaningfully on this learning. WPAs need to see the connections between civic engagement and writing and how building this awareness in students and faculty is a vital role we can play in the campus community.

How can WPAs build a first-year writing program that will help initiate students into this kind of engaged community? As is true in many things, previous engagement in the home leads to engagement in college; however, for those students who are not engaged at home, first-year courses need to model political practices and knowledge. In surveys of college students regarding their levels of engagement, "the two most powerful predictors of [political] engagement in college are parents (talking about politics at home) and schools (arranging for volunteer activities). Classes that require students to pay attention to politics and government also reap dividends" (Zukin et al. 2006, 153). Obviously, instructors of writing classes that are linked to political science classes can design writing assignments that engage students in elections, public policy, and local issues such as smoking ordinances; but even those writing classes not connected to political science can teach the practices of engagement: Alexander Astin (1999, 33) argues that "Comprehending democracy . . . includes the economy, corporate business, lobbyists, the manner in which political campaigns are funded, and especially the role of the mass media." Astin (1999, 33) continues, "Our educational system should help students . . . become better critics and analysts of contemporary mass media and of the political information they produce." The rhetorical grounding of the composition classroom makes it an ideal place to practice these skills.

At TAMU-CC, the interdisciplinary nature of the learning communities program facilitates community-building activities and learning about citizenship. Both of these educational goals were further developed and heightened when we joined the American Democracy Project (ADP), "a multi-campus initiative focused on higher education's role in preparing the next generation of informed, engaged citizens for our democracy, [which] began in 2003 as an initiative of the American Association of State Colleges and Universities (AASCU), in partnership with *The New York Times*" (American Association of State Colleges and Universities). ADP promotes both a civic engagement curriculum and service learning opportunities. A campus interdisciplinary team attended ADP conferences to gather information, to track activities, and develop interdisciplinary civic engagement assignments and activities. As a member of this team, I explored options for our learning communities program.

In 2005, ADP organized a "First Amendment Project" to promote learning specifically about the topic on a national level. Because I believed that the ADP closely aligned with the goals of the first-year learning communities program, I led an effort among teachers to develop writing assignments to pursue this initiative. After discussing possibilities, we adopted the "First Amendment" theme for the First Year Writing Program due to the breadth of possibilities for student research and interdisciplinary engagement with this one section of the Bill of Rights:

> Amendment I
>
> Congress shall make no law respecting an establishment of religion, or prohibiting the free exercise thereof; or abridging the freedom of speech, or of the press; or the right of the people peaceably to assemble, and to petition the government for a redress of grievances. (Charters of Freedom, 2008)

In fall 2005, we focused on the freedoms of religion, speech and press, and in the spring we focused on assembly and petition, figuring that the progress moved naturally toward greater commitment and action. At TAMU-CC, the writing sequence focuses on personal and research-based writing that broadens the civic awareness of students by connecting their lived experiences with academic concerns and social issues. Our assignment sequence asked students to first look at their own histories by writing a citizenship autobiography, optionally titled, "The past, present and future of my communities, my citizenship and my civil literacies." This reflective process was facilitated by an introduction to the constitutional documents, news articles related to civil liberties being currently debated, and the seminar class's discussions regarding transitioning from high school and defining life goals and values. Specifically in English we asked students to consider the various discourse communities of which they were a part and how those communities defined "good citizenship," and in what ways they did or did not meet those expectations. In this process, we connected the national with the personal, lived experiences of students.

After the citizenship autobiography, students wrote a multiple perspectives cause and effect essay that identified various communities and the causes and/or effects those communities ascribed to an issue or problem of the student's choice. At this point, each student moved into his own area of interest, but was required to use research to do so. In many cases students were asked to work within the theme defined by a learning community (such as, "revolution"), so the causes and/or effects might have to do with suffrage, for example, bringing in readings and research from both English and American History.

Our third writing assignment for the semester culminates the students' research with an argument to act, enacting in some ways the activism advocated by Zukin et al. (2006). This assignment was written in a multimedia genre and/or was enacted in a physical way, such as a protest or petition, at the First Year Celebration (discussed below).

Librarians were key partners who helped our instructors find and organize a wide range of materials related to the First Amendment, including online versions of the Constitution, Declaration of Independence, and First Amendment, as well as websites such as the First Amendment Center (www.firstamendmentcenter.org) and American Rhetoric (www.americanrhetoric.com). In addition, the professors teaching the American History, Political Science, and Sociology courses linked to our composition sections provided disciplinary perspectives on citizenship, engagement, power, oppression, and revolution. Our campus also subscribed to *The New York Times*, providing 100 copies of the paper per day available for pick-up free at the library. Many teachers used these by taking a set of 10 or 20 on a given day to class to find articles related to First Amendment issues to both facilitate class discussion and model engaged citizenship (reading the paper, keeping up with political news).

Spring assignments focused on making various arguments, both in text and visual media. Critical reading skills and the knowledge of how politics work were honed in the process of reading and writing various arguments.

Students' writing goes public when they present "arguments to act" at the end of the fall semester to everyone in the First Year Learning Communities Program and broader campus community at the First Year Celebration. This event is staged in the University Ballroom. Students choose one or more multimedia genres to make an argument regarding their chosen topic directed at an audience of college students, faculty, staff members, and sometimes community members and even family members. In addition to presenting, students in the First Year program are required to attend, to ask questions, and to fill out review sheets for the presentations they see. The types of genres chosen by students vary from the ubiquitous PowerPoint presentation or poster board to songs, dances, and sit-in demonstrations. Students collect surveys or create quizzes to capture their peers' attention. This event teaches civic engagement by teaching students to read arguments critically, especially what is presented in the media, as proposed by Astin (1999, 33), but also moves students into practicing the activities traditionally used to define "political engagement" (Zukin et al. 2006), such as encouraging peers to sign petitions, vote in particular ways, volunteer for political campaigns, and/or write to their political representatives. In many cases, their research has also taken them into the local, off-campus community, developing their skills and awareness of civic engagement (Zukin et al. 2006) as well.

BUILDING CAMPUS COLLABORATIONS

As WPA during this process, I frequently participated in campus discussions about civic engagement. When efforts were made at TAMU-CC by the administration to centralize these community-based projects, interesting things happened. Faculty got together to discuss their activities, but they did not want a centralizing effort led by upper administration. Instead, faculty have knowledge of each other's efforts by reputation, by "lore." These campus conversations occur less often now that faculty are operating "underground," as some of them have described it; however, with my connections with faculty in communication, business, political science, and history, I have collaborated on various teaching and publishing projects. I have also recognized some of the limitations of my position. One of the lessons I've learned from the professional writing service-learning program is that one cannot ask teachers to do "service learning" quickly or cheaply, either in terms of money or time. To be successful, a program coordinator spends a lot of time developing relationships, educating community leaders about the goals of service learning and the challenges and benefits of working with students. Given the established community network built by the professional writing coordinator who already has an ethos in the community and a history of civic engagement from that position, I would not start engaging students in service-learning projects at the first-year level because I would not want to interfere with or compete with the long-established relationships the professional writing coordinator has developed.

FYC AS A FOUNDATION FOR ENGAGEMENT/SERVICE LEARNING ACTIVITIES

Finding herself, as I have, in an institution where civic engagement and service learning are authentically valued by the faculty, staff, and administration, a WPA can structure her first-year curriculum in such a way so as to begin to acculturate students into that value system as a means to assist in that transition from high school. Recognizing the verticality of the students' experiences throughout the curriculum and what a WPA can do, can't do, and shouldn't do in this process, which will be different at each institution, is vital. In an institution with a climate of engagement and service learning, First-year composition can take the role of anticipating curricular experiences that will ask them to uphold certain values and develop certain understandings about engagement, service, and community.

One of the factors of enabling students' success is their ability, hopefully learned in their composition course, to recognize the expectations they will face in their coursework, within their majors, or in their careers. By initiating certain kinds of writing and exploring a shared value system, composition serves as an entry point in a student's legitimate peripheral participation in the community of practice that is an institution. As such, we are helping apprentice these students into the values of the community.

While I realize that every writing program is situated in its own unique context, elements of this civic engagement focus can be translated to other programs if they have a similar focus on the uses of writing that serve social aims and issues, including argument and argument analysis, and can work with linked learning communities to develop civic and political engagement. A definition of literacy that encompasses critical reading of written and visual texts and production of written expression of belief reinforced by evidence is a required component of citizenship that WPAs can facilitate in our administrative/programmatic choices. The interdisciplinary connections are important to this goal; it is helpful to show a general goal across disciplines of engaging students in meaningful questions, and the interdisciplinary understanding strengthens student learning. Discussions of the purposes of education and the structures and issues of a democracy can be incorporated into a first year writing course. Certainly, verticality of engagement requires a culture of engagement on a campus. A WPA who finds herself in such a community of practice might consider how her program can serve as a means of beginning to acculturate students to that community.

The intimate history of rhetoric with politics, as well as the public institution's relationship to government, and higher education and intellectual freedom's dependent relationship to democracy, requires writing program administrators to consider the relationship their curriculum has to the education and development of the next generations of citizens. However that curriculum might be shaped, consideration of both civic and political engagement should be a part of their deliberations.

REFERENCES

American Association of State Colleges and Universities (AASCU). American democracy project. *www.aascu.org/programs/adp/* (accessed 29 September 2008).

Araiza, Isabel, Humberto Cárdenas Jr., and Susan Loudermilk Garza. 2007. Literate practices/Language practices: What do we really know about our students? In *Teaching writing with Latino/a students*, ed. Cristina Kirklighter, Diana Cárdenas, and Susan Wolff Murphy, 87-97. Albany: State University of New York Press.

Astin, Alexander. 1999. Promoting leadership, services, and democracy: What higher education can do. In *College and universities as citizens*, ed. Robert G. Bringle, Richard Games, Edward A. Malloy, 31-47. Needham Heights, MA: Allyn & Bacon.

Beaufort, Anne. 2007. *College Writing and Beyond*. Logan, UT: Utah State UP.

Bringle, Robert G., Richard Games, and Edward A. Malloy. 1999. *College and universities as citizens*. Needham Heights, MA: Allyn & Bacon.

Cárdenas, Diana, and Susan Loudermilk Garza. 2007. Building on the richness of a south Texas community: Revisioning a technical and professional writing program through service learning. In *Teaching writing with Latino/a students*, ed. Cristina Kirklighter, Diana Cárdenas, and Susan Wolff Murphy, 135-144. Albany: State University of New York Press.

Charters of Freedom: Bill of Rights. 2008. www.archives.gov/exhibits/charters/bill_of_rights_transcript.html (accessed 16 August 2008).

Corpus Christi Daily. 2005. *www.corpuschristidaily.com/article_detail_new.cfm?id=2985* (accessed 29 November 2008).

DemographicsNow. 2006. Demographic Detail Survey Report. *www.cctexas.com/files/g5/CorpusChristiDemographics2006%2Epdf* (accessed 3 December 2009).

Kirklighter, Cristina, Susan Wolff Murphy, and Diana Cárdenas. 2007. *Teaching writing with Latino/a students*. Albany: State University of New York Press.

Paschal, Steve. 2006. American Democracy Project raises awareness of social issues at A&M-Corpus Christi. *A&M Systemwide. www.tamus.edu/systemwide/06/06/features/democracy.html* (accessed 29 November 2008).

Quintanilla, Kelly. 2008. Public Relations Techniques syllabus. *kellyquintanilla.com/student/sprtech.html* (accessed 29 November 2008).

TAMU-CC Planning and Institutional Effectiveness Office. Web Factbook Enrollment by College, Major, Level and Ethnicity. pie.tamucc.edu/ (accessed 3 December 2008).

Zukin, Cliff, Scott Keeter, Molly Andolina, Krista Jenkins, and Michael X. Delli Carpini. 2006. *A new engagement? Political participation, civic life, and the changing American citizen.* Oxford: Oxford UP.

7

WEARING MULTIPLE HATS
How Campus WPA Roles Can Inform Program-Specific Public Writing Designs

Jessie L. Moore
Michael Strickland

As Professional Writing and Rhetoric (PWR) concentration co-coordinators, we have drawn on other concurrent WPA experiences (Michael as Writing Across the Curriculum Director and Jessie as First-year Writing Coordinator) to take PWR student writing public. Our WPA roles, which are further defined by our participation on the Elon Writing Program Administrators (eWPA) committee, have prepared us for the challenges and rewards of extending student writing beyond the classroom to promote students' participation as citizen rhetors, to publicize the PWR concentration's programmatic goals, and to help students (re)construct their professional identities. Further, we believe that our negotiations of both our respective WPA roles and our efforts to extend and actively integrate multiple public writing projects in our undergraduate writing curricula are mutually supportive and enrich the role of writing on our campus.

The curriculum in Professional Writing and Rhetoric at Elon University is grounded in social-epistemic rhetoric. Our website notes, "Though distinctly not a pre-professional program, PWR prepares students to be more critically reflective, civically responsible communicators in their daily lives and, primarily, workplace contexts" (Professional Writing and Rhetoric, para. 2). This philosophy guides our efforts to take student work public through internships, senior portfolios, a public showcase of capstone projects, and our Center for Undergraduate Publishing and Information Design. All four of these categories of student projects support our programmatic goal for students to learn how to analyze, reflect on, assess, and effectively act within complex contexts and rhetorical situations, since these public projects introduce intricacies that rarely can be reproduced in situations created primarily by a professor in the context of a single course. Yet that complexity also requires PWR faculty to take some risks and release control over the final products that students take public. Fortunately, our experiences as writing program administrators have enabled us to develop strategies we and our colleagues can use to guide composing processes and frame cross-curricular and capstone public products in ways that support writers' development of rhetorical strategies while remaining attentive to the public image of our programs.

As faculty at a mid-size comprehensive university, we wear many hats. Our PWR concentration is housed in an English department with approximately 30 faculty and no graduate students, so to meet departmental and university needs, we often contribute to multiple areas of English Studies and writing program administration. Michael, for instance, was hired to develop the PWR concentration, but he also was later called on to direct the university's Writing Across the Curriculum program, and to teach an occasional literature course. Similarly, Jessie was hired to teach a course on supporting the needs of English Language Learners, primarily for students completing the department's teacher licensure option to pursue high school English teaching. Yet she also teaches in PWR and coordinates the first-year writing program.

One entity which helps us focus these diverse experiences, eWPA, meets monthly to discuss matters of import to any and all things writing at the institution, including programmatic, personnel, curricular, or even personal issues. The eWPA committee also includes the Director of the Writing Center, and we have made a conscious effort to create a unified identity on campus, often doing faculty development workshops together and representing each other at various events. We have found the resulting strength and support to be beneficial to all aspects of our professional lives. Furthermore, by consciously tapping our experiences across our teaching and administrative areas, we are able to enrich our work with our students, as we describe below.

Taking students' writing public deepens the learning experience in exciting ways and extends students' preparation for writing after college. Working with client-based tasks, for instance, often results in students encountering challenges that are hard to reproduce in classroom case studies but that are valuable experiences for students to negotiate—including what Thomas Deans refers to as "textured understandings of audience" (2000, 68). Authentic tasks also sometimes raise the stakes and prompt students to invest more time and energy into the projects because students clearly identify actual recipients of their work. For example, a recent PWR graduate developed a marketing campaign for a brewery as part of her senior capstone project. She heard the brewery's management discussing the need for a campaign and volunteered her services, requiring her to convince the management that she was capable of researching and developing a campaign appropriate for the brewery and their target audience. As a result, her reputation was on the line when the company agreed to work with her, and she was fully invested in the project. Furthermore, rather than attempting to respond to a fictional case study which might carefully scaffold her development of rhetorical strategies, she was responding to a real rhetorical situation that had the potential to change and transform as the project progressed.

To some extent, the public writing projects we describe in this also expose students to the "everyday and work literacies" that Jeffrey Grabill describes (2001, 117). Public projects like our PWR internships and independent capstone projects require students to become immersed in the communities that construct their interrelated institutional literacies (see Grabill 2001, 5 for an extended discussion of community literacies). Internships, in particular, introduce students to the everyday work tasks that often are not represented in constructed case studies but that are likely to inform institutions' or agencies' larger writing projects. Students often find themselves tasked with both daily writing activities, like requesting temporary foster housing for an abused animal, and larger-scale projects, like creating a PR campaign for the humane society's adoption program. While case studies might focus on one task or the other, authentic tasks at internship sites may require students to juggle the competing time demands and audience expectations of both tasks.

Although not explicitly service-learning or activist research, three of the public writing projects we describe also respond to Ellen Cushman's (1999) call to address the needs of both students and community members, as we as faculty work at the intersection of teaching, research, and service. Admittedly, our context at a teaching-focused institution makes this overlap more likely, but we do make a conscious effort to guide like-minded students towards public writing for community partners with a real need and to focus our scholarship on these teaching-service connections. These projects also lead to more specific learning challenges.

Public writing, for instance, challenges students' understanding of attribution systems, requiring them to consider the role of citations in building an argument or establishing credibility and to employ a citation system that works best for their readers. A recent senior was developing a volunteer handbook for assisted living facilities and recognized that she needed to attribute several ideas in the handbook to other people and facilities. In some cases, her attributions simply were a nod to ethical source use, but in many portions of the document, she also realized that citations would give credibility to unpopular policies or allow curious volunteers (like herself) to learn more about aspects of assisted living. At the same time, though, she felt that APA citations, which she frequently used in Human Services papers about assisted living, would interfere with the handbook's readability. Instead of using this academic citation system, she researched how other assisted living facility documents for non-academic audiences integrated citations and she opted to use an end-note system that met the field's conventions.

The same student encountered a challenge representative of another key learning experience that public writing projects sometimes present. When our students work on case studies in on-campus computer labs, they often have access to the latest versions of high end software. When they begin public writing for community-based clients, though, they often have to adjust their design strategies to the capabilities of whatever software the client has. The senior working on the assisted living facility volunteer handbook had hopes of using PhotoShop and other design software to apply visual design strategies she had developed through coursework; her client only had access to an old version of Microsoft Word, though, so she had to adapt her visual design strategies to the available software so that the client could continue to update her final product. These types of authentic tasks lead to learning experiences not always captured in classroom-based projects; as Deans notes, "students learn vital social competencies (reading audiences and work cultures, adopting professional codes, collaborating with peers and supervisors) and textual skills which will serve them well in their lives after college (adapting to new genres, employing concise language, and integrating text and graphics" (2000, 80). We would add that students also develop as flexible public writers, meaning that they learn to adapt social competencies and textual skills for the varied rhetorical situations they will encounter as students and as future professionals.

These types of public writing experiences not only give students practice developing professional writing products, but they also challenge students to reflect on their composing processes. Through the four public writing projects we describe below, our students learn to navigate challenges we would be hard pressed to reproduce in the classroom. They negotiate writing for clients whose expectations change as other aspects of the rhetorical situations shift. They learn to attribute information without using academically sanctioned citation systems and to implement rhetorical strategies using available means of production. Most significantly, they revise their identities as professional writers and rhetors as they progressively transition from student roles, to interns who are learning in professional settings, to professional writers and rhetors with increased independent job responsibilities. With each project throughout the PWR curriculum, they learn to negotiate more advanced tasks with less scaffolding and they renegotiate their self-identities as competent professionals. Collectively, these projects offer interwoven opportunities to respond to "real rhetorical situations in which to understand writing as social action" (Heilker 1997, 71) and to practice the "critically reflective, critically responsible" writing that we identify as a desired outcome of our curriculum (Professional Writing and Rhetoric, para.2). As a result, students encounter public writing as a central element of PWR regardless of when or where in the design sequence—they enter the curriculum.

INTERNSHIPS

Internships are an integral piece of the PWR curriculum, even without being required. Not one student has graduated from the program since its inception in 2000 without at least one internship experience, and most have had two or three. All PWR placements involve some combination of writing, editing and design, and students present their assignments to site supervisors, making them public documents within the organizational structure. PWR internships culminate in extensive portfolios which include documents produced for the organization, specific assignments for the academic aspect of the internship, and contextual narratives that analyze and reflect on these diverse rhetorical situations.

Internships have always been the foundational step in our programmatic plan. When our program was so new that we didn't have many course offerings and we had to send our students out to find electives in other programs like journalism and art, we still made internships an essential part of any student's curricular planning. Even without a diverse body of coursework in PWR, several well designed internships, book-ended by gateway theory courses and the intensive senior seminar could create a cohesive combination of theory and practice. And, because our program was small, we could give students personal attention in designing internship experiences that clearly advanced their personal goals. This is labor-intensive curricular work, but with clear payoff for individual students as well as for the program's success in placing graduates.

For example, if PWR students are interested in magazine writing, but don't want to major in journalism and take a hierarchical sequence of news writing classes, we try to get them internships in both local and national magazines. While this often results in students deciding to go another route because of what they learn about the magazine publishing industry, we have always felt such outcomes were positive aspects of experiential learning—shedding some light on idealisms and finding out what they do NOT want to do.

In these cases our roles as WPAs inform our approach to how internships in all fields should be structured and to how writing should be emphasized as a part of the internship experience. For example, while Michael directs most of the English department internships, even those that are not PWR, he also serves on the university Experiential Learning Advisory Board (ELAB), and as WAC director, he works closely with internship directors of other departments. In these capacities, he can observe best practices campus-wide, as well as influence other departments to focus on writing within their internship requirements, illustrating the WAC/community writing parallels that Deans (1997, 2000) anticipated in his reflection on the potential overlap between the two writing initiatives. While several departments have student internships that clearly require writing as a part of their on-the-job experience, other departments also have writing intensive aspects to their academic requirements for internships.

One of the aspects of going public with student writing that our roles as WPAs have fostered is reinforced by the process model of writing that eWPA clearly promotes from first-year writing to student work in the writing center to WAC workshops that encourage faculty to promote process writing in all their writing assignments. With our emphasis on writing-to-learn, staged, and scaffolded assignments for all disciplines, similar to what often is referred to in WAC as "vertical curriculum," it is a simple transition to include process work within internships. For example, when students are encouraged to reflect in an internship log and in weekly email reports to their faculty advisor, and they identify a problem or issue they observe on the job, they can be encouraged to explore problem-solving invention strategies that result in memos or short reports that might be addressed to the internship site supervisor. Even if these documents never actually get presented to the supervisor, the potential for such a public, high stakes audience can increase the level of engagement considerably. And often, with some careful guidance and editing with the faculty advisor, a document that does actually go to the supervisor can result. And the entire process, from initial observations in the log, to invention sketches, to drafts of the memo as it develops towards its final target audience can all be included as an entry in the student's portfolio.

As WAC director, Michael also oversees an interdisciplinary minor in Professional Writing Studies, or PWS. This program has a required internship, and the students come from majors all across campus. Again, our roles as WPAs recognized across campus lend ethos to other roles we encounter. Recently, for example, a journalism major returned from a year's tour of duty in Iraq and desperately wanted to graduate at the end of summer term so she could be on the job market for fall. She needed only a few credits over the summer to do so, and one of those had to come from an internship outside her major. She found an internship at a newspaper in Maine, but needed the academic credit to come from someone other than a professor in her field. While ideally this would have been a great opportunity to have her do an internship in cross-disciplinary writing, such as PR or even advertising, as a senior, she saw this newspaper internship as an excellent potential springboard into her serious job search shortly to follow.

Primarily because of his role as WAC director and experience directing internships at news organizations for both PWR majors and PWS minors, Michael's oversight of this vital last experience in this student's curricular path was approved. During the internship the student was encouraged to reflect on her academic studies and her experience in Iraq working as a military journalist as transitional elements and to try to map some cohesion onto this timeline. One thing she pointed out in a reflective report was that she probably could have learned all the essential skills in the Army, as she was given intense initial training and then "thrown to the dogs," writing almost immediately for Army publications; but the experience on its own did not support self-reflection about the writing process or meta-analysis of the context-driven written product.

While in Iraq, not only did she write daily for her assignments, but she also maintained a blog for readers back in the States. She was clear, however, that her academic studies had given her both a deeper perspective on the things she was writing about and a solid grounding in media law, history, and theory. "One thing for sure," she said of the writing-to-learn activities, reflective pieces, and the analysis of readings about journalists and journalistic practice, "this is not how we do things in journalism class. It was an interesting change!" Of course, this is exactly what we want to hear, whether wearing our hats as WPAs or as faculty in the Arts and Sciences: that our contributions to the education and experience of our students in professional programs have impact and influence. While this student was already quite adept at taking her writing public, she had not reflected too deeply on the concept of her identity as a professional writer beyond that of a working Army journalist now aspiring to a new position at a civilian newspaper. Therefore, her internship was critical for prompting this reflection.

Internships are now a long-established signature feature of our program, and English majors in other concentrations are also recognizing the value of such experiential learning. We have managed over the years to establish good connections with local and regional organizations that can utilize our interns, and our students have also been quite successful at landing national and international level internships during summer terms and study abroad semesters.

From an ideal perspective, it is almost never too early for students to start doing internships: the earlier they gain experience, the more engaged they typically become in their coursework. From a practical standpoint it is often better for students to have had several foundation courses so they can more effectively apply theoretical concepts to their experiential learning. Therefore, with often limited time and credit hours in students' weekly schedules, internships should be carefully designed into their curricular schemes.

CAPSTONE PROJECTS

A senior seminar in which students research a writing project and present their final analysis of their project and the corresponding composing process during a public showcase supplements a capstone portfolio and frequently extends or takes inspiration from students' internship experiences—or even motivates an additional internship. Student projects have ranged from the proposal for a brewery's marketing campaign, mentioned above, to a rhetorical analysis of self-publishing options. Students are responsible, though, for identifying a project that addresses a real rhetorical situation. After researching the context, purpose, and audience for their writing—a process which typically requires students to interact with the eventual users of their compositions—students and the senior seminar faculty member invite stakeholders and university community members to attend a showcase of their final projects. This showcase serves two learning goals: students must be able to explain their rhetorical choices to a diverse audience, and they publically share their final product with both their intended audience and a broader set of stakeholders.

By inviting campus and community audiences to the senior showcase, we consciously publicize our program's progress towards our goals for student learning. Students must be able to critically reflect on their writing and design process and communicate their assessment of both their process and their product to invested users of the documents, to faculty from other disciplines, to administrators who can inform hiring and budgeting decisions for PWR, and to other students.

Because the capstone project is a high stakes venture for PWR students and faculty, we take several steps to scaffold students and to shape our program's public image. We limit enrollment in senior seminar to 15 students so that the faculty teaching the course can offer intensive one-to-one support both within and outside the class. Students also work in small teams to support each other during the research and composing processes, meeting on their own as needed and at specified times for formalized peer review activities. We conduct a dry-run of the showcase the week before the actual event, inviting other PWR faculty to attend and offer feedback on students' projects and presentations-in-development. Students must "pass" this dry-run in order to participate in the actual showcase, and if students are on the border, they must demonstrate to the senior seminar instructor that they have made significant revisions and improvements in the interim week. The class does not meet the class session before the showcase (i.e., Tuesday, if the showcase is Thursday) so that students can devote the time to revising and editing or meeting with the instructor and/or their team members.

While students handle most personal invitations to the showcase presentation, PWR faculty also extend invitations to administrators, colleagues, and community partners who have supported PWR in the past or who might become contacts for future projects. As WPAs, we recognize the importance of maintaining these connections. We also advertise the showcase as part of the university's Celebrate! week and through the university's online calendar and digital displays around campus. These extra steps do not take much time and ensure that the students' projects really have a public audience during the showcase.

PORTFOLIOS

During the senior year, students also extend their internship portfolios and re-imagine them for an external, senior review and for use during their job searches by adding in carefully chosen documents that include class projects, production from all internships, and capstone projects. We facilitate a series of six one-hour workshops that guide students' development of their senior portfolios and emphasize a staged process approach to the portfolios which asks the students to Collect, Select, Reflect, and Edit in distinct phases. As public pieces, these portfolios prompt students to articulate connections among PWR courses and to make their writing processes transparent for the external reviewer—showcasing products and rhetorical process strategies.

One recent graduate, for instance, divides her senior portfolio into four sections: Writing in the Field of Law, Writing in the Field of Human Services, Visual Rhetoric and Document Design, and Putting it All Together. The first section consists of an extended rhetorical analysis of the documents she composed for a professional writing internship at a law firm; in essence, the section enables her to demonstrate to the external reviewer—and later to potential employers—that she can both write successfully for a new audience and unfamiliar discipline and explain the rhetorical choices she made as she synthesized, arranged, and shared information. The second section, "Writing in the Field of Human Services," showcases her ability to apply her professional writing and rhetoric skills to her minor, psychology with an emphasis on human services, and to her future graduate studies in social work. She developed many of the documents in this section during a second writing internship, this time at an assisted living community where she interviewed residents and created brief biographies to share with the residents and their families. Her contextual narrative for this project—a component that our students include for each item or set of items in their portfolio—details the challenges of adapting interview strategies for residents with dementia and adjusting writing styles for audience members with poor vision and diminishing mental capacities. Although she provides samples of the biographies, her analysis and discussion of her writing process makes her use of rhetorical strategies transparent to the external reviewer and other readers of her portfolio.

The final sections of this portfolio reflect the student's efforts to master one rhetorical strategy and to demonstrate to her audience that she can apply multiple strategies to a single project. The third section, "Visual Rhetoric and Document Design," showcases her visual design skills by making her design process public for two projects. She includes early drafts of both projects, details the feedback she received, and explains how she responded to feedback as she designed subsequent drafts. Her portfolio readers see not only the final, polished copy, but also the messy process and rhetorical decisions that led to the product. Similarly, in "Putting it all Together," the student showcases a writing project she completed during her senior year and provides an extended analysis of the multiple rhetorical strategies she employed while composing the document. While students are often initially hesitant to reveal this messy part of writing in a public document, by making both the product and the process public, they better demonstrate their deliberate use of rhetorical strategies—strategies that often seem invisible when we look at a polished final document. As WPAs wearing multiple hats, we recognize that a clear and intentional focus on students' processes is both a natural culmination of their preparation and a result of our shared and collaborative visions for our writing programs. For students, it helps them articulate the strategies they carry into future careers, a characteristic that our external portfolio reviewers often identify as a strength; for us, it exemplifies and unites the stated goals of all our campus writing programs.

As co-coordinators, we balance supporting students' development of their senior portfolios with representing our program through them. To meet these competing goals, we routinely draw on experiences— from our other WPA roles—as mentors and as the public faces for writing programs: facilitating student learning, highlighting programmatic strengths, and contextualizing areas for continued development within the history, growth, and goals of the program. Jessie frequently draws on previous experience as a mentor when she offered workshops for fellow graduate students on creating teaching portfolios. Replicating activities from these earlier workshops at Purdue University, she presents students with a variety of strategies that they can try at different stages in their development of their portfolios. During a meeting on organizing portfolio materials, for instance, she walks students through invention activities that encourage them to explore a variety of organization schemes and to select one that they think best supports the identity they wish to portray through their portfolio. In essence, as we would do in faculty development sessions with first-year writing teachers and faculty across the curriculum, we offer research-informed strategies, but we encourage students to implement the specific strategies that allow them to best represent their identities as PWR students. Our administrative styles inform our teaching styles as we work with students on the verge of becoming full-fledged fellow professional writers and rhetors.

By emphasizing to PWR students, from their introductory classes on through to senior seminar, the importance of the senior portfolio, we encourage them to begin to design class projects with later inclusion in their portfolios in mind. Such class projects are (as often as possible) designed with actual or perceived public clients in mind, and current or recent internship experience has shown students how writing for the workplace functions with all its contextual contingencies. So, while the senior project is explicitly designed for both an actual client as well as public presentation, students begin to see the efficacy of viewing all writing as having multiple audiences, whether explicitly public in intent or not.

Although we have experimented with supporting seniors' portfolio development within the PWR senior seminar, we now prefer to offer stand-alone portfolio workshops that we can space throughout the senior year. This scheduling gives students more time to develop, select, and reflect on materials for their portfolios, but it also reinforces that the portfolios should represent their identities as PWR students completing a degree program, rather than the work they produce for any single course. Offering portfolio workshops also enables us to invite sophomores and juniors to attend so that they begin thinking about their portfolios before their senior year. Furthermore, the workshop format helps us reinforce that the senior portfolios present another rhetorical situation which students must consider as they compose their final products.

CENTER FOR UNDERGRADUATE PUBLISHING AND INFORMATION DESIGN

The Center for Undergraduate Publishing and Information Design (CUPID) serves as a hub for projects that take student work public. We established a signature space on campus that serves as classroom during the day and working publications lab for students after hours. The lab contains 22 computers, plus an instructional station, with 20 of the computers distributed in pods of five. Each pod also has a large plasma screen on which students working in the pod can display their documents, facilitating group composing activities and peer response. CUPID houses digital cameras and video cameras, as well as external hard drives and other peripherals that students can use while completing PWR coursework, internship projects, their senior portfolios, and other projects that originate directly from CUPID.

PWR faculty have pieced together these resources using budgeting strategies that we developed and honed while wearing our other WPA hats. While we make annual budget requests to support CUPID, we also look for collaborative opportunities that could stretch our funding, as well as grants and special initiatives. For instance, Michael and a colleague secured the external hard drives through a technology grant for special teaching projects. When students working on a CUPID project for the dean's office had to go to another lab to access necessary software, we used their experience to support a funding request for software upgrades. Similarly, when the university's technology department decided to upgrade computer platforms, we requested that they fund any software upgrades necessary for compatibility with the new platform.

In essence, the other projects that take student writing public helped us demonstrate a need for a publishing and design lab, and in turn, the developing space enabled our students to do more with their internship writing, capstone projects, and portfolios. The symbiotic relationship between CUPID and these projects (see Figure 1) also highlights the progressive nature of our public writing opportunities, both for our students and for our program. Internships help students learn to read and respond to a specific work-place context, while also giving students' early access to CUPID as a place where they can compose their public pieces (as an extension of writing they do onsite). Internships also give students a chance to test the rhetorical strategies they will further hone for their capstone projects. CUPID then becomes the primary site for planning, composing, and revising capstone projects, with students using the collaborative writing tools in the lab to seek and offer feedback on their work in progress. This collaboration is extended during the portfolio development process through regular peer-editing group meetings in CUPID. Without CUPID, our students would have had much more limited access to key resources for public writing that occurs as part of their

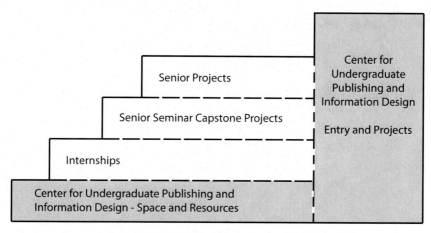

Figure 1. Symbiotic development of CUPID

internships, capstone projects, and portfolios; in turn, without these three categories of public student writing, we could not have successfully argued for this facility.

On a university campus that emphasizes engaged learning, CUPID is becoming the epitome of hands-on experience. All the projects produced in CUPID require students to examine the rhetorical situation and to use the rhetorical techne introduced through PWR coursework to respond with an appropriate public piece. CUPID therefore reinforces our programmatic goals and becomes a central example of how we support the university's mission to *"put knowledge into practice, thus preparing students to be global citizens and informed leaders"* (Elon University Mission Statement).

Once CUPID began to develop its own identity as a venue for student publishing, we were able to justify hiring a colleague who could focus on expanding the number and scope of CUPID projects for university and community clients. This new colleague is helping PWR students develop branding for CUPID and coordinates public writing projects designated as CUPID projects. In her first year at Elon, she guided students through a redesign of the department's newsletter, which will now be an ongoing CUPID publication, and mentored students who composed a program book for a week-long university celebration of student scholarship and performance. She has begun fielding requests from other university departments and from off-campus non-profit organizations who would like to use CUPID's student-provided publishing and information design services. As a result, students can pursue CUPID public writing projects, in addition to the three categories of projects described above, and they can begin them early enough in their academic careers to integrate them into their portfolios or to extend them as capstone projects. In essence, the more CUPID develops as a self-supporting publishing and design lab, the more it extends the symbiotic opportunities with the other avenues for public writing.

As WPAs, we extend our new colleague's efforts by introducing CUPID to faculty across the curriculum, remaining attentive to cross-campus requests for writing and publishing expertise during WAC faculty development initiatives and general studies meetings. Through our roles in WAC and first-year writing, we often have access to university meetings that we would not otherwise tap as PWR faculty; therefore we take advantage of our multiple hats to extend the opportunities we can provide our PWR students.

Developing CUPID has required patience, but by tapping one-time resources and persistently lobbying for larger budgets, PWR faculty have been able to incrementally create a lab that supports students' taking writing public and that has become a central home for members of the PWR community. Since CUPID is used as both a classroom space and a publishing center, students are familiar with the resources and continually refine their abilities to use the available technology. The pod formation further encourages collaborative writing, and the plasma displays help students get used to sharing their work early and often. Finally, having a faculty coordinator for CUPID should enable us to streamline our efforts to keep the space up-to-date and to support CUPID projects.

TRANSFERABLE STRATEGIES FOR GOING PUBLIC

The types of public writing we have described above have been successful in our context because we could develop them progressively, with each building on the prior types of writing. From a programmatic perspective, adding one project at a time ensured that we could adequately support our students' public writing. From a student learning perspective, this step-by-step approach also enabled us to identify the potential these projects hold for helping students construct and revise their professional identities as professional writers and rhetors. We strongly recommend that readers interested in implementing these types of projects in their own contexts take a long-term perspective and consider how they might introduce the projects incrementally to reach 5- or 10-year goals for student writing.

These progressive steps also ensured that we maintained curricular cohesion. Each time we add or extend a public writing project, we consider how it contributes to our program mission and our goals for student learning. Taking time to review curricular connections enhances the likelihood of success for new public writing projects, since this reflection prompts faculty and program administrators to consider how they might build on existing projects and activities. Readers pursuing new public writing projects should take time to reflect on what they already do that could be extended in interesting ways as a foundation for future public writing.

We also cannot emphasize enough the importance of persistent, if small, steps. None of our public writing projects developed overnight—or even in the course of a semester. Our confidence in the quality of our students' internship, portfolio, and capstone project experiences is a reflection of taking a leap of faith and continuing to tweak these projects over eight years. CUPID remains a work-in-progress that assumes a more defined identity with each semester, as we continue to request more funding for the lab's structural bones, pursue grants for CUPID projects, and even host painting parties to make our mark on the visual identity of the lab. The key lesson from our experiences is to start somewhere and to take persistent steps towards long-term goals.

Finally, successfully taking student writing public requires a growing network of stakeholders. We've found that starting with small projects for colleagues, deans, and community organizations often leads to larger, on-going opportunities for students' public writing. Yet, we also rely on our WPA connections to identify prospects for PWR students. An unexpected benefit of being forced to send our students outside our program for course electives in our early years was being more overtly linked to sister programs in digital art and computer science, as well as journalism and communications. These days, while our students still have options to find electives in those departments, and many still do, the proliferation of our own offerings has made this occur less often. Without our roles as WPAs, the vital connections with these departments might naturally begin to drift. However, because of the necessary links of the first-year writing coordinator and the WAC director to the concerns of these departments, our relationships are able to continue—one major benefit of these relationships that were bred by necessity, but nurtured by the mutual goals of campus-wide writing programs. Communications colleagues are more likely to be receptive to the particular needs of our students if they see the first-year writing program adopting pedagogical approaches that emphasize rhetoric and argument over literary analysis, benefitting their own majors. As Art History faculty become more familiar with us as WPAs and with our majors who bring certain rhetorical skills and perspectives into their art courses, these colleagues become more engaged in WAC activities and offer more writing-intensive art courses. What's more, retaining these connections with faculty across campus allows us to volunteer CUPID's services and to identify additional opportunities for CUPID projects—transforming the parallel WAC/community writing initiatives into an intersection of WPA roles and scaffolded, student public writing.

Of course we realize that one key aspect of our approach—the unified identity of our eWPA roles—is hard to replicate at many institutions. We understand how job descriptions and duties vary widely, reporting lines diverge, and often budgetary lines will place, for example, the Writing Center under one dean, the first-year writing program under the English department, and WAC under General Studies. We too, wearing our many hats, have our own complex web of interconnectedness. Our point is more that such effort towards unity can be very beneficial. When WPAs can push the campus-wide concept of taking student writing (and other forms of student work) public, their own efforts to establish public venues for writing within their home majors can only be strengthened. Writing becomes an imbedded part of helping students develop a professional identity, regardless of discipline or major. Departments more readily see the value of writing as a way to assess and showcase student learning. And writing instruction assumes a more essential role within the larger institutional mission.

REFERENCES

Cushman, Ellen. 1999. The public intellectual, service learning, and activist research. *College English*, 61(3): 328-36.

Deans, Tom. 1997. Writing across the curriculum and community service learning: Correspondences, cautions, and futures. In *Writing the community: Concepts and models for service-learning in composition*, eds. Linda Adler-Kassner, Robert Crooks, and Ann Watters, 29-37. Washington, D.C.: American Association of Higher Education.

Deans, Tom. 2000. *Writing partnerships: Service-learning in composition*. Urbana, IL: National Council of Teachers of English.

"Elon University Mission Statement." (n.d.). *www.elon.edu/e-web/visit/about_elon.xhtml* (accessed 8 August 2008).

Grabill, Jeffrey T. 2001. *Community literacy programs and the politics of change*. Albany: State University of New York Press.

Heilker, Paul. 1997. Rhetoric made real: Civic discourse and writing beyond the curriculum. In *Writing the community: Concepts and models for service-learning in composition,* eds. Linda Adler-Kassner, Robert Crooks, and Ann Watters, 71-77. Washington, D.C.: American Association of Higher Education.

"Professional Writing and Rhetoric." (n.d.). *www.elon.edu/pwr* (accessed 29 July 2008).

8

STUDENTS, FACULTY AND "SUSTAINABLE" WPA WORK

Thia Wolf
Jill Swiencicki
Chris Fosen

Despite several cycles of reforms spanning the last fifteen years, we three composition colleagues were unable to achieve widespread student engagement in our required one-semester writing course. At California State University, Chico, the WPA oversees faculty development and program assessment for a first-year writing program that serves 2700 students each year with over 100 sections of first-year writing. Several different WPAs experienced fatigue as they undertook challenging and often unproductive work: resisting an outdated California State policy on the aims and goals for General Education, including what constitutes appropriate aims for writing courses; revising notions of student writing that are too tied to the "modes" and views of information literacy that end in exercises rather than in the activity of scholarship; developing and delivering assessments whose findings frequently conflict with budgetary, ideological, or departmental constraints; and promoting the complex underlying assumptions of our work despite widespread and reductive beliefs about the writing capabilities of first year students.

As Bruce Horner and many others have chronicled, for most readers, the avalanche of challenges we have just listed is nothing new and may seem like "business as usual" for program administrators who work in composition studies. We borrow the term "business as usual" (BAU) from climate change researchers Steven Pacala and Robert Socolow because of an analogy we see between climate scientists' battles with "normal" but harmful environmental practices and WPAs' battles with normal but harmful institutional practices. For Pacala and Socolow, BAU "refers to a whole range of projections" about carbon emissions levels, "all of which take as their primary assumption that emissions will continue to grow without regard to the climate" (qtd. in Kolbert 136-7). BAU establishes a trajectory for levels of carbon in the atmosphere if current emissions trends continue unchecked for ten, twenty, even fifty years out. In addition to charting the rapid destabilization of the Earth's atmosphere, BAU is also in itself a powerful argument in favor of the status quo. Because there is currently no direct or immediate cost to emitting CO^2, and because many of the proposed mitigations or "wedges" seem inadequate to the scale of the climate change problem (Kolbert 141), calls for action can be subsumed by stall tactics and feelings of helplessness. And unlike many other fields, the BAU scenario in climate modeling is much more serious and pressing to experts than to laypeople. In an interview with Elizabeth Kolbert, for example, Socolow notes with some irony that while nuclear scientists are far more relaxed about the potential for Chernobyl-type radiation leaks than the public is, "in the climate case, the experts—the people who work with the climate models every day, the people who do ice cores—they are *more* concerned. They're going out of their way to say, 'Wake up!'" (133-4). BAU is both a direct and a symbolic measure of the effects of a human preference system on the environment, one which mitigates against seeing long-term damages to the environment and girding ourselves properly for the deep paradigm shifts in thinking and acting that are needed to adequately meet the climate crisis.

While research on global climate change is not equivalent to our challenges in articulating a sustainable model for writing instruction, Pacala and Socolow's model is inspiring to us as literacy workers because it represents a way of collaboratively intervening in large-scale, seemingly intractable, institutional practices using available methods and resources. It also helps us parse the current, real-time effects of historical assumptions about student writers and writing. For us, BAU represents a constellation of staggering state budget cuts, crippling ideological divides about writing instruction, and an increasingly problematic framework for managerial efficiency-and-accountability models of teaching and learning. The most recent material effects of these have been, in part, individual and group failures to move course caps below 27 students; lost reassigned time for WPA work involving TA supervision and program coordination; and the closing of our Writing Center. While it might prove difficult to map the trajectory of these issues linearly along a graph, as climate researchers do, or to plot their direct effects upon the university "environment," it is clear to us that we've reached a steady state in which, doing all of our usual work, everything is slowly getting worse.

California's budgetary woes are driving the writing course in predictable ways, and our arguments about class size, the important contribution writing makes to learning, and so on no longer have rhetorical weight. As with the public debate about climate change, dissensus reveals the differences in perspective between laypeople and experts. As faculty trained in literacy, writing, and teaching, we believe the situation is far more serious than do non-experts, who don't recognize BAU writing instruction as a problem. As with carbon emissions, there might be no appreciable "cost" for continuing with BAU in this fashion that anyone but writing experts could measure.

According to Pacala and Socolow, stabilizing carbon emissions is possible through the use of available strategies and technologies. The idea is to reduce toxicity, to reduce what is problematic by changing the trajectory of carbon emissions to more sustainable levels—first to a holding pattern and then in the direction of a reduction. By "ramping up" energy-efficient technologies and deploying them on a grand, cooperative scale across nations, the pair argues that we buy ourselves needed time for developing the more substantial changes in technologies and human practices that are ultimately needed, changes that reduce emissions and evidence a changed "preference system" from destructive to more ecologically informed practices. Socolow and Pacala's development of wedge theory provides a two-stage process whereby a system is first held in check so that no increased damage is done, and then shifted in the direction of a new system, undergirded by changed understandings of humans' eco-behaviors, eco-impacts, and eco-responsibilities. Wedges are an ordering of new constellations of human practices, relying on cooperative uses of available resources in new/broader ways, and thus providing room and time for technological innovations that address global warming by "substituting cleverness for energy" (Socolow and Pacala 52); and for an altered "planetary consciousness" where "humanity will have learned to address its collective destiny—and to share the planet" (57).

We argue that "business as usual" (BAU) writing program administration is not sustainable and cannot lead to robust engagement or agency for the stakeholders involved—faculty, staff, or students. Our chapter details the "stabilization wedges" we are putting in place to enable progressive literacy work—integrated, coherent curriculum that enables identity formation focused on engaged scholarship—on behalf of first year students. We understand that the wedges—for us, as they revolve around civic writing pedagogy—provide us room and time to respond purposefully to the crisis now while we seek more radical, structural and bureaucratic changes for the long term. In the pages that follow, we analyze the set of very recent conditions and actions that allowed us to engage in meaningful, authentic WPA practices.

In his book *Defending Access*, our colleague Tom Fox rightly characterizes the period of WPA work in the 1990s at Chico State as "a coordinated practice" where literacy reform happened "simultaneously across multiple programs and sites" (71). Starting in 2000, as our composition faculty grew in number and some took on duties outside the English Department, the First-Year Composition Program's WPA became for a period more isolated and pressured to work individually. While filling this WPA position at Chico State, Jill's determination to change the nature of this work was enabled by her closest colleagues' locational shifts across the university that happened in the fall of 2006. These shifts opened up the possibility of productive new exigencies and communities in which to do curriculum development in the first year and enabled the fluid and emergent structures for collaborating on this work. The changes resulted in new understandings of how administrators collaborate, how communities of literacy workers are created and supported, and how all this work is made public and institutionally supported. For us, these three elements guided the formation of "stabilization wedges" supporting our shift away from "business as usual" models of campus literacy work.

Our use of wedges helps to address and alter BAU models of teaching and learning, moving away from current-traditional assumptions about students as malleable objects and teachers as certifiers and to an insistently interactive, public-oriented model of teaching and learning involving variously situated participants. In this model, teachers, staff, students and administrators all exist first and foremost as learners; learning occurs through ongoing inquiry and participatory dialogue, such that all learners engage in identity work focused on participation in a democracy. Our example of the first-year composition program's Town Hall Meeting as one wedge helps us outline new notions of practice and identity by which we might build a bridge away from business-as-usual models of administrative compliance and toward more institutionally-sustainable WPA work.

INITIAL INTERVENTIONS

Three interrelated changes helped us to build a bridge from BAU models of administrative compliance to more institutionally-sustainable WPA work: changes to our positions in the university, our mission statement, and the structure of the composition course itself. These changes all brought campus and community leaders into more direct contact with compositionists, creating new partnerships with the potential to change WPA work and writing instruction. First, when we situated ourselves differently in the institutional hierarchy, the meaning of our collaborations changed dramatically. When Chris became Chair of the General Education Advisory Committee (GEAC) he began to research and write about the history of general education, comparing that history with our present goals and working with the Dean of Undergraduate Education (UED), William Loker, and GE faculty to create a coherent vision of general education for the campus with writing taking a central role. Thia became the university's director of the First Year Experience Program (FYE), and began researching liminality, identity formation, and learning communities in the transition from high school to college. Inspired by that research, in collaboration with the UED, she launched a pilot restructuring of a portion of the first-year curriculum. This curriculum featured an emphasis on teaching-teams, with teams comprised of faculty from across disciplines and students serving as Peer Mentors working together to create an integrated thematic approach to course development. An introduction to civic inquiry formed the backbone of the entire curriculum revision effort. Jill's work as WPA at the time had been to pilot a more streamlined version of first-year composition (English 130), one that mainstreamed remediation and rested on an inquiry-driven curriculum.

Although we didn't know it at the time, a crucial shift in our BAU approach to administration occurred when the three of us, through our new roles, agreed to collaborate on a pilot syllabus focused on civic literacies. We agreed to do most of this work in the summer months. Prior to doing this work, Jill spent the spring semester listening to the speakers invited by the university to lecture on civic engagement initiatives at the college level, and became concerned about a number of aspects of the discourse of civic engagement: the centrality of the identity of citizen; the focus on appreciating U.S. democracy rather than critically engaging with its most intractable problems; the maintenance of the noble citizen narrative—individuals who persevere and achieve the promises of the American dream by doing good for others. Jill knew that campus initiatives like civic engagement could be little more than the campus branding itself amidst an increasingly competitive educational marketplace. Her fears were allayed when she saw this articulation of engagement at Chico State:

CSU–Chico Mission Statement

We see civic engagement and sustainability powerfully linked as a way to help students understand that democracy must be actively created and nurtured and as a way to work with others to build and live in the community . . . Believing that each generation owes something to those who follow, we will create environmentally literate citizens who embrace sustainability as a way of living. We will be wise stewards of scarce resources and, in seeking to develop the whole person, be aware that our individual and collective actions have economic, social, and environmental consequences.

We understand how context-specific this definition is, and how strange it might seem to other compositionists interested in advocating engagement. Chico State's identity is being actively reformed from "the party school" to "the sustainability school," and in under five years, its effects have been real and powerful for our campus and city community.[1] We appreciated the complex understanding that community was less something to celebrate than something to actively make and remake; that the notion of being engaged required historical knowledge of who did what before you, and why; the tacit assumption that all education should be clearly relevant to the present time; and a notion of scholarly identity that had embedded in it an ethics of living, a notion that what you think becomes what you do, which then becomes "a way of living" that has resonance and consequence. If we were hemmed in by BAU practices within our college of Humanities and Fine Arts the mission statement

---

1. Some of CSU, Chico's sustainability plaudits are the following: having been awarded the 2007 Grand Prize by the National Wildlife Federation for efforts to reduce global warming; recently being ranked rank as #8 on a top green colleges and universities list by *Grist*; CSU, Chico faculty such as biologist Jeff Price, Department of Geological and Environmental Sciences, who is one of the authors of the Intergovernmental Panel on Climate Change report that received the 2007 Nobel Peace Prize; our "This Way to Sustainability" conference, the nation's largest sustainability conference of its kind; and our Rawlins Endowed Professorship of Environmental Literacy, which has the responsibility to prepare all students of all majors, across the campus, for dealing with a world environment by working with faculty from across campus to integrate the concepts of sustainability into the curriculum.

allowed us to link to a new set of values for our literacy work, and build wedges into our location's BAU from there.

We three had all used rhetorical approaches to writing instruction: writing for real audiences, purposes, issues, and genres that students have a stake in. With that focus, we saw an opportunity to put into practice the campus civic engagement initiative, and to involve the college President and Provost as co-literacy workers. With Jill and Chris taking the lead, we designed a first-year composition syllabus focused in the areas of civic pedagogy and engagement and responding to these declared relationships, practices and values. It became a challenging and creative process to author and implement curriculum in dialogue with these campus-wide aims with faculty, students, staff and administrators who wanted this kind of integrated vision front and center in the curriculum. Thus our first crucial collaboration-toward-change occurred when we set ourselves an administrative goal, but responded to that goal by thinking and working as teachers. With civic inquiry the guiding focus of our curricular writing work in the first year, we were persuaded by the work of Susan Wells that engaged writing is "not always found in the clichéd public act, such as the letter to the editor, but in the relationships and practices that a person *engages in* to recast their prior knowledge and do something with that knowledge." For Wells, who draws on Jurgen Habermas, public writing is communicative action, "a relation between readers, texts, and actions" in engaged stances (338):

> Public discursive forms . . . require a reconfiguration of the writer, and of agency, beyond the figure of the modernist scribe. Communicative action is an attempt by speakers and writers to coordinate plans, to come to agreement, to 'make up the concert." . . . Habermas's definition of communicative action does not require a warm bath of mutual understanding or respect. It does not require shared styles of communication. All that is required is an agreement to undertake reciprocal action, based on shared problems and possible solutions (336).

The above description captures our aims for students' experience in first-year composition: writing to identify problems, researching to understand their complexity and possible solutions, and reciprocating with other stakeholders in working for change. This approach also captures the stance of learner-as-inquirer that defines the way we engage in collaborative WPA work; as Wells puts it, "it might be helpful to see public speech as questions rather than answers" (327).

In our "Writing for the Public Sphere" syllabus, students undertake the work of an assignment sequence that assists writers in generating the top public issues they are curious about, developing a research question, and tentatively answering it through database and internet research in collaboration with their peers. The aim of this work, amounting to about six weeks, is clarity on the past and present issues related to the question, as well as an understanding of proposed solutions.[2] After coming to individual notions of what is assumed or valued in question, students then co-create a public sphere called the Town Hall Meeting (THM). The THM is essentially a series of roundtable groups in which purpose-driven discussion creates multiple kinds of engaged literacy practices. It is a three-hour event that starts with a welcome in our large conference center and then moves to two one-hour sessions. In the first session, students meet with those who researched the same or similar question and exchange ideas about the history of their question, stakeholders in the conversation, and possible solutions to problems. In the second session, they break into smaller groups of people with similar assumptions or interests to decide what kind of "impact work" they might undertake based on their research to date, or follow up on aspects of the prior conversation with the help of "consultants" who provide feedback and encouragement from their own experiences because they are living the questions the students are researching. After the THM, students write their major research paper which synthesizes the scholarship they've examined with the enriched discussions of the issue and impact work coming out of the THM. The final writing project is a reflection on their experience in the course as it relates to the development of a public, scholarly identity.

Invited to participate in these roundtable discussions are faculty, staff, administrators and students, along with members of the community. Students who have completed the THM claim that they felt taken seriously as thinkers and researchers, that they felt clearer about their academic interests and goals, and that they saw clearly that their opinions can matter and can make positive change. One student, Chris Scott, stated,

> In the past six months, I have been in and out of the library more times than I have in the last six years. The notion that there is an ongoing conversation

---

2. Wells argues that "the public requires . . .an understanding of what is assumed—and therefore available as value—by all speakers and writers: of what is universal without being foundational" (335).

out there in the world pushes me to find something to add to it. During the course of my research, I realized how important it is to hit a topic from every angle. Not only does doing this make my writing longer, but it gives me credibility that I leave my bias at the door; and after having been to the Town Hall Meeting, I am well aware everyone has their own opinions.

Writing in this class gave my work a sense of purpose; it became more than a paper written, graded, and handed back. Who knew that what I said would be taken seriously by those higher up the academic food chain than I? This fact also encouraged me to step up my writing game knowing that my research was actually leading me somewhere. I enjoyed writing with the thought in mind that my research is not going to ever be complete; it is going to continue to change and progress.

Another, Amy Casperson, stated:

At the first Town Hall [roundtable] discussion about education, there was a man in a suit defending the local educational system, and an ex-assistant principal calling him out, and graduate students bringing up recent issues in the education system. My friend and I kind of looked at each other and just remained quiet until the discussion was over. It was at that one discussion that a little part of me grew up. I realized I now have a voice in the community. I am an educated adult and if I want, I can debate with men in suits over issues that affect me.

Wells argues that there is a

simultaneous sense of exclusion and attraction that marks our relations to the public as students and teachers: our sense that the broadest political arenas of our society are closed to us, inhospitable; and also our impulse to enter them, or approximate them, or transform them. I have never known a writer, student or teacher who wanted a smaller audience, or a narrower readership; I have never known a writer who was unproblematically at home in the discursive forms of broad political or social address. (332-3)

As we see in Amy's response, our syllabus couples students' literacy work with inquiry into felt moments of exclusion, using writing to propel us to those moments of attraction.

The enthusiasm of students and teachers following the first THM led to a remarkable increase in the number of teachers (and therefore students) participating in the second THM—from 150 student participants and 55 faculty, staff and community member participants in fall 2006 to a total of 300 participants in spring 2007; the largest THM to date took place in fall 2008, with over 700 participants. Assessments of students in Town Hall sections in comparison with students in other sections of ENGL 130 and in other first-year courses also revealed that students' attitudes toward academic work and their likelihood of seeing themselves as civically engaged members of the campus and community improved if they participated in a THM section of ENGL 130. A campus-wide direct assessment of student writing from ENGL 130 courses showed that students in THM sections ranked significantly higher than other students in summarizing and responding to sources in their writing. In this assessment, we also learned that Educational Opportunity (EOP) students, who three years ago had the highest failure rate of all first year writing students (23%), had a failure rate of just 6%. A growing number of students even became "Town Hall alumni," returning for each THM and frequently serving as volunteers during the events; and beginning this spring some will serve as more capable peers, helping currently enrolled students with their research. The growth of the THM, the sudden and spontaneous movement toward better multi-section uniformity in ENGL 130, and the positive assessments and student narratives arising out of the Town Hall Meetings convinced us that we should put our accumulated energies into continued support for the Public Sphere writing course.

Watching our students succeed in negotiating this exclusion/attraction pull that is at the heart of endeavors of engagement and agency has emboldened our notion of collaborative WPA work. Around what kinds of campus practices, structures, and ideas do we feel excluded? What kinds of responsive literacy work attract us to those very points of exclusion? How do we locate ourselves differently—in relation to structures, students, and campus personnel—to create possibilities for transformative change? To break from the exclusion/attraction dynamic and into reciprocal action on shared goals for first-year students? Jeanne Gunner's call to "decenter the WPA" continues to remain relevant for us and the field, especially when scholars such as Carmen Werder find that the "master narrative" in WPA scholarship is not our work and how it's enacted but ourselves and our relationship to power. Despite recent attempts to recast power talk along more egalitarian lines, Werder argues that the emphasis remains not on situated action, but on individuals maintaining, wielding, and even yielding their own power in order to overpower or persuade others. "Such talk," she finds, "implies that we conceive of our professional identity mostly in terms of individual charisma, rather than in terms of situated, collective expertise" (9). Discourse focused on personal power, status, and influence reveals our limiting perspective on work, "for none of these three terms enables us to describe a dynamic where mutual agency—not control—is at the center of the relationship" (11).

By constructing WPAs as individual actors, then, we reproduce a binary script of the oppositional teacher or administrator hero courageously resisting encroachments into private space by hegemonic structures of the institution. Work, as the product of individuated labor, becomes a zero-sum game of control over resources, disciplinary status, or recognition, as power, commodified into artifacts like scholarly articles or student evaluations, is won or lost through crises outside of local control. Linking agency with the individual efforts of faculty and students thus contributes to the over-determined nature of solitary and disaffected WPA work. Social psychologist Carl Ratner argues that agency is a social habitus, a project that takes place and is given meaning in a historical moment, within a particular sociopolitical framework. Enhancing it can only be accomplished by strengthening the social relations that constitute it, by going beyond agency to focus on bonds, rules, and relations in a community of practice. "The more one narrowly focuses on changing agency by itself," he argues, "the more agency will conform to [existing] social relations because these constituents of agency have remained intact" (425-26). To focus on agency as personal decision making is thus to encourage alienation of people—students and faculty—from their own labor. This focus guarantees that BAU holds sway, much as nationalistic assumptions about energy production maintain narrow, inadequate views of our climate crisis and prevent the development of a shared paradigm for addressing catastrophe.

CURRICULUM, COLLABORATION, AND STABILIZATION WEDGES

After years of struggling to make sense of the Academic Writing Program—and to make it make sense to others—how had we emerged into this place of personal and administrative energy, collaboration, and widespread involvement on the part of our students? How had we escaped some of the problems attendant in the BAU approach to writing program administration? Most important, how could we understand and maintain a pedagogical innovation that so evidently served—and apparently transformed—many of our students? To ensure ongoing development and support for the Town Hall Meeting and Public Sphere syllabus, we needed to understand how to make room in our university for a different way of regarding students, teaching and learning, and literacy practices. Pacala and Sokolow's work with sustainability wedges suggested itself to us because we knew we were facing a long-entrenched set of institutional practices that (re)produced teacher-centered class-rooms—in spite of our university's stated goals of developing student-centered approaches to instruction. Their model gave us a way of under-standing how major change may occur despite pervasive, systemic pat-terns that do harm in the guise of supporting BAU as the university's "normal and neutral" state.

Originally, we developed the idea of the Town Hall Meeting in order to transform civic literacy as course content into civic literacy as social practice. Jill posed the possibility of a public Town Hall Meeting where students could have meaningful interactions with others around their scholarship. The embedded public event, in which students discuss their research and learn ways to make a meaningful impact, supports students' political/civic engagement as well. The public space of the THM became an important wedge, then, in a series of wedges developed strategically to support a transformed and transformative pedagogy and set of administrative practices in both the composition program and the FYE program.

In Pacala and Socolow's work, a wedge serves as both a scaled-up tech-nology aimed at reducing "carbon intensity" (para. 9) and as a strategic response working in cooperation with other strategic responses. A single wedge, no matter how thoughtfully implemented, can have no impact on mitigating the large-scale problem of global warming. A local, strate-gic response to large-scale destructive practices only becomes a "sustain-ability wedge" in the company of other wedges. Our goal for sustainable literacy instruction became linked to a broader, more pervasive goal: altering the way students are constructed by the institution. We see stu-dents as capable beginning scholars; we see scholarship—of faculty and of students—as engagement in the world.

This approach moves away from conceptually and geographically bounded classrooms, situating students in virtual and live realms to meet one another beyond individual classroom boundaries, requiring students to collaborate with unknown others who share areas of inter-est, and providing students with an entrance into public life. Pacala and Socolow's vision helped us see that institutional change support-ing student engagement would clearly have to extend beyond a single person, program, or institution. Intervention by the WPA to produce an engagement-focused model of education would require multiple partnerships, resource commitments, and ongoing mechanisms for including students' voices and insights in every facet of Town Hall Meeting development and delivery. To provide for the possibility of change, "wedges" would have to be created that could, in concert with other wedges, alter the university's BAU model of writing instruction and the underlying notion of students as underprepared and undeveloped. And to effect lasting change, enough wedges would need to operate for a long enough period of time to allow many people in collaboration the space and time to change their own preference systems—and to offer up these changed systems to others as compelling models for lasting change.

In designing a workable method to affect global warming, Pacala and Socolow argue that any seven wedges from a list of fifteen they provide will produce a steady-state trajectory that holds carbon emissions at an even rate while approaches are developed to reverse the harmful trend. Using the idea of wedges, we have adapted their idea in our work for institutional change. Below we list eight wedges we are working to implement, but do not argue that a particular number will reliably achieve the preferred trajectory; our use of this theory is, of course, conceptual. We cannot quantify the effect of our wedges in the same way climate scientists quantify the physical impact of theirs. We do assert, however, that multiple wedges are needed to alter the momentum of the BAU in a large system such as a university.

POSSIBLE WEDGES

In our approach to changing institutional culture around the meanings and practices of "teaching first-year students" and "providing literacy instruction," we build wedges by constructing strategic community-building relationships, involving an array of people from within and beyond the university in meaningful interactions with first-year students. These interactions include all of the following characteristics in order to count as a "wedge":

- Individuals from more than one program, institution, or site must participate, and members' statuses within hierarchies must be varied;

- "Participation" within a wedge means a dialogic approach to program development and delivery where each participant is positioned to make meaningful contributions toward change; responsibility for development, delivery, review and maintenance of the new preference system requires involvement on the part of all participants;

- Participants' reasons for working within a wedge or multiple wedges vary according to individuals' background, situatedness and public and private agendas, such that participants' view of the meaning of "engaged scholarship" remains a contested space, open to debate, ongoing review and construction, and new insights.

Wedge 1: Using Public Sphere Curriculum

Our initial intervention in our university's BAU was the rewriting of curriculum to move students and their coursework into the public domain. This approach to working with students rests on the beliefs that the scholarship of first-year students matters; that students come to understand the potential larger impact of their work when that work reaches constituencies beyond the classroom; that John Dewey's notion of democracy as dependent on dialogue holds true; and that students come to understand the possible relationships of their scholarship to public work through dialogue with invested, interested others.

Currently on our campus, public sphere pedagogy informs both our introductory writing course and our "Introduction to University Life" course (delivered through the First-Year Experience Program). Our adoption of public sphere pedagogy in first-year courses involves the participation of faculty, administrators and students engaging in dialogue each semester about the impact of this pedagogy on all participants. Faculty report that this pedagogy enlivens student inquiry, and students report that public sphere work contributes to their first experience a sense of belonging and contributing to an academic community. Administrators focused on assessments that support this pedagogy because of heightened student engagement in both academic and civic contexts.

Wedge 2: Forging New Institutional Relationships

From our various vantage points in the university, we engage in dialogue about ongoing and future curricular reforms that increase student engagement in the first year. Meetings occur each term among the WPA, the English Department Chair, the First Year Experience (FYE) director, and the Deans of Humanities and Undergraduate Studies focused on recognizing BAU practices and imagining and engaging in curricular reform. In the last six months, the V.P. for Student Affairs, the Provost and the President have also become involved in these conversations.

Support for curricular reforms has arisen through these dialogues in a variety of ways: faculty meetings have given way to longer gatherings in homes, where extended conversation happens over potluck meals; students and administrators have traveled together to civic engage-ment-related conferences, establishing new kinds of relationships as they make public presentations about this curriculum to regional and national groups; the President and provost have each featured the work of the Town Hall Meeting in particular in their work with commu-nity members, educators, and interest groups—such as the American Democracy Project.

Wedge 3: Producing Public Sphere Events

Our Town Hall Meeting must be "produced" as a public event through many kinds of arrangements and negotiations, and additional public sphere events linked to our UNIV 101 course are also produced each fall. The FYE director and her student staff oversee most of the nuts and bolts work of staging the public space, publicity, and so on. The alignment of THM values and goals with the President's stated mission, to provide undergraduate education that prepares students to work as informed citizens in a democracy, assisted the director in arguing for long-term support of the THM by the FYE program. This wedge involves the practical end of public events work, but the practical work assists in the students' development of new institutional identities—as scholars, as Peer Mentors, as program assessors, and as Town Hall "alumni."

Wedge 4: Acting as Members of the Community

Students, administrators and teachers all participate in community outreach in connection with any public sphere event on our campus, publicizing the Town Hall Meeting and inviting people with interests in specific subjects under discussion to attend. The WPA, assisted by our campus's Civic Engagement Director, devotes time each semester to con-tacting faculty and community members with expertise in the subjects that students are exploring, inviting them to attend student exhibits and/or the Town Hall Meeting and to meet with smaller student groups during the closing reception. Students generate lists of community guests they hope will attend their sessions and request ongoing contact with community members they have met in the context of public events. The WPA and faculty work to create pathways between community participants and students desiring ongoing dialogue, as students frequently request further conversation with consultants, and consultants frequently contact us searching for a student they met with whom they want to follow up.

Wedge 5: Creating Responsive Administrative Roles

When the budget crisis in California rapidly depleted the English Department's funds, effectively eliminating the Composition Coordinator position and moving it into the hands of the Composition Committee, the Dean of Undergraduate Education proposed and created the position of "Town Hall Coordinator." While the primary work of this position is to oversee the ongoing curricular and faculty development needs of the THM, as well as taking on some parts of THM production work, the invention of the position provides our campus with a recognized site for discussion of Town Hall/public sphere pedagogies in relation to other courses and/or campus projects with administrators, faculty and students from a variety of disciplines/organizations.

In FYE, new work roles have been created for students and recent graduates with public sphere experience. Students' work roles connected to the first-year writing course and to the introduction-to-university course have become more professionalized, including some clerical and administrative duties, but mostly assessment and research tasks. Recently, students who frequently return to the Town Hall Meetings have begun to organize as an official Town Hall Alumni organization, with seed funding provided by FYE and training for classroom mentoring roles provided through the English department.

Wedge 6: Committing to Responsive, Ongoing Revision

To ensure that the THM undergoes review and revision based on multiple perspectives, the Town Hall Coordinator and FYE director hold debriefing sessions post-THM and have initiated a relationship with Chico's City Council as we look for ways to put students' scholarship and the THM event itself in dialogue with the surrounding community. Faculty retreats conclude each semester; here we revise syllabi based on faculty and student feedback, as well as students' written and public work. UNIV 101 undergoes yearly revision (it is offered only in the fall) to align itself more fully with public sphere pedagogy, to review faculty and student experience, and to include the expertise of staff who work with first-year students (e.g., counselors, alcohol educators, advisors).

Wedge 7: Sharing the Model

Small-scale efforts have been made to share the public sphere model of instruction through a small "VIP" program for visitors from other campuses/organizations who come to a THM and experience a day of dialogue with students, teachers, staff and administrators involved in it. One visitor to the Town Hall Meeting, Emily Edwards of Montana State University, has implemented it in her campus's introduction to university life course. We are in the early planning stages of working with area high school teachers wanting to explore this model, and it is now being re-created to enhance the student inquiry work in the entry-level political science course on campus. The goal of this wedge is to shift the regional and national views of students' identity, of academic literacy instruction, and of student and faculty engagement.

Wedge 8: Legitimating the Model

When a combination of direct experience attending Town Hall Meetings and positive assessments convinced the Dean of Undergraduate Education that the public sphere model of instruction made a positive difference in the lives of students, he enlisted the help of the campus director of Civic Engagement. Together they wrote a grant proposal requesting funds for design and production efforts from the "Bringing Theory to Practice" project sponsored by AAC&U and the Charles Engelhard foundation. This grant was awarded to support redesign work in the University Life course, in CourseLINK (block-enrolled courses for first-year students), in the Academic Writing course, and in some residence life co-curricular programming. The receipt of the grant brought the THM syllabus into relief for faculty from across the disciplines who were informed that the THM writing course would be the culminating experience of a one-year curriculum redesign for first-year students. Faculty and students from across campus come together multiple times in the spring term and summer months to develop a coherent first-year curriculum with the THM as a guiding culminating event for all curriculum planning. In addition, Jill, Chris, and Thia have presented on the Town Hall Meeting and the concept of public sphere pedagogy at the National FYE Conference, and have written articles for publication about various aspects of the Town Hall. The public success of the activity contributes to its stability during a period of deep financial—and therefore programmatic—instability.

CONCLUSION

Wedge theory allowed us to understand how to move forward in a systematic way to put civic inquiry at the heart of our first-year students' experience at CSU, Chico. The Town Hall Meeting began, not as a conscious 'wedge' against business as usual WPA work, but as a pedagogical innovation. Our core insights as administrators, then, came from our work as teachers. One can build all sorts of programs within a university without truly keeping students in mind; we avoided this mistake by asking ourselves what could make a writing course matter to students enrolled in it. What we most wish to stress is the value of connecting students' work to the larger world through a variety of public sphere experiences that take students seriously and require them to behave as participating members of a democracy. We learned how we wanted to practice the work of Writing Program Administration by seeing the transformative effect on our students in a literacy system that gave preference to the research and writing of first year students, listened to their work, and promoted their transformation of writing into public action.

As Pacala and Sokolow put it, what we are trying to initiate is a changed "preference system" around literacy work on campuses. Their research in the field of engineering is influencing how the climate crisis is being addressed internationally, and they are committed to solving it through mitigating and lowering carbon emissions, a most daunting and—until their relentlessly pragmatic theory of stabilization wedges— an almost unimaginable task. Socolow says he asked himself, "What kind of issue is like this that we faced in the past?":

> I think it's the kind of issue where something looked extremely difficult, and not worth it, and then people changed their minds. Take child labor. We decided we would not have child labor and goods would become more expensive. It's a changed preference system. Slavery also had some of those characteristics a hundred and fifty years ago . . . [A]ll of a sudden it was wrong and we didn't do it anymore. And there were social costs to that, [but w]e said, 'That's the trade-off; we don't want to do this anymore.' So we may look at this and say, 'We are tampering with the earth.' (Kolbert 143)

We tend to think of a preference system changing in single, dramatic moments created by lone, long-suffering agents of change. In some ways, Socolow reinforces this notion above when he simplifies exactly how the change in preference happens. He sees it as a tipping point, one where people awaken and see the system they took for granted in a new light. It is the supposed moment where it appears that the various stakeholders all come to a single conclusion through a single motive. While making change on the scale of global economies and cross-cultural ethics requires that stakeholders come to a single conclusion, it does not in fact require a single motive. Major shifts in systems require dialogue and action around the notion of values and morals. What motivates a shift from business as usual to a new, more ethical, responsive system? How do we negotiate our varied and sometimes competing motives for the change we collectively want, and move to what Wells calls "reciprocal action"?

Compared to climate change and abolition, the scale of the problem for writing program administrators is clearly less severe. Still, we see WPA work as existing on an ethical continuum with these problems, as it is helping students negotiate their emergent identities through scholarship in ways that produce whole, agential, socially conscious, engaged human beings. The work of critical literacy development is, for us as literacy teachers, the crucial component in this endeavor. It is the value we described to the stakeholders we work with: students, deans, grant-funding agencies, departmental curriculum reform initiatives, program directors, teachers, and staff. What we are learning in the very early stages of enacting this changed preference system is that it has little to do with sole, heroic agents like WPAs, and everything to do with relationships and practices strategically positioned to develop and enhance student writing, identity, and the creation of the very kinds of learning environments that represent engaged work for faculty, administrators, and students.

We know this because in spring 2008 our dean discontinued all assigned time for WPA work due to the massive budget cuts the State of California is undergoing, cuts that will become even more severe in the coming years. What amazed us when we processed this news was that it this change did not alter our ability to continue with our work in '08-'09. WPA work is now done by the composition committee, and the THM work is supported by assigned administrative time provided through the grant one semester and through FYE the other.

The focus on civic engagement and sustainability did not arise initially through our own personal commitments, but as our response to an exciting, emerging rhetoric on our campus. Through this experience, we have come to see the "WPA against the university" power struggle narrative as a WPA version of BAU and learned that we could actually accomplish our legitimate goals and authentic purposes for the writing programs by "engaging" with the "engagement discourse." Now, even without a figure called a WPA at Chico State, we are finding that the change needed to happen through dialogue on the proclaimed values of the campus culture—in our case, sustainability and civic engagement—to push them toward the formation of a socially progressive vision of literacy work and literacy workers.

REFERENCES

Fox, Tom. 1999. *Defending access: A critique of standards in higher education.* Portsmouth, NH: Boynton.

Gunner, Jeanne. 1994. Decentering the WPA. *WPA: Writing Program Administration* 18 (1/2): 8-15.

Horner, Bruce. 2000. *Terms of work for composition: A materialist Critique.* Albany, NY: SUNY Press.

Kolbert, Elizabeth. 2006. *Field notes from a catastrophe: Man, nature, and climate change.* New York: Bloomsbury USA.

Letter from the Director. Institute for Sustainable Development. Chico State University. *www.csuchico.edu/sustainablefuture/letterDirector.shtml* (accessed 9 December 2009).

Pacala, Stephen and Robert Socolow. 2004. Stabilization wedges: Solving the climate problem for the next 50 years with current technologies. *Science* 305 (5686): 968-972.

Ratner, Carl. 2000. Agency and culture. *Journal for the Theory of Social Behavior* 30: 413-34.

Socolow, Robert. 2004. Stabilization wedges: Solving the climate problem for the next half- century with technologies available today. Laboratory Energy Research and Development Working Group, Washington, DC, November 16.

Socolow, Robert and Stephen Pacala. 2006. A plan to keep carbon in check. *Scientific American* 295(3) September, 50-57.

Wells, Susan. 1996. Rogue cops and health care: What do we want from public writing? *College Composition and Communication* 47 (3): 325-341.

Werder, Carmen. 2000. Rhetorical agency: Seeing the ethics of it all." *WPA: Writing Program Administration* 24(1/2): 7-26.

9

THE WRITING CENTER AS A
SITE OF ENGAGEMENT

Linda S. Bergmann

In this chapter I will discuss how writing centers can be important sites for engagement with larger academic and civic communities and with other institutions seeking to work with the university. One of the reasons that writing centers become sites of engagement is that people looking for various kinds of help, knowledge, and interaction with projects related to writing and literacy often contact effective and visible writing centers. They may not know who else in the English Department or the university to contact. Moreover, writing center administrators may sometimes be more able than other WPAs to respond to such contacts because they have traditionally held mixed commitments that efface some of the boundaries that other faculty and even other WPAs have a greater need to remain within. Because of their irregular place in the academic landscape, writing centers are sometimes seen (or see themselves) as marginal or marginalized; their institutional roles and practices include features that set them outside of at least some of the exigencies of academic life: courses, semesters, grading, and sometimes departmental affiliation. This can make writing center administrators feel marginalized—and because many writing centers are under-funded and under-respected, these feelings are often accurate. (See, for example, Waldo, "Relationship"; Grimm.) However, as some writing center researchers have noted, (Clark and Healy; Bringhurst, and most recently the authors of *The Everyday Writing Center: A Community of Practice*), life on the margins can offer opportunities to experiment and change, can open up some time and space with which to develop new ways of thinking, learning, and interacting, and can foster engagement with institutions outside the university. The interactions that come with engagement, I argue, are not only ways of extending our expertise to the community, but also opportunities for us to question our ideas and practices and to incubate new ways of working with students, clients, and the community.

This ability to step over traditional academic boundaries has allowed writing centers to create alliances and find funding sources outside of conventional departmental channels. Like other writing center directors, I tend to look for trends favored by deans and to make myself aware of key terms in our university's strategic plan in order to seek opportunities for the Writing Lab to participate in and sometimes help shape new initiatives. When "engagement" emerged as an important and often-invoked goal at Purdue, I sought ways for the Writing Lab and its various staff members (graduate tutors, undergraduate tutors, faculty, and other staff) to participate in what has become a growing body of engagement activities. This outreach is valuable because engagement offers distinctive learning experiences for our staff, and it has been possible for us to pursue because I sought engagement initiatives that promised funding that would allow us to work with the community without diverting substantial resources from our primary work of supporting student writers. As I suggest below, participating in engagement has provided interesting opportunities for Writing Lab students and staff, and it has fostered the development of knowledge and skills that I consider to be very important to the Writing Lab staff (including me). What follows is a description of how the Purdue Writing Lab has built on its longstanding work with Writing Across the Curriculum and Writing in the Disciplines (Harris, "De Facto") and on its longstanding commitment to build and maintain an excellent Online Writing Lab (OWL) as we moved into projects that took us off campus and into the community.

I am using the term "engagement" very carefully here because it can be a slippery term, and at a time like the present, when university administrators seem smitten with the idea, it is easy for everything to become engagement. At Purdue, "engagement" became an important term in the early 2000s, as the newly-appointed President Martin Jischke was setting goals for his presidency and involving large bodies of faculty and administrators in the strategic planning process. President Jischke had been a member of the Kellogg Commission, whose report *Returning to Our Roots* (2000) stressed the importance of engagement to the mission of land grant and state universities. In Purdue's strategic plan, the traditional missions of the university—teaching, research, and service— were identified with new terms: learning, discovery, and *engagement*. In part, the semantic shift from "service" to "engagement" was an attempt to rehabilitate the concept of service and to extend it beyond mere voluntarism. I have trouble with the concept of voluntarism, because it too often involves using unpaid labor to address needs that should be part of an ongoing budget, thus hiding the actual costs of necessary work. Moreover, because service has normally received more verbal approval than tangible rewards in most research-oriented institutions, it can be hard to make faculty and administrators really value its contribution to a university's functions. However, in a land-grant university like Purdue, "extension" has a longstanding and respected place, particularly in the very powerful College of Agriculture; and the various Engineering schools have long-established ties with local and regional businesses, corporations, and government agencies.

The larger and more prestigious term, engagement, then, can be used to denote ongoing, important work, valuable not only as a teaching tool (as in "service learning"), but also as an extension relationship, which has for generations been associated with fostering scientific and scholarly research, applying it in the community (to business, government, and non-profit organizations, as appropriate), bringing resources into the university, and offering the university's resources to a wider community. Lasting engagement facilitates an exchange in both directions, and this bi-directional (or multi-directional) exchange is what makes engagement not only a *good* thing to do, but also a practical endeavor for a writing center. At best, this exchange of resources involves an exchange not just of work, but of knowledge. It increases our knowledge and understanding as well as those of our partners, clients, and collaborators outside of the university. It adds to our resources as much as it takes from them.[1]

LEARNING FROM INTERNAL PROJECTS: IDENTIFYING ELEMENTS OF SUCCESSFUL ENGAGEMENT

Over the past five years or so, the Purdue Writing Lab has become affiliated with several engagement projects. I use the term "affiliated" by design, since these projects have seldom been formal initiatives

---

1. I am here drawing upon the as yet unfinished dissertation research of two of my students, H. Allen Brizee and Jaclyn Wells, which is described later in this chapter. As is often the case in close collaborations, our thinking about these issues is intertwined; moreover, it has been heavily influenced by the published work of Ellen Cushman (1996), Paul Heilker (1997), and Eli Goldblatt and Steve Parks (2000), and by our attendance at presentations about engagement at Purdue, particularly that by Rosemarie Hunter of the University of Utah in October 2007.

enhancing our primary goals, but instead loose collaborations developed by specific Writing Lab staff with various groups outside the university. In these projects, we have tried to foster a teaching-research-service interface that can sustain them beyond the initial flurry of interest. Staff members are currently working in various capacities with several such projects, including a community literacy initiative, an affiliation with the local historical association, an international tutor exchange, and a training program for the Indiana Department of Transportation (INDOT). Many of these projects involve developing instructional materials for the Purdue Online Writing Lab (OWL), which we have been updating, expanding, and digitizing at the same time as we have worked with the projects I describe here.[2]

The way we undertake these projects has been greatly influenced by our understanding of project planning and management gained from earlier collaborations within the university. I see our recent efforts in the direction of engagement as having begun with our efforts to develop collaborations with other programs in the English Department, which Tammy Conard-Salvo and I described in Bill Macauley and Nicholas Amauriello's collection, *Marginal Words, Marginal Work?* (2007). These initial efforts were directed toward establishing stronger working collaborations between the Writing Lab and Purdue's first year composition and professional writing programs. The strategies and skills we learned from establishing productive relationships with our nearer colleagues prepared us to carry out projects with other departments on campus, and ultimately to extend our efforts to engagement with institutions outside the university.[3]

An early project within the university but outside the English Department was a Writing Across the Curriculum project conducted with Purdue's Department of Child Development and Family Sciences (CDFS). Part of the impetus for this project was our need to generate funds for content development for the OWL, particularly in response to

---

2. With over a hundred million hits in the 2007-2008 school year, the OWL can be seen as an engagement project in its own right. My colleague Michael Salvo and I are working on a project that considers it in this way. For a brief history of the Purdue OWL, see *owl.english.purdue.edu/owl/resource/612/01/*.

3. Of course the Purdue Writing Lab was well-known for outreach projects, particularly in Writing Across the Curriculum, long before I became its Director in the fall of 2003. See, for example, Harris, "A Writing Center without a WAC Program" (1999). The connections between WAC and writing centers have been close since WAC programs were first developed, as described in Waldo "The Last Best Place" (1993) and throughout Barnett and Blumner's collection of essays on this topic.

my ambition to develop more discipline-specific material and a stronger WAC section for this resource. In this project, graduate student instructors from the Writing Lab worked with faculty in CDFS to develop writing instruction for their majors and graduate students. This department, like many at Purdue, assigned a considerable amount of writing in its component disciplines (including economics, psychology, and sociology), but its faculty devoted little time to writing instruction. Not surprisingly, the faculty were not happy with their students' written work, and they called me for advice. In our initial meeting, we discussed possible curricular changes they could make, although we all knew that someone would have to work to develop the course materials in disciplinary writing that we all felt they needed. Because neither their department nor the Writing Lab had funding to pay for this work, we agreed to look for grants that might pay for it. When a university educational technology grant turned up, we proposed a project for developing materials for writing instruction in several CDFS courses which would be used in those courses and then made more widely available on the Purdue OWL. When we received the grant, Writing Lab staff, primarily graduate student assistants, worked under my direction with CDFS faculty to develop better assignments and to produce annotated sample papers, grading templates, etc. that would help instructors teach students to do the writing demanded in their major. The English graduate teaching assistants, recruited from the Writing Lab staff, were paid hourly for their work which included developing materials, advising faculty in CDFS how to use them successfully, and giving presentations in CDFS courses. One CDFS faculty member and I were given summer salary funding to supervise the project and assist the students who worked on it. I mention these financial details because they turned out to be an important aspect of my learning about engagement: people remain committed to a project when they have a stake in it, and that stake is strongest when it is a material stake, such as salary and/or the potential for publication.

This WAC project was formative because it helped members of the writing center staff, including me, see some of the elements that have come to be important for subsequent external engagement.[4] Four elements that were discovered (or maybe, more accurately, stumbled upon) in this project have become ongoing features of later projects, internal

---

4. I am adapting the term "formative" from assessment studies because it emphasizes how these projects have constituted an ongoing learning process, not simply a list of purported accomplishments.

and external, and I believe they have been crucial to making our later engagement work possible. First, we established the practice of not only solving an immediate problem, but giving our work residual value by putting it on the OWL web site. Putting the materials developed for these specific courses on the OWL gave them a permanence they might otherwise not have had, due to the constant change typical of most university departments and programs: students graduate, faculty shift from course to course, faculty initiating projects leave for new positions, and new faculty who were not involved in creating the materials are hired. Putting the materials on an established and well-known web site, however, ensured that they remained accessible beyond the initial funding, and that at least some of the knowledge gained from that year of hard work could be extended beyond the direct participants in the project to later faculty and students in that program. Second, we were convinced that even materials produced for such a specific audience, with its well-articulated needs and requirements, might also be useful for a more general audience or for students and faculty in other institutions with similar needs. The materials produced for this project can be accessed at owl.english.purdue.edu/handouts/WAC/CDFS/.

Third, we learned to separate the Writing Lab general operating budget from funding for special projects outside the English Department. We could not afford to use Writing Lab funds[5] to develop materials for a program in another college in the university, and CDFS did not have funds available to pay for what they fully agreed they needed.[6] The project was held in abeyance until we found funding for it. Although I was not fully aware of the significance of this decision at the time, we established the precedent that although Writing Lab staff must be paid appropriately for their work, few if any Writing Lab funds should be diverted to WAC projects, and later to engagement projects. Though the students working on this project were for the most part affiliated with the Writing Lab, this was additional work for them, not part of their English Department assistantship positions. This loose relationship not only provided them with much-appreciated extra income, but also kept me from having to decide how much time could and should be diverted

---

5. Except for direct funding of the OWL, most staff positions and other expenses are part of the English Department budget, and we are clearly not in a position to support WAC without a broader funding base.

6. I considered making this a course project for one of my graduate seminars—a kind of in-house service learning project—but I suspected (correctly) that part of a single semester would not be sufficient time to do the necessary work.

from our main work of one-to-one tutoring and other essential Writing Lab work (workshops, conversation groups, etc.) to other worthy and intellectually enriching (but not as central) endeavors.

These first three elements might appear to place an unseemly emphasis on funding and logistics. However, the project showed me and the students working with me how important those elements are. Unlike faculty and students in the sciences, for whom funding is an omni-present concern, humanities faculty and students who are not involved in administrative work often ignore what their work costs or how it is paid for—and I am trying to argue that such practical ignorance endangers the sustainability of such projects. It can also, as Jeffrey Jablonski argues, undermine the value placed on our expertise. In *Academic Writing Consulting and WAC* (2006), Jablonski argues that writing programs should not sell their expertise short. He calls for a consulting model of collaboration that eschews the idea of amateurs learning together across disciplines in favor of a model that envisions experts bringing discipline-specific knowledge to a project. His argument has reinforced my own developing belief that WPAs, writing center directors, and experienced writing center tutors have definable expertise, needed by people outside the university; and it has enabled me to think about engagement not as "volunteer work," but as sustainable collaborative effort. For an engagement project to be sustainable, the participants must be willing and able to produce work of high quality; the product is important, not just the process. One of the reasons that "service learning" projects are difficult to sustain is that students may not have time in a single course to develop sufficient expertise to do really effective work; the process of service learning may be more valuable to *the students* than what they do or produce is for the client. Effective, ongoing engagement needs to rely on considerable expertise, not just good intentions.

Situating this engagement work outside students' regular responsibilities to the Writing Lab and the English Department also changed my relationship with the students in some interesting ways: In addition to being their Writing Lab director, and in some cases teacher and/or dissertation director, I became a co-consultant, sometimes one who knew *less* about some particulars of the project, and more about others, than they did. In this way, engagement served a professionalization function for the writing students, helping them to see themselves as acquiring and using definable expertise to collaborate with other experts and building their confidence about their understanding of teaching writing.

The fourth element was that we learned to listen—to *really listen*—to our collaborators, in order to understand their needs, their potential, and their limitations. Engagement involves the exchange of knowledge in both directions, and so it can demand considerable effort in learning to understand how other institutions work. For example, early in the project with CDFS, I learned that the graduate students were drawing ire from faculty with whom they were working by using terms like "collaboration" and "consulting" to describe their relationship. For people in these fields (primarily psychology and sociology), these terms denote paid work—and a considerable amount of it. Since only one faculty member in that department was paid out of the grant, they considered *her* to be the consultant and collaborator and themselves to be recipients of our work. Although we were asking very little of them, our language made them feel that we were asking for a major contribution without compensation, and this they resisted in order to protect their time.

Once I understood this, I advised the graduate students (also being paid) to think about their vocabulary, to reconsider their work to maximize the unpaid faculty member's understanding of what the student consultants were creating, and to be sure to protect the faculty member's time from minor tasks of the project. We discussed what we really needed from the larger body of CDFS faculty and decided that we did not really need them to think of themselves as equal (but unpaid) partners (a contradiction in terms, in any case); what we did need was for them to use the materials we developed and to help us improve them as they used them with their students. The Writing Lab graduate students more fully discussed with the CDFS faculty what they meant by the terms they had used earlier, but they also modified their language to make it more familiar to them. The CDFS faculty, in turn, were very generous with their time, because they really did want to improve the quality of their students' professional writing, and because they were confident that their own time would be respected and well-used. They collected their students' papers for our project, reviewed the Writing Lab staff's annotations of those papers for accuracy, and helped us understand the criteria by which they evaluated their students' writing. Instead of haggling over terms, we worked together to figure out what CDFS students needed to learn about writing in order to efficiently and effectively do the writing they were assigned.

MOVING OUTSIDE THE UNIVERSITY

Although in retrospect I think that our work with this large WAC project and several smaller ones led to our engagement projects with institutions outside Purdue, and certainly helped us develop the expertise
we needed to pursue external engagement, I am not going to offer a
chronological narrative of Writing Lab engagement, since many of our
cross-institutional and engagement endeavors have overlapped in their
beginnings and progress over the past two or three years. Instead, I am
going to focus on two specific engagement projects in which we applied
the elements learned in earlier ventures. The first project was self-lim-
iting and is now finished; the second involves dissertation research still
being undertaken. A fifth element emerges in these accounts: the vital
need for a well-though-out assessment strategy.

The first engagement project that took us outside Purdue University
probably came to us because of several years of high-profile promotion
of our services, which resulted in a direct link from the Purdue home
page to the Writing Lab. This project involved a training program we
developed for the Indiana Department of Transportation (INDOT).
Planning for the program began in the Fall Semester 2007, and the
project was carried out during the Spring and Summer Semesters of
2008. The project began with an inquiry from a civil engineering manager at INDOT, who was looking for help teaching four members of his
engineering staff (all Ph.D.s in Engineering for whom English was a second language) to write better. He was frank about the fact that he had
neither the time nor inclination to continue doing the extensive editing that their written work (primarily proposals and reports) needed.
However, he was not simply looking for editorial assistance; he particularly wanted his engineering staff to improve their own writing, both
for their development as professionals and for the success of his department. Although I was impressed with his stated intentions, based on my
previous experience with the ways apparently common terms can be
differently defined in different disciplines, I was very careful to establish
from the beginning of our planning sessions a common understanding
of key terms in the project, particularly "tutoring," "editing," and "consulting," to make sure that we shared a common vocabulary.

I was interested in pursuing this project because of my longstanding interest in and work with WAC and Writing in the Disciplines and
my desire to offer Writing Lab staff the chance to work with high-stakes

workplace writing. However, even more clearly than the project with CDFS and other academic departments at Purdue, this work was outside the Writing Lab's budget, and it was also beyond our collective expertise. Because it involved working to improve the writing of professional engineers, not engineering students, I knew that I had neither the time nor the expertise to carry it out with only Writing Lab staff. However, because the Writing Lab had previously collaborated with faculty from the Professional Writing and First Year Composition programs on a number of projects, I was able to find sufficient faculty and students willing and able to take on the project. In this case, then, the Writing Lab served as a catalyst for a project that drew on a wide range of expertise from across the English Department.

In developing this project, I drew on the four elements described above. I planned to develop materials that would have a direct impact on the engineers we were working with, but also to end the project with materials that could go on the OWL for future users at INDOT and similar agencies. The managers at INDOT understood the value of making the materials developed for them available to users beyond the project, particularly on our OWL, a web site with its long history and substantial body of users. Moreover, coming from a field that is used to collaborations among experts, they were willing to seek funding for the project. Based on earlier experiences with WAC projects within the university, several considerations went into our proposal. We needed faculty consultants with the expertise and experience to develop and present effective workshops for this audience. Although this work could offer valuable learning experiences for the Writing Lab staff and Professional Writing students involved, I anticipated that only a few graduate students would be prepared to help develop the necessary materials and to successfully conduct the necessary high-level tutoring and editing with professional engineers. Therefore, we needed sufficient funding to find and hire advanced students who would be successful at the work, and who had considerable expertise and time to put into the project. However, we wanted to bring into the project some less-experienced students, particularly undergraduates, for whom this would offer a rare chance to view and participate in an advanced level of workplace learning.

Clearly, this was a project closer to "extension" than "service learning." It was not sufficient for the participating students to learn "something" and INDOT to get "something" from this project; if it were to be successful, it had to meet the expressed and urgent needs of the professional engineers requesting our help, in the present and in the future. As we worked with this project, I came to understand more fully how *engagement* (as compared to service learning) must meet the needs of all of those involved: students, faculty, and in this case our INDOT engineer clients. However, as I will discuss in more detail later, I neglected an aspect of the project that I should have anticipated from the outset: assessment of such projects needs to be planned from the beginning, not added on later as an extra chore at extra cost. If good assessment is not factored in from the start, it may never take place.

In adapting to the needs of both Writing Lab and INDOT staff, the project changed as it took shape. The project was initially designed to involve writing faculty, graduate students, and undergraduates, to draw on the students' different levels and kinds of expertise, and to develop them in new directions. However, because the INDOT calendar was different from the Purdue academic calendar, funding approval was delayed until after the beginning of the spring semester, making it more difficult to recruit students than it would have been a month or two previously. The undergraduate student who had planned to work with us realized shortly into the project that she was too over-committed to participate; and so instead of a project in which undergraduates and graduate students were working and learning together, we had only two graduate students, paid hourly, to participate in the work. Because these were experienced students with a well-developed interest in and knowledge of professional writing, we were able to meet our commitments to our INDOT partners, but we were not able to provide the broader apprenticeship for our undergraduates that we had hoped for.

As the project developed, the English department writing faculty maintained direct contact concerning the content and progress of the workshops with the INDOT engineers and managers and supervised the graduate students who worked with their texts as tutors/editors. The English faculty served as workshop presenters, with the graduate students as assistants. The graduate students also worked as one-to-one technical editors with the INDOT engineers, with the expectation that they would not merely edit the engineers' work, but also provide instruction in language and editing that would supplement the workshops.[7] The graduate

---

7. In spite of this pedagogical aspect of the editing, this is not the kind of tutoring normally done in the Purdue Writing Lab or other college and university writing centers, which is another reason why we needed to maintain this project's distinction as an engagement project loosely affiliated with the Writing Lab, not part of its normal

students helped to create workshop visuals and handouts and to revise the PowerPoints, worksheets, and annotated sample materials to be put on the web for future use (*owl.english.purdue.edu/owl/resource/727/01/*). The workshops were initially designed for a small group of INDOT managers and engineers; however, with our agreement, the agency invited Purdue Civil Engineering faculty and graduate students to participate in the workshops, which increased not only their size, but also (and more importantly) their interactivity, in what seemed to be very positive ways. These faculty, graduate students, and professional engineers exhibited considerable interest in discussing what they wrote, and how, and why they made particular rhetorical and stylistic decisions.

From what I can see, this project was beneficial to the engineers, the English faculty and graduate students, and to the Civil Engineering faculty and graduate students who participated; but our failure to provide for systematic assessment makes it impossible to move beyond anecdotes or to document what knowledge our engineers gained and how valuable and valued it was. This was, as I said earlier, a lesson learned, because not only were we left without specific evaluations of the work, we also lost the data and assessment methodology that can make local projects and program assessment the foundation of larger research programs, and the research potential of an engagement project should never be underestimated. While teaching projects are perhaps the most obvious way for a writing center to become involved in engagement projects, research is a crucial means of sustaining them. As Goldblatt and Parks also observe, tying engagement to research is a necessary means of establishing and maintaining long-term relationships between university programs and community institutions, because research projects can last for a long time, drawing new faculty and graduate students into the work, and the knowledge gained increases with the length of the project and the amount of information the projects supply.[8]

---

operation. For these practicing engineers, who were writing real grants and reports that would be acted on (or rejected), the product was more important than the process of their improving as writers, even though they were highly motivated to pursue that improvement.

8. This point was also strongly emphasized by Rosemarie Hunter, Special Assistant to the President for Campus-Community Partnerships and Director of University Neighborhood Partners at the University of Utah, in a talk given at Purdue in October 2007, and it has served as a touchstone for my work with engagement activities in the Writing Lab since then. See www.partners.utah.edu for information about that well-established program.

Most importantly, engagement projects rooted in research do not depend on the good will or volunteer time of participants from the university, but are deeply embedded in work considered highly important and productive to the university and to faculty and graduate student careers. This assumption underlies another project loosely tied to the Writing Lab, the dissertation research I mentioned earlier, which is the work of two Purdue graduate students, Jaclyn Wells and H. Allen Brizee. Their project also involves teaching, but their focus is research into how to develop successful materials for adult education, how success can be defined and measured, and how those materials are actually used. Wells and Brizee are preparing adult basic education materials for a local adult literacy organization with which they had previously done a service learning project in a Professional Writing course. For their dissertations, they will test these materials for usability, adapt them accordingly, and study how the engagement process works for both the Writing Lab and the adult literacy center.

The project is connected to teaching, but it is framed as a research project; although it started with a service-learning project, the participants have extended it into an ongoing, sustainable collaboration with a community adult literacy program. In the process, they have incorporated the elements I described earlier: they learned to calculate the *cost* of their work as well as to articulate its less-tangible value, to find ways of funding it that kept participants involved without draining our budget, and to work on both the immediate problem of testing materials developed for the agency and on the creation of a resource that can be more broadly used. Working with administrators and volunteer teachers at the adult literacy agency taught them to see and to work with issues of funding and logistics; it has allowed them to see and understand that engagement is grounded as much in institutions as in good intentions. They have learned much about material practices of sustaining engagement work, including finding funding, setting budget priorities, and working within the varying regulations and needs of both the university and the program they are assisting. Like INDOT, the adult learning agency with which they are working operates on a different calendar than the university, and their own work had to be adjusted accordingly. Unlike either INDOT or the university, the agency educates many people who are unwilling or unable to commit to regular class meetings and sessions, and this lack of continuity must also be accommodated.

Where we will go with engagement in the future is hard to predict. Because our Writing Lab is quite visible to the campus and the general public, we regularly get requests for participation in many projects, and we certainly cannot participate in them all. The projects we become involved with tend to be those that arouse the interest of particular students or staff who work here, and those interests change over time. Like other writing programs and academic programs in general, we have limited funding and many regular obligations that must be met. Nonetheless, engagement has enriched our writing center intellectually in important ways, building a body of experience, knowledge, and methodology that has grown from project to project and that is passed along both informally and through publications like this. It has also helped us re-create our Online Writing Lab and re-envision its potential uses and users.

These benefits notwithstanding, I am not trying to argue that *all* writing centers can or should serve as sites of engagement. A writing center's priority must be its work within the institution to help students develop as writers, and many writing centers operate on barely sufficient (or insufficient) resources to meet even the basic needs of their students. I am fortunate to direct a writing center that is more than thirty years old, with strong support and funding from the English department and the university in which it is situated. The Purdue English Department has a graduate program in Rhetoric and Composition that provides a vital group of students interested in pursuing the kinds of projects I describe. Many other writing centers, however, are hard-pressed to survive in even the best of times, and may not have resources to spare to even pilot engagement projects. My purpose, therefore, is to suggest what might be done and to describe what we have done, (illuminated with the understanding that comes from hindsight). Moreover, I am not arguing that writing center administrators are the *only* WPAs who can or should direct engagement projects. Purdue has engagement projects in its Professional Writing and Creative Writing programs, elsewhere in the Department of English, and throughout the university.

However, certain features of writing center theory and practice lend themselves to engagement efforts when sufficient resources can be found. Writing center administrators are different from administrators of other writing programs because they tend to be more loosely tied to university departmental structures, calendars, and restrictions (Ianetta, et al.). While this freedom can lead to marginalization, it can also offer room for experimentation. While few writing centers can offer serious funding for engagement projects, many can offer a few hours of time, a meeting place, and maybe space on a web site—resources that can serve as a seed bed for grant funding. Because writing centers tend to promote a more collaborative culture than other parts of English departments and universities, they sometimes have the flexibility to incubate projects that would be difficult to start elsewhere. Moreover, over time, writing centers tend to become an acknowledged presence in the university. People both inside and outside the university, looking for help, advice, information, and collaboration, learn to call the writing center. Students interested in engagement activities gravitate toward our Writing Lab as they generate their ideas. Most importantly, insofar as writing centers are ongoing concerns, they can develop and maintain the knowledge gained from project to project, learn from successes and mistakes, and pass along that knowledge as individual participants change over time. The "we" I refer to throughout this has been made up of a shifting body of people, but the knowledge we gained is stored in our annual reports and shared files as well as passed along in our conversations. This collective knowledge provides a flexible but ongoing institutional and intellectual base that lets us learn from and build on past experiences to start and maintain collaborative relationships with other programs and groups.

I like to think that our commitment to *listening* to clients contributes to this strength. Writing center literature fosters a commitment to listening closely to clients and sharing the process of setting agendas (see, for example, Murphy; Newkirk). More traditional writing programs, like first year composition or professional writing, often need to establish quite firm definitions of and boundaries around what they do, and rightfully so; otherwise, they would be inundated by demands from other departments. But writing center theory and practice promote commitment to listening to clients and responding to clients' and collaborators' expressed needs with patience, if not always with acquiescence. Writing centers develop in their staffs a powerful combination of empathy and expertise that works particularly well when extended to stakeholders in larger engagement projects like the ones I have described. Engagement, then, as Eli Goldblatt has shown, extends the range of inquiry and practices already established in many writing centers.

There is a danger to engagement that should be apparent from how I have described our projects. Rosemarie Hunter of the University of Utah impressed us with the idea that sustainable engagement projects with community agencies require clear understanding of those agencies' felt needs, and a stronger commitment to them than to pursuing our own agendas, however well-intentioned we may be. This can mean giving up language that we would otherwise use, making us redefine, at least for the terms of a project, words and concepts that have deep roots in our literature and research. It can mean conflating editing and tutoring in ways that writing center directors have been fighting since the early years of writing centers. It can mean putting a much greater focus on the products of our work rather than the process. I think, however, that these dangers are good dangers for our students and staff to encounter. They demand that we question and test our beliefs, and I anticipate that they will lead us to more and better empirical research into how writing is learned. (See, for example, Johanek.) They give us opportunities to learn from people in other disciplines, to work with experts in other activity systems and I would hope to investigate how writing functions in places outside our corner of the university. The literature of writing centers tends toward an idealized view of writing, from Andrea Lunsford's idea of the writing center as fostering Kenneth Burke's "conversation of mankind" to the playful view of writing in *The Everyday Writing Center* (Geller et al.). When we work with people outside English departments and outside the university, people who have an urgent and practical need to write, we often find much greater concern for writing as a means of getting important work done than for writing as a source of personal satisfaction, and I think we can use these interactions to gain a more complicated understanding of what successful and unsuccessful writing may mean to the people who do it. Finally, working with agencies and institutions outside the university offers rich opportunities to disseminate the very real understanding about writing that has emerged in Rhetoric and Composition in the past two decades to publics outside the university. Writing centers, I believe, are in an excellent position to pass along this knowledge, even as we enrich it by learning from our friends and collaborators outside the university.

REFERENCES

Barnett, Robert W., and Jacob S. Blumner. 1999. *Writing centers and writing across the curriculum programs: Building interdisciplinary partnerships.* Contributions to the Study of Education Number 73. Westport, CT: Greenwood Press.

Bergmann, Linda S., and Tammy Conard-Salvo. 2007. Dialogue and collaboration: A writing lab applies tutoring techniques to relations with other writing programs. In

Marginal words, marginal work? Tutoring the academy to the work of the writing center, ed. Bill Macauley and Nicholas Amauriello, 183-196. Cresskill, NJ: Hampton Press,

Bringhurst, David. 2006. Identifying our ethical responsibility: A criterion-based approach. *The writing center director's resource book*, ed. Christina Murphy and Byron L. Stay, 281-90. Mahwah, NJ: Erlbaum.

Clark, Irene L., and Dave Healy. 1996. Are writing centers ethical? *WPA: Writing Program Administration* 20 (1-2): 32-38.

Cushman, Ellen. 1996. Rhetorician as an agent of social change. *College Composition and Communication* 47 (1): 7-26.

Geller, Anne Ellen, Michele Eodice, Frankie Condon, Meg Carroll, and Elizabeth H. Boquet. 2007. *The everyday writing center: A community of practice.* Logan, UT: Utah State UP.

Goldblatt, Eli, and Steve Parks. 2006. Writing beyond the curriculum: Fostering new collaborations in literacy. *College English* 62 (5): 584-606.

Grimm, Nancy Barbara Conroy Maloney. 1999. "The way the rich people does it": Reflections on writing center administration and the search for status. In *Kitchen cooks, plate twirlers, and troubadours: Writing program administrators tell their stories*, ed. Diana George. Portsmouth, NH: Boynton/Cook.

Harris, Muriel. 1999. A writing center without a WAC program: The de facto WAC center/ writing center. In *Writing centers and writing across the curriculum programs: Building interdisciplinary partnerships*, 89-104. Westport, CT: Greenwood Press.

Heilker, Paul. 1997. Rhetoric made real: Civic discourse and writing beyond the curriculum. In *Writing the community: Concepts and models for service-learning in composition*, ed. Linda Adler-Kassner, Robert Crooks, and Ann Watter, 71-77. Washington, D.C.: American Association for Higher Education.

Ianetta, Melissa, Linda Bergmann, Lauren Fitzgerald, Carol Peterson Haviland, Lisa Lebduska, and Mary Wislocki. 2006. Polylog: Are writing center directors writing program administrators? *Composition Studies* 34 (2): 11-43.

Jablonski, Jeffrey. 2006. *Academic writing consulting and WAC: Methods and models for guiding cross-curricular literacy work.* Cresskill, NJ: Hampton Press.

Johanek, Cindy. 2000. *Composing research: A contextualist paradigm for rhetoric and composition.* Logan, UT: Utah State UP.

Lunsford, Andrea. 1991. Collaboration, control, and the idea of a writing center. *The Writing Center Journal* 12 (1): 3-10.

Murphy, Christina. 1989. Freud in the writing center: The psychoanalytics of tutoring well. *The Writing Center Journal* 10 (1): 13-18.

National Association of State Universities and Land-Grant Colleges. 2000. *Returning to our roots: Executive summaries of the Reports of the Kellogg Commission on the Future of State and Land-Grant Universities.* Washington, DC.

Newkirk, Thomas. 1989. The first five minutes: Setting the agenda in a writing conference. In *Writing and response: Theory, practice, and research*, ed. Chris Anson, 317-331. Urbana, IL: NCTE.

Waldo, Mark L. 1990. What should the relationship between the writing center and writing program be? *Writing Center Journal* 11 (1): 73-81.

Waldo, Mark L. 1993. The last best place for writing across the curriculum: The writing center. *WPA: Writing Program Administration* 16 (3): 15-26.

10

NOT POLITICS AS USUAL
Public Writing as Writing for Engagement

Linda K. Shamoon
Eileen Medeiros

A writing program faculty member approaches the WPA with a new course proposal: WRT 327 Public Writing. The WPA is pleased. At the last faculty meeting she had asked program members to suggest one or two new courses for the writing program, courses that would get students doing "publicly engaged writing."

The faculty member explains in WRT 327 Public Writing, each student would be targeting a local political or social issue, and each student would be required to pursue that issue in an activist manner, writing and sending out letters, hooking up with a local activist group, and promoting the work of that group on and off campus. "Now that is publicly engaged writing," enthuses the faculty member.

The WPA takes a deep breath. Could she successfully usher such a course through the curricular approval process? Should she usher such a course through the process? Her enthusiasm turns to ambivalence; ambivalence turns to doubt.

From our perspective, public writing is exciting and timely for our discipline. It empowers students to engage with communities beyond the classroom around the issues they—and we—care about, issues of social justice, the environment, peace and more, and it connects our discipline's oldest roots in the rhetorical tradition with its most recent directions of writing in the streets and cultural awareness. As enthusiastic as we are about public writing courses, we also recognize that such courses raise difficult issues for WPAs, as suggested by our opening scenario: issues of definition, intra and inter-departmental friction, and institutional concern. In this paper, therefore, we will argue for public writing as an excellent option for WPAs who want to promote writing for engagement, and we will offer an approach to public writing we believe could flourish in a program committed to writing for engagement, an approach that mitigates public writing's possible complications.

WHAT DO WE MEAN BY PUBLIC WRITING?

Public writing is one form of engaged writing and as most writing scholars would agree, engaged writing literally gets students out of the classroom, or as Paula Mathieu refers to it, writing "in the streets" (1) and engaging with others about topics, issues and differences in life circumstances beyond the classroom. One recent development in this type of writing is the place-based writing class in which students "take on issues of public concern" and "write about . . . places where they live" (Mathieu 4). In the place-based writing classroom, students go "out into their neighborhoods to record stories about local places and people by drawing on techniques of narrative, cultural studies analysis, historical research, and oral history" (4). Service-learning, however, is probably the best-known and most widely practiced form of engaged writing in composition. Service-learning is a type of experiential learning that connects community service to academic coursework by integrating students' service into the academic curriculum. Service-learning also provides "opportunities to use newly acquired skills and knowledge in real-life situations in their own communities" and "enhances what is taught in school by extending student learning beyond the classroom." It also helps "students develop a sense of caring for others" (Commission on National and Community Service, qtd. in Deans, 1). Importantly, these goals are achieved through acts of reflection prompted by various kinds of writing, especially journal writing.

Public writing as we envision it should share these same qualities: the students' attention and much of their course-related activity should be in the local community; students' writing should be a primary means of engaging with that community; and writing along with reflection should prompt students' learning—be it learning about themselves, about writing (or other disciplinary themes and skills), and/or about the diverse community beyond the classroom.

Public writing, however, focuses squarely on another common goal of writing for engagement, namely writing for civic and political engagement in the community. According to the Campus Compact, a national nonprofit that promotes community service, civic engagement, and service-learning in colleges and universities, many service-learning organizations embrace civic responsibility or the development of social responsibility and citizenship skills as an important outcome of the community engagement experience. The University of Michigan's Ginsberg Center offers a prominent example of the centrality of this goal. This service-learning organization's mission is, ". . . to engage students, faculty and community members in learning together through community service and civic participation in a diverse democratic society." In addition, some scholars like Bruce Herzberg, place an emphasis on an increased awareness of the disparities and injustices that play along the lines of race, class, and gender as a pathway to political engagement ("Community Service and Critical Teaching"). Other composition scholars seek to heighten the focus on issues of social injustice by linking community engagement writing courses to political consciousness raising (Bickford and Reynolds), to patterns of activism by 30's radicals (Welch), and to a theme-relevant activist experience (Spigelman). Thus, whether the instructor's or program's goals include civic participation and increased citizenship skills, on the one hand, or the development of a politically-aroused critical perspective, on the other, political engagement beyond the classroom is a widely-proclaimed objective of the writing for engagement movement.

Public writing fully embraces this objective. In fact, in our view public writing starts with a prioritized commitment to writing for political engagement, often along with the other forms of community engagement. From our perspective, public writing turns the established engagement experience on its head, and in some cases public writing may be said to start where other kinds of writing for engagement courses may end. Public writing starts with a heightened sensibility that something is awry within the community and that each of us as members of that community have a responsibility and a right to seek a remedy through political engagement. Public writing starts with that sense of urgency. Within a course setting, public writing positions students firstly as citizens in a democracy who have the potential for political agency. Public writing aims to embrace that potential by providing students with the framework, analytical perspective, and writing activities to raise, debate and/ or promote solutions to social and political issues of importance to them and to a particular community.

Finally, while we compositionists may turn to the rhetorical tradition as providing a framework for politically engaged writing courses, several writing scholars have turned to public sphere theory as a particularly fruitful framework for public writing (Wells, Welch, Ervin, Ward, and Weisser). Public sphere theory focuses on the nature of public discourse on social and political issues, and in Jurgan Habermas' formative work in this area, it identifies those social conditions, locations and normative behaviors that enable rational public deliberation and even consensus-building on all kinds of public issues. In Habermas' account, these normative social conditions are: free and open access to—and participation in—the public debate in informal, everyday settings, for any person regardless of race, class or gender, without fear of social or political reprisals.[1]

Now, Habermas presents these normative conditions of public political engagement in Western societies as based on both historical and empirical evidence, and we acknowledge that this line of argument has encountered fierce criticism in a number of disciplines from philosophy, to political science, to women's studies. Nevertheless, major elements of the theory still have an appealing quality even among those in our own field who agree with much of the criticism. We too agree that, in general, ordinary individuals' lack of access to the political public sphere is sometimes insurmountable, and that a unified public sphere (if it ever existed) has long ago splintered into disparate, disjunctive public spheres. As writing teachers, we also know too well that the lack of expressive equality among our students sometimes reinforces their exclusion from many sites of political public debate. Yet, we still find the underlying concepts appealing because the conditions Habermas elaborated—free and equal access for all, places to meet and debate anything without fear of reprisals—are the conditions which seem to spawn political agency for each person in a democracy; and because the theory focuses squarely on *participation in public debate*—rather than, say, pulling a lever in a voting booth—as a central activity in a democratic political public sphere. In addition, from a writing for engagement perspective, if the conditions of public political engagement and participatory discourse for ordinary individuals are available anywhere, they are often available in local public spheres, which are the sites of the community

---

1. While Habermas emphasizes that these conditions initially adhered only to debate on cultural and social issues apart from politics, most theorists see the topics available for public debate inevitably extending to political and more politically sensitive social issues ("Public Writing and Rhetoric . . ." 244). Habermas argues that the historical conditions that initially gave rise to the idea of a political public sphere—namely a capitalist economy independent of governmental authority and a social life independent of court life—changed the nature of the public sphere into a location that is now a privatized, legally protected *for*-profit zone of consumerist activity.

engagement experience. Thus, the kinds of discursive practices that public sphere theory tries to elucidate and promote are the kinds that lead naturally to actual engagement in the political public sphere.

In answer to our question, then, "What do we mean by public writing?" we respond that public writing is one form of engaged writing that gets students out of the classroom communicating with others about difficult social and political issues. In our formulation, public writing courses should focus on writing for civic and political engagement in the community, and they should position students firstly as citizens in a democracy who have the potential for political agency. Finally, public writing courses should draw significantly upon public sphere theory to provide a framework, an analytical perspective, and writing activities for students to actually use their writing to promote social and political change.

WHAT DO PUBLIC WRITING CLASSES LOOK LIKE?

Public writing as derived from public sphere theory has gained a lot of attention in composition studies thanks to provocative articles by Wells, Welch, Weisser, and others, and a few of these scholars have also shared their course designs. Their work is particularly helpful because they suggest different ways to draw on public sphere theory while guiding students to use their writing for actual political engagement beyond the classroom.

Christian Weisser is one composition studies scholar who has explored public sphere theory extensively. The course he derives from this theory focuses on the close-up study of actual public discourses on a widely debated issue, such as the environment, combined with critical analysis as preparation for students to create their own public discourse on the issue. Specifically, the course, called "Environmental Discourse and Public Writing," has students study U.S. environmental writing to help them become "more aware of the degree to which gender and other factors influenced what these authors wrote as well as how their writing was construed in public spheres as a result of these social factors" (*Moving Beyond* 113). Weisser explains that these readings provide "students with the background they would need to speak with authority and competence necessary to enter public discourse about the environment." The course also asks students to create "their own public discourse" (114) on environmental issues of their choice. Some students wrote letters to the local paper or to their Congressional representatives, others wrote articles for activist groups and composed interviews with "developers, contractors, and builders." Some students took a more service-learning approach with their writing and worked with several environmental organizations producing mailers, newsletters, and "other forms of counter public discourse" (114).

Elizabeth Ervin, in her textbook *Public Literacy,* suggests another model for a public writing course, a model that draws heavily on the concept of public spheres as the sites where public political discourse actually occurs. The text explains that each site of public debate entails broadly-defined literacy practices (which Ervin calls "literacies") that individuals know (or should know) if they are to participate in that pubic sphere. In this course, students first examine the conflicting meanings of terms like "the public," "public sphere," and "the public interest," and then they consider the purposes, locations and literacy practices of four public spheres (the national, the global, the local and the everyday). Students are then guided to select an issue and a genre that they will use to pursue the issue in a specific public sphere. Throughout the text, there is a tacit understanding that students will use their writing to enter an identified political public sphere, and most of the examples in the book show students working outside of the classroom, learning and using appropriate public literacies.

Weisser and Ervin illustrate two approaches to public writing courses, each drawing on a particular aspect of public sphere theory. Weisser's approach emphasizes attention to actual political discourses as these have taken shape historically, along with critical analysis, as a framework for public political engagement through writing, while Ervin emphasizes kinds of public spheres and literacies combined with genre study as preparation for writing and engagement. We, however, focus on other elements of public sphere theory as the basis for a public writing course, namely the theory's description of communicative interactions among participants in public debates on difficult social and political issues, and its special conception of publicity, or the degree of openness and inclusiveness of those interactions.

Drawing on public sphere theory through communicative interaction and publicity prompts us to focus on the demands participants make of each other when they are exchanging views, experiences, and assumptions about difficult social and political problems. This exchange, which may be face-to-face but also in writing, can be the means by which participants discover the full range and the nature of their positions on an issue, and the means by which they discover others with whom they agree, as well others with whom they no longer agree. This back and forth process, with its questions, challenges and confirmations from others, lies at the heart of the political in a political public sphere, forcing participants to be public with their stances, allowing them to find like-minded others, and keeping them focused on the actual circumstances, causes, and effects of the problems being debated.

Critics of this rendering of communicative interaction in the public sphere say such a portrait is idealistic at best and that such debate (for a variety of reasons) usually winds up reinforcing the status quo. Radical democrats and participatory democracy theorists who follow this emphasis on communicative interaction in public sphere theory reply that the back and forth in a genuinely political public sphere must be across lines of difference, be it different stances, different economic or social circumstances, different racial or ethnic experiences, or other difficult divides. Without the element of difference, there will not be the genuine back and forth of debate.

As writing teachers we are attracted to this line of thinking because it turns our attention to the nature and process of debate on the difficult public issues that already is the focus of some of our writing classes, such as in classes focused on argument, the essay, and even academic writing. Many of our students in such classes are ready to make public statements on issues of concern to them, issues ranging from stock issues like gun control or abortion to local issues like campus parking. The deliberative process outlined above, however, requires them to more than merely espouse a stand. It requires them to listen to and engage with those who disagree with them, and also to listen to those who are undecided or do not find the existing stances convincing. This deliberative model also focuses attention on the quality of questioning and the quality of challenges to those who hold strong, long established positions, and it especially makes room for the perspectives, questioning, and analyses of those who might not usually be heard from and those who feel left out. In this deliberative model, all of these perspectives must be accounted for and responded to, just as they should be in the wider political public sphere where these issues are similarly debated.

At the same time, merely encouraging this kind of encounter with diversity in students' research and debate on public issues is not the same as engaged writing or even "public writing" in the sense we focus on in this essay. What we are seeking is writing for actual engagement outside the classroom. Writing for engagement in the political public sphere turns our attention to the concept of publicity. Habermas's notion of publicity seems to be a complex socio-political idea concerning the degree to which the public is engaging with an issue, or better yet, the degree to which there has been extensive public debate on an issue (as well as debate on its solution). Some theorists add that the debate should be across lines of difference (Bohman). An issue may be said to fail the test of publicity if it is not widely debated or when a solution is put into place without extensive debate. In a democratic public sphere the test of publicity on political debate should be extremely high since the public must live with (or live under) the outcomes of such debate, namely the rules, laws, or administrative decisions by which the issue is resolved.

As writing teachers, we find this concept of publicity particularly helpful when we view publicity as a process—a process by which more and more individuals are drawn into the public debate on an issue and on its solution. By focusing on the process, we inevitably focus on the activities by which our students are drawn into expressing themselves publicly on an issue, as well as on the means by which they engage in the public debate on the issue. As writing teachers, our focus is on having our students enter public debate on any issue through a wide range of written documents. Thus, letters to the editor[2] and letters to elected officials are clearly a means by which students can participate in the public debate (a means they themselves often suggest), but so are written texts of speeches at meetings, blogs, campaign materials like political pins and bumper stickers, a policy paper at a web site, or even an issue brief for a local politician, plus an array of other documents by which individuals at varying levels of involvement in an issue may participate in the public sphere. Usually, too, we see that individuals who are heavily engaged in a high level of public debate on an issue do, indeed, use a wide variety of writing to make their stances public, and they stick with an issue over time, seeking enough momentum for their issue so that

---

2. We are aware of the reservations in the discipline about letters to the editor. Not only does Gary Olson call such assignments "simplistic . . . assignments of the past" that could be effective but more often than not are completed simply to meet class requirements (in Weisser, *Moving Beyond* . . . x, 94). Welch also labels them as "stultifying" (475). Herzberg calls them "hollow" assignments ("Service Learning" 397). On the other hand, Medeiros has found that letters to the editor are one of the genres members of activist groups use to enact citizenship and foster social change; perhaps we should reconsider how we might use them in a public writing course in a way that is effective, that isn't simplistic, that isn't stultifying, and that isn't just another assignment students complete to pass the course.

it may be resolved through legislative or administrative action, and not expecting that one piece of writing or one act of publicity is enough to bring a widely debated issue to closure. Indeed, from a public sphere perspective, the true purpose of their writing is to insure that their issue attains a high level of publicity.

From the perspectives of the WPA and the writing teacher, this view of publicity means that there are multiple ways for a class to be engaged in the political public sphere. At a simple level of publicity, even a one-time personal public statement like a letter to the editor is a form of writing for engagement if—*if*—it genuinely adds to the public debate on an issue, *if* it is sent to a publication that is likely to publish the letter, and *if* that publication is part of a political public sphere in which that personal public statement is likely to have some consequences for the individual. However, as the public sphere model of participation suggests, generating one piece of public writing hardly signifies as engaging in publicity on an issue. Instead, public writing on an issue should demand multiple acts of publicity on an issue, including engaging with different kinds of audiences through different kinds of writing that, if published, become part of the public debate on the issue. For example, the student who sends out a letter to the editor on a selected issue should also do extensive research to generate a policy paper or an issue brief for publication (at least for circulation among appropriate officials or concerned individuals). At the same time, the student might also maintain a blog or respond to other's blogs on the same issue, while also locating and writing a speech to a sympathetic organization, activist group, civic organization, or local board that might actually offer a venue for oral presentations. Importantly, such acts of publicity should not always be to like-minded audiences, but should reach across lines of difference, sometimes seeking to create dialog and response and sometimes seeking to bring an issue to closure.

In a more service-learning mode, students may engage in public writing while working with an activist organization dedicated to a particular cause that is of concern to them. Students may also have opportunities to write a variety of documents that contribute to the public debate on an issue when they participate in an internship with a public service organization or legislative body or even with a newspaper or other publication, as long as these venues bring students into contact with like-minded audiences and with those who hold different stances, identities, and values.

Within one writing class, instructors may offer an array of opportunities centered on writing for engagement in the political public sphere. As we have explained, the class on public writing we are describing, which is taught by Linda Shamoon, is thoroughly shaped by concepts of publicity and communicative interaction. One main goal of the course is for students to use their writing to gain access to and participate in a local political public sphere in order either to raise and address a local public on a problem or issue, or to participate in the already on-going public debate.

The syllabus for Shamoon's course follows this sequence. Students identify an issue of concern to them and others in a local public sphere, and they identify actual publication sites and audiences that would welcome their writing on that issue. Such venues include local newspapers, blog sites, organizational newsletters, web pages, or meetings of those organizations where they may be able to make an oral presentation or speech. As we move through the semester together, students are challenged first to develop short personal position statements on their selected issue. They then form into "activist" groups for collaborative in-depth research and writing, again aimed at developing documents that could actually be submitted for local publication. Their research includes interviews with those in the community who hold a variety of experiences and stances on the issue, reading, and even conducting surveys (if possible) of those affected by the issue. In addition, they conduct an analysis of where their issue is in terms of its publicity. Has the issue attracted any amount of public debate, is it already widely debated, or has it attracted the attention of elected leaders or administrators who are proposing ways to take action and resolve the issue? This kind of analysis prompts students to identify those publics that need to be drawn into the public debate if the issue is to achieve a momentum for change, and it helps students think strategically about how to interact with a selected public—through which genre and publication site—for the purposes of securing their allegiance to the issue and their participation in the public debate.

Within such boundaries, students have pursued a wide array of issues, including issues like an effort to end the practice of euthanasia of feral cats in a town's animal shelter, or an effort to promote the development of a wind turbine on campus to provide electricity for one academic building, or an effort to initiate an investigation by a university-town coalition into the leases given to students for rental property in the town. Not all students in this class manage to get their writing into a local political public sphere, but many do. Most send their letters to newspapers and elected officials, some deliver speeches to like-minded organizations or local boards, others post their longer documents on appropriate internet sites or place them in the hands of appropriate committee members and officials. Even those who do not succeed in entering the political public debate on their issue through their writing (or speaking) do participate through their research activities.

By the end of the semester, most students dramatically deepen their understanding of their selected issues, and they appreciate how the concept of publicity can strategically guide their communicative interactions with others as they work to raise public debate on a local public problem and seek a legislative solution. Students certainly come to understand that their initial personal public stances were insufficient to account for or to respond to the range of experience and stances among the many other individuals who are also affected by the problem. Almost all students develop a more nuanced stance by actually by engaging in the give and take of public deliberation (or in the preparatory activities for that give and take). By the end of the semester most students also agree (or at least understand) that their issue should be widely debated among diverse publics before it is resolved through legislative or administrative decisions. Furthermore, students also understand that the process of publicity has to happen to create the momentum for social and political change and to mitigate the ability of powerful institutions or agents to dominate the available options to resolve the problem or to strike back against those who disagree.

WHERE DO WPAS GO FROM HERE?

We opened this essay with a scenario that portrayed the excitement one faculty member could have for a course in public writing and the understandable hesitation that a WPA might have in response to such a proposal. When a new course is proposed for a program, a WPA should always be concerned about its disciplinary integrity, its appropriateness for the program and for the institution, as well as the ability and interests of other writing faculty to support and teach the course. In addition, a course in public writing that requires students to get involved with political issues outside of the classroom and that draws on disciplinary materials germane to political science, philosophy and communication studies, should be of concern to WPAs. We believe, however, that WPAs should embrace public writing as an important offering in a program committed to writing for engagement. Through its emphasis on involvement in public deliberation, the course offers students a chance for a special kind of writing for engagement that is sometimes not available through other writing for engagement courses, and it helps students gain political agency, which is so crucial to them, our communities and our democratic society. Furthermore, we know that if the course is framed appropriately, most of the problems intimated by the scenario can be avoided.

Among the most urgent of the concerns hinted at in the scenario is the question of disciplinary integrity, a question that raises the issue of sustainability within the writing program, on the one hand, and the issue of approvability beyond the program, on the other hand. Within the writing program, WPAs want to make sure that the course really represents program interests and directions, and that enough faculty embrace the class so that it may be offered consistently. In addition, most WPAs do not want to institute a course that is so specialized only one faculty member can teach it or that one faculty member "owns."

A public writing course based on publicity and communicative interaction like we've described has full disciplinary integrity and is absolutely appropriate for a program committed to writing for community engagement for both disciplinary and practical reasons. First, students' engagement outside the classroom is a defining element of the class. Second, public writing is derived from public sphere theory, which is one line of disciplinary inquiry pursued in composition journals and scholarly books. Third, the course's core activities are writing activities usually combined with rhetorical and discourse analysis and genre study.

In a practical mode, while the framework for the course is highly theoretical, the syllabus and lesson plans are faculty friendly. The course does not require scholarly expertise on a particular topic or public problem. Any faculty member can bring a particular issue to the course, *if* the issue chosen by the faculty member is recognized as a problem in an available local community and *if* the issue invokes a sense of urgency for both the faculty and the students. On the other hand, the students and teacher, together, could decide the topic and the teacher can be a co-learner, or individual students or small groups of students can decide the issues they want to pursue, as they do in Shamoon's class. In this way, the course is not "owned" by any one faculty member.

Another reason our model of public writing is sustainable is because it inevitably involves two areas familiar to many composition faculty, namely genre and rhetoric. During the course, students write in an array of genres most of which writing teachers know, letters to the editor, argumentative essays, informative articles, web pages, blog posts, press releases, flyers, and so on. In addition, each document written should be aimed at a particular public, a demand which calls for familiar rhetorical analyses of audience and purpose. Furthermore, the publicity framework lends a sequence to the writing assignments. Students start by researching and analyzing their issue in the context of its publics: Who is currently part of that public? Who still needs to be drawn into the public debate to achieve a momentum for change? Students then work with the genres that help them engage in the real debate occurring in the community.

With respect to sustainability, however, public writing raises another question: what about faculty who are hesitant to support or teach such a course because they believe it is too political or is promoting a particular kind of radical politics? A public writing course by its defining principles is political, but it does not promote or presuppose a stance on any particular issue, nor is it focused on politics as protest—although protest activities might occur, depending on the issue and community circumstances. However, a public writing course based on publicity focuses on writing for public deliberative purposes—to broaden the amount of public discourse about an issue, to draw a wide variety of people into concern for the issue and debating a preferred solution, and through those means to effect social and political change. Thus, even those faculty who do not engage in organized political activity themselves should be able to appreciate the broadly democratic nature of the class, and, perhaps, to trust their own ability to guide students' selections of relevant issues, to direct students' research on the publicity of their issues, and to help them strategize about appropriate genres and publication sites.

Issues of disciplinary integrity beyond the writing program raise their own set of questions. In particular, could such a course be ushered through the approval process? As we know, writing courses are sometimes a lightning rod for criticism. A curriculum committee may object to a public writing course because it does not seem to focus on the "basics," or because it may seem to overlap or call for an expertise in political science or other disciplines. However, we believe a public writing class based on publicity is easily approvable. By sharing the syllabus and disciplinary materials, WPAs can confidently show others that the course is a *writing* class and has elements of rhetoric, discourse analysis and genre study. Furthermore, since the course aims to have students use their writing as everyday citizens and work within the normative political spectrum of open and free debate on difficult social issues, the course may supplement lessons from other disciplines like communications studies and political science. Finally, because students are writing for actual publication and real audiences, they and their teacher may well pay extra attention to the basics—to correctness and clarity. We have found that students actually take their writing more seriously when writing for the "real world."

However, sustainability is not a WPAs only concern. Scalability raises another set of questions. How many sections of public writing should a program offer? Is public writing best seen as one among a number of offerings in a writing program or can it be means of expanding the program through the offering of many sections and variations?

Obviously, a course in public writing could be one course among many in any writing program that offers courses beyond the basic level, such as in a program that offers specialized second semester writing courses or advanced courses. We also think that public writing should be part of a menu of offerings in programs focused on writing for engagement or in programs that focus on any of these specialties: rhetoric, argumentation, American studies, critical studies, and literacy.

At the same time, public writing can be more than one course among many. Public writing can be the mode to which other writing courses are adapted. Argument, rhetoric, community-based writing, and issues-based writing could easily be adapted to our public writing model. For example, a class in argument or applied rhetoric adapted to public writing could ask students to focus on local issues, on local publics and on ways to expand the publicity of an issue. A course in American studies could follow Weisser's model of close-up historical study of public discourse on one issue as preparation for students to enter into that discourse. In addition, a public writing course could be paired with courses in other departments to enhance and supplement the learning in both classes. Natural pairings include Political Science; Communication Studies; American Studies; Sociology; Social Psychology; Environmental Science and variants like Marine Science; Women's Studies and similar classes like Peace Studies, African American Studies, and Latino Studies.

Nevertheless, we do not see public writing as adaptable to all courses or as driving the growth of a whole program. Technical, professional, and academic writing, as well as creative nonfiction, for example, tend to be very situation- and/or genre-specific and may be weighed down with too many demands and expectations inside and outside of the writing program. But in a program committed to writing for engagement, public writing should be a crucial, maybe even required, course. As we have argued earlier, public writing provides a kind of writing for engagement that is too often intimated but not experienced in other forms of community-based writing classes.

In the final analysis, even if a WPA believes that public writing has disciplinary integrity, is sustainable and may be appropriately scaled, the WPA may encounter institutional or administrative resistance. After all, the course requires students to engage in political action off campus. This is a legitimate concern. Students who take up a cause outside of the classroom may see themselves as acting on their own concerns and expressing themselves as individuals, but others within the organization and beyond, such as a deans, other administrators, or the neighbors see these students as inevitably "representing" the institution, not by speaking for the institution but by being a member of it and being associated with it. Thus, the students' activities do redound to the institution, for better or for worse. Furthermore, if the student is trying to take action against the institution, then the institution could respond in an exercise of power that can be alarming.

In response, we acknowledge that writing for social and political change can be risky, and while we cannot offer a guarantee that difficulties will not arise, if students have followed the steps and options available through a course based in publicity, they will not be campaigning alone, they will have anchored themselves with likeminded others in the community. They will have explored all kinds of ways of working for change. If students are working in that responsible manner, the institution can take pride in their courage and commitment.

REFERENCES

Bickford, Donna and Nedra Reynolds. 2002. Activism and service-learning: Reframing volunteerism as acts of dissent. In *Pedagogy: Critical approaches to teaching language, literacy, composition and culture* 2(2): 229-252.

Bohman, James.1996. *Public deliberation: Pluralism, complexity, and democracy.* Cambridge MA: MIT Press.

Campus Compact Website. Campus Compact. www.compact.org/ (accessed 3 October 2008).

Deans, Thomas. 2000. *Writing partnerships: Service-learning in composition.* Urbana, Illinois: NCTE.

Ervin, Elizabeth. 1997. Encouraging civic participation among first-year writing students; or, Why composition class should be more like a bowling team. *Rhetoric Review* 15 (2): 382-399.

————.2003. *Public literacy.* 2nd ed. Boston: Longman.

The Ginsberg Center. Division of Student Affairs. University of Michigan. *ginsberg.umich. edu/.* (accessed 10 October 2008).

Habermas, Jürgen. 1989. *The structural transformation of the public sphere: An inquiry into a category of bourgeois society.* Cambridge: MIT Press.

Herzberg, Bruce. 1997. Community service and critical teaching, in *Writing the community: concepts and models for service-learning in composition,* ed. Linda Adler-Kassner, Robert Crooks, and Ann Watters, 63-75. Washington, DC: American Association for Higher Education.

_____. 2000. "Service learning and public discourse. *Journal of Advanced Composition* 2: 391-404.

Mathieu, Paula. 2005. *Tactics of hope: The public turn in English composition.* Portsmouth, NH: Boynton/Cook.

Spigelman, Candace. 2004. Politics, rhetoric, and service-learning. *WPA: Journal of the Council of Writing Program Administrators* 28 (1-2): 95-113.

Ward, Irene. 1997. How democratic can we get?: The Internet, the public sphere, and public discourse. *JAC: A Journal of Composition Theory* 17 (3): 365-380.

Weisser, Christian. 2002. *Moving beyond academic discourse: Composition studies and the public sphere.* Carbondale: Southern Illinois UP.

_____. 2004. Public Writing and Rhetoric: A New Place for Composition. In *The private, the public, and the published,* ed. Barbara Couture and Thomas Kent, 230-248. Logan, Utah: Utah State UP.

Welch, Nancy. 2005. Living room: Teaching public writing in a post-publicity era."*College Composition and Communication* 56 (3): 470-492.

Wells, Susan. 1996. Rogue cops and health care: What do we want from public writing? *College Composition and Communication* 47 (3): 325-41.

11

COMING DOWN FROM THE IVORY TOWER
Writing Programs' Role in Advocating Public Scholarship

Dominic DelliCarpini

*While there still is, and probably always will be, a particular class
having the special business of inquiry in hand, a distinctively
learned class is henceforth out of the question. It is an anachronism.
Academic and scholastic, instead of being titles of honor, are becoming
terms of reproach.*

John Dewey, *The School and Society*, 1907

*The term "ivory tower" designates a world or atmosphere where intel-
lectuals engage in pursuits that are disconnected from the practical concerns of everyday life. As such, it has a pejorative connotation, denoting
a willful disconnect from the everyday world; esoteric, over-specialized,
or even useless research; and academic elitism, if not outright condescen-
sion by those inhabiting the proverbial ivory tower. In American English
usage it ordinarily denotes the academic world of colleges and universities, particularly scholars of the humanities.*

"Ivory Tower," Wikipedia, 2007

Ideally, scholarship can serve both academic and civic interests; yet in
an American culture of persistent anti-intellectualism, going public is
no easy task for those of us in academe—as predicted by John Dewey
and as eerily fulfilled by the public sentiment expressed in Wikipedia
exactly a century later. Writing programs that seek to invest students
in the public goals of writing cannot help but be wary of the double
bind we face: When we concern ourselves only with "academic" matters,
we are seen as disconnected from other publics—as "anachronistic,"
"esoteric," "useless," and "elitist." But when we refuse to build our programs on narrowly "academic" matters, and instead contextualize writing pedagogy within larger civic and social goals, we are often attacked

as politicizing the classroom and being neglectful of our "real" jobs[1]—
teaching right grammar and offering writing skills easily transferrable to
future classes and to the workplace. The degree to which writing programs complete that utilitarian work has increasingly become the public's measure of success in a time when the Department of Education
has expanded its concerns from K-12 to K-16 education and when the
National Commission on Writing has dubbed writing "a ticket to work—
or a ticket out." If writing programs are to venture from the familiar
environs of the ivory tower to enter into the vagaries of the larger polis,
how, then, are we to respond to public sentiment that sees the necessarily political work of civic engagement as somehow extraneous to the
work of "teaching writing?"

Furthermore, we should recall that writing programs that venture
into those public geographies are not doing so alone; we take our
students, and their writing, with us. And our students face an equally
tough audience out there. After all, the long-standing town/gown
divide has suggested that not only the professoriate, but the students
who people our ivory tower, are neglectful—perhaps even injurious—
to the surrounding community.[2] Like the professoriate, college students are often treated as elite members of a world that is isolated
from the day-to-day lives of the cities and towns that contain those
institutions. In a time when advancing one's professional standing is
the primary reason for attending college, when the media amplifies
each campus scandal, and when younger generations are already seen

1. Not only the very public attacks upon Linda Brodkey's "Writing about Difference"
   course at University of Texas at Austin in 1990, but also the existence of sites like
   NoIndoctrination.org, a site created by parents of college students, continue to attack
   political *topoi* in classrooms as liberal indoctrination. This concern is addressed by
   Elizabeth Ervin, in her call for "publicism without partisanship." Noting that "'public' services and institutions such as schools are increasingly associated not only with
   waste, incompetence, corruption, and dependency, but also the soft paternalism of a
   quasicommunist nanny state," she describes a condition that can apply specifically to
   public perceptions of the "distinctively learned" class predicted by Dewey. By inviting
   her students to frame their writing within "interested publicism," she provides them
   with both motives and outlets for their writing.
2. The town/gown divide, as it affects not only faculty but students, is certainly not a
   new phenomenon. For a discussion of the history of this uneasy set of relationships,
   see Laurence Brockliss, Stephen D. Bruning, et al. and Loomis Mayfield. For a discussion of recent attitudes toward college students from community perspectives, see for
   example David Crary and S. L. Davidson. These sources were provided by one of the
   students enrolled in the first-year writing course described in this essay, Erica Robak, as
   part of her research into town/gown relationships; her historical study can be accessed
   through our class Wiki at *wrtifl.pbwiki.com*.

as disengaged from civic life, asking them to establish a public voice is no easy matter.[3]

This essay describes efforts by York College of Pennsylvania's first-year writing program that are designed to bridge this divide, engaging students in civic deliberations that ask them to consider their *future* roles as professionals and as citizens of the wider community through the lens of their *present* role as academics. That is, rather than accepting the dichotomy of "academic" versus "public" writing (and the concomitant narrative of a disconnected 'ivory tower"), our program has sought to legitimate the academic research and writing done in first-year composition as crucial preparation for the work of the larger polis. I first address the false choice that the academic/public dichotomy sometimes forces upon writing programs, arguing that accepting the frame of that dichotomy (that either a program is committed to teaching academic discourse *or* it is committed to public/civic writing) keeps us from claiming a space for academic writing *within* the larger polis. I then briefly describe a pilot course developed in conjunction with our Honors Program which helped students treat their academic research and writing as a way to consider the intersections among their roles as student, future professional, and citizen of local and national communities. Finally, I detail the larger programmatic changes that have led our program, and our students, to treat public writing as a culmination of academic research, rather than as a substitution for it.

REVISITING THE "CATEGORY MISTAKE" OF ACADEMIC WRITING

As should be evident from the introduction to this essay, one central premise informs the curricular decisions described here: Writing programs have an obligation not only to *teach* argument, but to *make* arguments. These arguments have two important audiences: The first audience is our students, whom we are helping to prepare for their current and future work as citizens. To them, we are arguing the relevance of academic, disciplinary research as a way of fulfilling their role as active (and activist) citizens, citizens that base their decisions on reliable information. And second, we speak to the publics that surround, contain, and fund our writing programs, publics that exist both within and outside of

---

3. The Center for Information and Research on Civic Learning and Engagement (www. civicyouth.org) provides a wealth of studies on attitudes of, and toward, recent generations, who are dubbed "dot-nets" by Scott Keeter, in reference to the technological saturation of their formative years.

our ivory tower; to them, we assert that the deliberations that go on in academe, and the products of those deliberations in academic writings, do in fact have both indirect and direct value to the larger community.

Perhaps even more pointedly, I suggest that curricular decisions are always already arguments—arguments that indicate to a variety of stakeholders what it is that we value (and, at least to some extent, what we devalue). As higher education undergoes an increasing degree of public scrutiny, paying attention to *all of the messages* that our curricula send to those stakeholders is even more central to the work of program administration. For example, consider the implicit message of Douglas Downs and Elizabeth Wardle, who argue that our claims to teach academic writing are a "category mistake." They assert that programmatic claims to teaching academic writing "beg the question" as to *which* "academic writing" we are claiming to teach amidst the various forms of writing that are used in disciplinary discourse communities. They also contend that

> when we continue to pursue the goal of teaching students 'how to write in college' in one or two semesters—despite the fact that our own scholarship extensively calls this possibility into question—we silently support the misconceptions that writing is not a real subject, that writing courses do not require expert instructors, and that rhetoric and composition are not genuine research areas or legitimate intellectual pursuits. (553).

This set of implied messages is clearly of importance to writing program administrators as we continue to seek legitimacy for our own discipline, our practices, and our research areas.

However, negating the public expectation that first-year composition prepares students for the academy also has the potential to send some unintended messages—not only about our work as teachers, but about our work as academics—to stakeholders both inside and outside of the academy. First, it can suggest that one key *raison d'être* of our work, preparation of students for the writing that they do in the academy, is an impossibility. But to what degree is this true? Downs and Wardle themselves acknowledge that "some general features of writing are shared across disciplines," and in particular, that academic genres share the "view of research writing as disciplinary conversation" (556). Though there is little doubt that we cannot "cover" all types of discourse in first-year writing, these other important purposes—such as helping students to see academic writing as a conversation into which they are entering—are glossed over a bit too quickly. Students entering college, like entrants to the dialogue described in Kenneth Burke's famous parlor metaphor, need guidance on how these conversations work and how they can become part of them. That role of first-year writing remains crucial and should not be abandoned in whole because it can be fulfilled only in part.

In light of the already negative views of the liberal arts/humanities, if we give up on this important, if imperfect, public purpose, it may say just the wrong things about us. To the larger public, denying this tangible purpose in favor of introducing students to our own discourse community (as Downs and Wardle suggest) can perpetuate perceptions of the ivory tower as filled with insular knowledge silos—only one of which we seek to call our own. Further, as Joshua P. Kutney notes in response to Downs and Wardle, there is no real evidence that learning about our discipline will transfer to an understanding of other disciplinary conversations, nor that it will encourage other types of disciplinary research. In short, claiming the "impossibility" of "teaching a universal academic discourse" (553) only has merit if we take that to mean teaching students how to *deliver* specific styles of academic discourse in ways that transfer directly across curricula.

Clearly, studies of knowledge transfer from first-year writing to other academic courses demonstrate that the portability of specific, disciplinary writing skills is shaky at best.[4] Even the authors of the WPA Outcomes Statement for First-year Composition felt it necessary, within each category of outcomes, to place responsibility upon teachers in all disciplines to complete this transfer by supplying more specialized understandings of discipline-based writing.[5] Our program, however, looks beyond narrow definitions of transfer that measure abilities in specific disciplinary writing, and instead aims at helping students transfer higher order academic habits (both as readers and as writers) to their role as active citizens. After all, giving up on the general concept of "academic discourse" might seem, to important stakeholders and to the wider public, like giving up on the category of the "academic" altogether. Instead, writing curricula need to resist definitions of "academic writing" that frame the work of scholarship as a set of closed *topoi* without public implication,

---

4. See, for example, recent studies of transfer by Wardle, "Understanding Transfer," Bergmann and Zepernick, and Dively and Nelms.

5. Each category of learning outcomes expected by the completion of first-year writing courses included in the WPA Outcomes statement is followed by a statement that "Faculty in all programs and departments can build on this preparation by helping students learn . . ." specific disciplinary techniques.

helping students embrace the role, and the responsibility, of the public intellectual. In fact, doing so is at the heart of both the liberal arts and rhetorical traditions. Further, holding on to the category of academic writing, rightly understood as a mode of learning and knowing, need not (as Downs and Wardle suggest) denigrate the role of rhetoric; to the contrary, it can resituate rhetorical processes as crucial to the types of structured deliberation necessary to both scholarly and public writing.

In sum, going public by abandoning our role as teachers of academic research and writing worries me for two reasons: 1) it further isolates us from other disciplines instead of demonstrating that rhetoric is embedded in all of them and 2) it subtly, but substantively, suggests that we agree that academic writing has no inherent value. The self-deprecation of the ivory tower can inadvertently affect our relationship with wider publics as well. For example, Ellen Cushman's landmark "The Rhetorician as an Agent of Social Change" challenges individual writing teachers—and perhaps writing programs—to act in concert with communities to avoid "overlooking" those communities from our ivory tower. While Cushman works hard to avoid devaluing the intellectual work of the academy, she still accepts the frame that applying "our theories" is a "top-down" rather than "bottom-up" articulation of the town/gown relationship (23-24). Accepting that frame, however inadvertently, solidifies the notion that intellectual work is not *real* work, originating instead from some higher (and so detached) perch atop the ivory tower. That is not to minimize the material realities of Cushman's argument that "the very power structure of the university makes it difficult to establish, and maintain, dialogue and solidarity" with its surrounding communities (19). But at the same time, the message that we may be sending about intellectual or "academic" work is that public depictions of the isolated or irrelevant scholar—especially in the humanities—remain accurate unless we tear down the ivory tower and instead deal with the "reality" that, according to Paolo Freire, "does not take place in ivory tower isolation" (qtd. in Cushman 11). This nearly automatic association of "ivory tower" with "isolation" is a frame that writing programs need to resist if we are to continue to value academic work.

Linda Adler-Kassner and Heidi Estrem also confront the seemingly isolated nature of academic writing, offering pedagogies that ask students to identify specific purposes and audiences for their work within wider communities as a substitute for the "monolithic research paper." In doing so, they overcome one of the key problems with the disconnected research paper by offering a public forum for multi-genre student writing through their now well-established "Celebration of Student Writing." Students in this program reported a new confidence in their research abilities, including increased dexterity in "using a variety of research sources" and in "using evidence and ideas from other sources in writing" (126). Perhaps even more telling in terms of the transfer of knowledge from FYC is the fact that over 80% of students "said that they believed the writing strategies emphasized in the course would help them in later courses" (126). But while the research-to-public-delivery method has similarities to the curriculum I describe below, using negative terms such as "monolithic research paper" already says things about the research methods of the academy that we might not want to say, and bypasses some of the positive values of ivory tower deliberations.

Together, Downs/Wardle and Adler-Kassner/Estrem seem to be responding to a similar problem, though providing very different solutions: that the academic research *paper*, at least as it exists in first-year writing, is a false category. And in many contexts, it can be. Most students, and many writing teachers, seem to believe that at best, the genre is one that is useful only in academe, and at worst, that it is a disposable genre whose use will wither away once collegiate research is completed. Giving in to these impulses to denigrate the genre of the "monolithic research paper," however, can have deleterious side effects: it can teach our students that the *methods* associated with academic research lack longer-term use; it can reinforce stereotypes of the ivory tower by suggesting that the types of essays that academics write are indeed only useful for those in the tower; and it can send a new generation of citizens, our students, out into the polis with that same set of beliefs.

Our curriculum is meant to mount different arguments: that academic research and disciplinary-based academic essays do in fact have value, and that it is important that educated individuals go public by using the expertise that they develop as they write in those academic genres. That is, it suggests that the first products of academic research, the academic essay and the disciplines it represents, are crucial heuristics, providing students with a process and format for writing whose methodologies are important for obtaining reliable results. By configuring research as an academic "exercise" and a form of "disciplined" thinking—in the most positive senses of those words—it suggests the value of the sustained and disinterested research that informs the peer review system of the academy as preparation for civic activism. The alternative—accepting the impossibility of teaching the methods of our own genre, academic writing—does not truly counter Dewey's concern about the "learned class"; instead, it subjects that class to possible erasure. Not only does this undermine our own interests as academics, but it also represents both civic and pedagogical irresponsibility on our part. In a time in which every special interest has its own "institute," paid experts whose work resembles the types of sophism decried by Plato, it is our civic responsibility to assert the importance of *disinterested* research and richer understandings of rhetorical deliberation for well-reasoned decision-making. In doing so, we can re-assert the importance of scholarly research as central to the work of liberal education: training future civic leaders. Our culture can ill-afford a new generation of students who rely upon the types of arguments created by partisan and corporate "research" or who define rhetoric as style without substance. After all, one only needs to look at recent historical events to see the effects of bad information upon civic decisions.

PILOT EFFORTS: ACADEMIC WRITING AS DELIBERATIVE RHETORIC

> *There's nothing about being an English Professor that exempts you from the normal obligations of citizenship. In fact, you have an increased obligation, because you know how to do research.*
>
> Elaine Scarry, *New York Times* interview

> *A popular Government, without popular information or the means of acquiring it, is but a Prologue to a Farce or a Tragedy or perhaps both. Knowledge will forever govern ignorance, and a people who mean to be their own Governors, must arm themselves with the power knowledge gives.*
>
> James Madison, Letter to John Jay

In 1997, Professor Elaine Scarry took it upon herself to investigate the possibility that the 1996 crash of Flight 800 off Long Island had been caused by electromagnetic interference (EMI) from military planes. Though her report's findings have been "considered extremely unlikely" by government authorities, they did have their effect, finding their way onto the first page of a NASA study of the effects of EMI. Why would a Victorian Literature scholar take on this unlikely task? The author of the *NY Times* article concluded that her work was based upon "an almost alarmingly well-developed sense of civic duty."

It is this connection between the ability to "do research" (even outside of one's comfort zone) and civic responsibility that our first-year writing program seeks to instill in students. Rather than treat scholarship as an autonomous or partitioned field of endeavor, our goal is to remind students that they are obligated as citizens to bring the scholarly habits that they are developing in college to bear upon a culture that relies upon solid and reliable information. That is the key connection which first our pilot programs, and then our larger programmatic efforts, have sought to establish: that academic writing and civic activism are not, as the negative depictions of the ivory tower suggest, mutually exclusive. To the contrary, our curriculum is meant to establish clear connections between students' academic learning and their civic obligations.

The need to reinforce scholarly habits of deliberation is driven by recent studies of civic engagement. Research by Zukin et al. has suggested that recent upswings in civic engagement among young people when measured by volunteerism have not been accompanied by a concomitant upswing in political engagement, i.e., the willingness to participate in the civic decision-making. Further, though levels of volunteerism continue strong when measured by percentages of citizens involved, the level of *sustained* civic and political action by individual citizens is less encouraging, and has in fact been called a "leaky bucket" by the Corporation for National and Community Service: Robert Grimm reports that though citizens continue to become involved in volunteer activities, more than 22 million (one in three) also dropped out of the volunteer efforts. The findings point out "how important it is for organizations that use volunteers to treat them as valuable assets, give them meaningful assignments, and use best practices in volunteer management." Though this study points to the responsibilities of the *organizations* to engage volunteers in "meaningful assignments," I would suggest that it also indicates the need for *participants* to come to the organizations with deeper expectations and knowledge—not merely to fulfill a pre-existing role in a pre-existing organization. After all, full engagement comes from believing that one can make a significant contribution through the use of one's unique knowledge and talents. As such, civic engagement, as our curriculum has sought to define it, involves the use of deliberative abilities that are at the heart of both political and rhetorical engagement.

The pilot course we developed was meant to give students the motive and the tools to use their own talents, goals, and academic interests to spur this deeper level of civic engagement. That is, we were more interested in developing students' habits of mind than in measuring the number of hours they spent in community activities, believing that sustainable public service would follow from deeper intellectual engagement. The pilot course was offered to our Honors Program students, and was team taught by myself and the coordinator of our Information Literacy Program.[6] We began by developing a course theme that would ask students to consider, in ways that would be meaningful to them, the relationship between the privileges and the responsibilities that came with their status as college students; and it acknowledged the real and potential problems that exist when the ivory tower interacts with the larger polis. In this way, as noted in the introduction, we were able to show why we as professors and they as students were facing similar divides from the larger community. To that end, our course was described on our syllabus as follows:

> Our course theme this semester is a question: In what ways can an institution of higher learning become a productive element of the community within which it is situated? In this course, we will be using writing as a way to explore both our collective responsibilities as a college and your individual responsibilities as a citizen of this college and this city. As such, we will explore topics that bring together our goals as individuals and our responsibilities as citizens of the various communities to which we belong—civic, professional, and private. We will act as a community of scholars, relying upon critical thinking, reading, and responsible research to inform our ideas and our writing. And by "scholar," as we'll discuss, we mean a person who values reliable, credible, and relevant information as the means to decision making and acting as a productive citizen.

The curriculum was specifically designed to exercise key tenets of deliberative rhetoric by creating not only a community of citizens, but also a community of *scholarly* citizens.[7] While the immediacy of town/gown relationships helped students base their work in actual *kairotic* occasions,

---

6. The Information Literacy program at York College provides students with skills recommended by the American Library Association for "finding, evaluating, and incorporating information." The course description can be found at *www.ycp.edu/library/ifl/etext/ethome.html.* Results of our pilot course are detailed in DelliCarpini, Campbell, and Burkholder.

7. This approach to scholarly community is similar to that of Stephen Fishman and Lucille Parkinson McCarthy who forward a model based in Dewey's "cooperative inquiry" opposed to the concept of the "contact zone."

our larger goal was to encourage them to treat disciplinary, academic scholarship as a key methodology for addressing civic needs. The curriculum was also designed to encourage students to treat their available contributions to civic life as a function of their own areas of projected and actual expertise, drawing upon concepts discussed in John Dewey's pragmatism, which treat one's "occupation" as "a life's work" rather than merely a way of making a living.[8]

To engage students, we broke down the larger issues related to the separation of the academy from its environs into a more local and manageable one—how *our* academy and *our* town interacted, how (and why) it didn't, and how we might deliberate upon deficiencies and possibilities. We began the course with two central, shared points of inquiry: "What is the responsibility of a college, its professors, and its students to its surrounding community? How can what we do here and now help to serve those responsibilities?" Though the first question led to a great deal of speculation and discussion, it was in fact the second question that was the most difficult—and in the end, the most productive—largely because it required students and their teachers alike to define what it is that "we do here." We spent quite a bit of time contemplating that question at the outset. And the answer to that question was, in short, this: we *deliberate* here. Focusing upon the importance of the scholarly setting as a place of disinterested deliberation provided many key connections between rhetorical processes, research, and action/activism. Since deliberative rhetoric attempts to persuade others to take necessary action, its intent was to move students beyond the belief that civic engagement meant participation in already-existing service programs, and instead to use their academic learning and research toward proposing actions upon which the college and community ought to be collaborating. It also reinforced the notion, as noted in the syllabus materials, that "we will ourselves act as a community of scholars, relying upon critical thinking, reading, and responsible research to inform our ideas and our writing." That is, rather than see the ivory tower as isolationist, it treated the protected space of the academy as fruitful—as a pre-condition for doing *motivated* research that was at the same time *disinterested* (in the positive senses suggested by sound research methods). Academics, we told them, are cranky—but cranky for important reasons.

---

8. For a full treatment of this Deweyan pedagogy as translated into classroom practice, see my *Composing a Life's Work: Writing, Citizenship, and Your Occupation*

Rather than frame academic research in ways that accepted the Wikipedia view of such work as detached (an attitude we might inadvertently portray when we accept academic writing as a "category mistake"), we worked explicitly to show why withdrawing for a time from the vagaries and special interests of the larger polis can in fact breed better, more reliable, results, framing the processes of academic research as follows:

> Academic research papers teach you very important skills; but when the process is a mechanical one, one that does not fully engage you in real problem-solving, your work is not as effective as it could be. As we see it, research is not a mechanical process by which you produce "a paper with 6-8 sources" that you incorporate into your paper, sometimes in very superficial ways. Research is a process that begins with curiosity (a desire to know more or to solve a problem) and ends with the writing of an essay that would interest others, and that you feel would benefit them in specific ways. So in this period of the course, it is your job to find a topic that you sincerely care enough about that you'll want to educate yourself (and others) on by using methodologies that allow you to obtain reliable results.

While this description tries to motivate the processes of academic research in ways that overcome more superficial versions that are deeply engrained from secondary education, in hindsight, it is clear that it still begs key questions about the value of the product: the academic essay itself as a genre. This is a crucial question because charges of elitism, I suggest, may stem not only from anti-intellectualism, but from the roots of a specifically American anti-intellectualism. Simply stated, citizens of a country whose *ethos* is so centrally democratic and pragmatic have put to us a question about academic genres that sounds something like this: Aren't specialized, scholarly essays meant largely for a closed circle of experts in the ivory tower, in effect, anti-democratic? Our programmatic answer: yes and no.

The genre of the academic essay becomes anti-democratic when it becomes a parody of itself. What I mean by "parody" occurs when academic essays, both in the hands of professional academics and in the hands of students who are doing their best to imitate what they see as the impenetrable language that academics seem to write, lose their true generic purpose. Conversely, the *prototypical* academic essay is not meant to be difficult for difficulty's sake; it is difficult because it is attempting to deliver arguments about complex concepts and content; and it is especially difficult for outsiders, since it engages in insider, disciplinary language. At its most useful, the academic essay forms a template for clear and "disciplined" thinking and allows disciplinary discourse communities to deliberate through the common grounds established by the preferred genre. This, of course, returns us to Downs and Wardle's argument about "which academic writing" we are claiming to teach in first-year writing, because stripped of its community of discipline-specific scholars, the academic genre certainly loses much of its purpose. The question then becomes, at the first-year level, if any of the generic conventions of "academic writing" (broadly understood) are worth retaining. The answer our course attempted to supply is this: we should retain only those facets of academic writing that have benefit for its audience. If the audience is, from the start, the wider public, then the academic essay can seem obsolete. However, if the audience is fellow student/ academics in whom we are attempting to nurture scholarly habits and from whom we are forming a scholarly community, then the academic essay can retain much of its importance. This is the reason why we treat the academic essay as a genre meant for those of us in our class's scholarly community; it is a chance to teach one another the rhetorical art of deliberation as a precursor to going public as experts whose ideas have been vetted.

FROM ACADEMIC TO PUBLIC GENRES: THE UNDERGRADUATE AS PUBLIC INTELLECTUAL AND ACTIVIST

Our pilot course accomplished the purposes of a pilot—it showed us many of the strengths and weaknesses of our plan. On the positive side, though our students were of course not yet ready for truly public roles as leaders, they were indeed "out there," interacting with members of the community in ways that showed the effects of their new knowledge. They were able to establish relationships with local businesspeople, community leaders, city council members, social service agencies, and other community leaders as they completed their primary research. For example, a political science major interacted with members of our City Council to consider a program through which Student Senate members would attend Council meetings; a sports management major worked with community athletic groups to consider whether our new sports and fitness center could contribute to a more fit community; a psychology major developed potential programs to contribute to community mental health; and an education major developed possible shadowing programs to help urban youth better understand college life. What each of these topics had in common is that each proposed *new* possibilities for the community's deliberation, rather than merely participating in existing programs. This approach, we believe, nurtures a sustainable "activist" rather than merely occasional "volunteer" mindset. (See our class Wiki to view the work of class members at (*wrtifl.pbwiki.com/*). But as we moved from the pilot course to programmatic revisions of our curriculum, we became aware that our class theme was too limited and limiting—students grew tired of linking all our work in the course to the problem of town/gown relationships. We knew that such a theme could not work on a programmatic level, as it would not only limit various teachers, but it would flood the community with first-year students seeking access to information from community leaders. As such, as our new curriculum was devised, we abandoned the idea of a course theme in favor of asking students to develop research topics based upon their own majors and/or areas of interest as they impacted the greater good of various communities.

One of the successes of the pilot program, conversely, was the use of oral presentations and discussions delivered by students as they proposed research topics, which became a required feature of our revised curriculum instituted in fall 2007. Students, we found in the pilot program, had learned a great deal about deliberation through their oral reports, which provided a forum that forced them to defend, and in many cases rethink, the potential efficacy of their proposals. These class dialogues demonstrated the value of this limited public sphere, geographies within which academically *insulated* but not *insular* discussions could take place.

To encourage such scholarly discussions, students in all sections of our Academic Writing course are required to present their proposed area of research to the class (after they have done initial research), simulating scholarly practices of first a conference-type presentation (from which they could gather feedback from their peer group) before writing a paper that incorporated those suggestions, caveats, and limitations. This part of the course was once again designed to demonstrate to students the value in the processes of academic, scholarly research and deliberation, as expressed in our curricular materials:

> Researchers rarely work in isolation. In fact, researchers in various fields gather regularly at conferences to present their work-in-progress and to

solicit the feedback of others on this work—feedback that can then inform continued research. Your oral presentation will give you the opportunity to present what you've learned about your topic so far and to get feedback from your classmates and teachers.

Students' 10 minute presentations, which are enhanced by visual components such as PowerPoint or handouts, are followed by about 10-15 minutes of discussion in which instructors and classmates are given the opportunity to question the plan for the paper and the validity and relevance of the sources. Instructors model for the students how to challenge the presenter in civil, but serious terms, helping students to see the value in the peer review process that informs scholarly work. Assessment of these reports was based upon:

- The clarity with which the presenter explained the topic and purpose
- The clarity with which the student explained his/her findings to date
- The student's ability to invite feedback and discussion, and to respond to questions
- The quality and usefulness of the students' visual aids

Class members are reminded that, since the quality of the discussion following presentations affects the assessment of the presenter's oral report, they are obligated to provide serious and challenging feedback. And this spur, along with our modeling of deliberative methods, creates an environment within which challenging the assumptions and research methods of the presenter is considered helpful rather than rude.

But the key challenge that remained involved the genres of delivery. The oral presentations helped students to work within a (albeit idealized) polis—what Rosa Eberly, drawing upon Jurgen Habermas, has called a proto-public sphere and what John Dewey called a type of "laboratory" that transformed the scholastic space into a testing ground for civic deliberations. [9] And student's work in the pilot class's Wiki, rather

---

9. Eberly's concept of the "citizen critic" is based in the concept of an individual who "produces discourse about issues of common concern from an ethos of citizen first and foremost" (1) and discusses ways in which this *ethos* is nurtured in proto-public spheres. Susan Wells (338) also suggests that the classroom can be treated as a public sphere if it is preparation for more public writing. Dewey, drawing upon Charles Pierce, suggests

than existing in an isolated classroom space, made their work public, largely to each other but also to wider publics, since it was accessible via the web.[10] These features allowed for simulated public delivery largely within the classroom space. But the pilot version of the course also highlighted the need to bring academic research into a richer set of public forums if we were to complete a strong programmatic argument that defended the intellectual space of our ivory tower as preparation for full civic engagement. Thus, as we planned our new curriculum with the dual goals of scholarly research/writing and civic engagement, we remained keenly aware that if kept between student and teacher in our ivory tower, the work of the scholarly community was less likely to truly help students become active participants in civic discourses. To bridge this divide in the pilot course, we (much like Adler-Kassner and Estrem) felt the need to water down the genre of the "monolithic" academic essay in order to make it palatable for public purposes; to do so, we hybridized the academic genre with the genre of a proposal for civic action. But what we were left with was neither academic fish nor public fowl, serving neither audience particularly well. (After all, how many public genres feature citations and notes?) Still, we were not willing to throw the (academic) baby out with the bathwater, conceding that the work of scholarly writing could be bypassed altogether in favor of more palatable public genres; indeed, our pilot course demonstrated that the goals of the ivory tower and its commitment to research were not so divorced from civic action as Wikipedia might have it—and in fact, that the ability to do research brings further civic obligations, as the story of Elaine Scarry demonstrated. The activities of this course, conversely, demonstrated that positive civic action could be rooted in serious and purposeful research, in deliberation and contemplation, and in public purpose.

Our programmatic solution was to create a sequence of assignments that *first* asked students to produce a paper in academic format as part of their classroom community, and *then* to go through the process of

---

that this "laboratory habit of mind" be "every area where inquiry may fruitfully be carried on" (Dewey, "What Pragmatism Means" 100).

10. To accomplish both internal dialogue and external delivery, the class made use of a Wiki. We treated this standard form of Web 2.0 technology as a method of sharing work within our scholarly community and participating in public dissemination of the products of their academic research. Though this technology allowed us a limited form of "going public," its greater value was for internal dissemination of materials for the community of scholars within the class.

translating the knowledge they had gathered and vetted into a form that would be fully palatable for public uses. The academic essay itself was framed as a natural outcome of the course activities that preceded it, a moment to write up the results of an interactive process of scholarly research and dialogue with their classmates rather than a canned and isolated genre:

> The researched essay's main goal is to make an argument based upon the research conducted; it is not enough merely to report on that research. Since we'll have had many conversations about your research in advance of your writing the paper—in writing, conferences, and the oral presentation period—your purpose and argument should be relatively clear before you write your essay, though your opinions and directions are likely to change somewhat as you interact with class members.

By framing the research paper as an argument—and by using activities such as the oral presentations that keep the element of argument in play throughout the process of scholarly writing—students were asked to consider the academic essay as the culmination of those discussions with their scholarly peers, who also represented the audience for those academic papers. As we attempted to frame it, scholarship is about working through ideas in disinterested but motivated ways, first within the ivory tower, and then going public with the results of those deliberations with that same academic public. We were quite pleased by the results as they reflected high levels of commitment to a topic/cause, public arguments that were bolstered by serious and accurate data, and confidence that the public presentation was the tip of an iceberg of further understanding. That is not to say that the students were true experts on their topic; but, as we told them, they were experts in that they likely knew a great deal more about their topic than most of the people who argued about it in the public. In that way, we suggested that *gnosis* indeed informed *praxis*, and that the process of scholarship informed *gnosis*.

The final assignment in our revised curriculum, which is variously dubbed the "alternative genre" or "public genre" assignment, supplied a solution to the either/or dilemma of public versus academic genres that forms the subject of this essay. It also served as a reminder to faculty in the program that the work we do as teachers also carries obligations, obligations related to our roles not only as intellectuals, but as *public* intellectuals. That is, not only did this assignment make a programmatic argument to our students and the public, but it served as a reminder to the professoriate teaching the courses that, as Scarry put it so aptly, "There's nothing about being an English Professor that exempts you from the normal obligations of citizenship." One such obligation is the preparation of deliberative citizens.

As such, we asked students not only to complete the act of scholarly deliberation, but to simulate the ways in which the fruits of academic research and discussion could then be transferred to a wider public. Our curriculum continues its argument with students:

> Scholarly research often also has public purposes—to solve a social problem, improve upon the work of an organization, help to build better communities, and so forth. In the "public genre" project, you will apply the expertise you have gained in your researched essay to public purposes by putting it into a form that best suits its rhetorical situation—its topic, purpose, and audience. After all, most public writing is not presented in the form of an academic essay (though informed public writing is bolstered by that kind of research).

This change in audience and purpose also asked students to consider genre amidst the possibilities of multi-modal composing. They were told on the assignment that:

> This assignment will give you the chance to mount a public argument based in the knowledge base of your scholarly research and discussions using the various media that are at the disposal of 21st century writers, and to use those media to serve a real social purpose. For some, the public genre might involve writing an op/ed piece for the newspaper; for others, it might mean constructing a website, blog, or wiki. If you have the know-how and the tools, you might develop a video presentation—a Public Service Announcement, for example. If you're more interested in paper texts, you might create a brochure. If you love visual presentation, a poster or an advertisement might be for you. The possibilities are very wide.

To reinforce the transfer of knowledge from scholarly to public purposes, students were asked to also produce a cover memo that described their process of making genre choices to fit the rhetorical situation, what they hoped their public genre would accomplish, and, perhaps most centrally to our goals, *how they used the rich learning facilitated by their academic, scholarly paper to inform the public genre*. This project was assessed by:

- The appropriateness of the genre to the purpose and audience

- Students' ability to employ the research from their previous project in ways that are palatable to a more public audience (but which still provide the key information)

- Students' creativity in developing this alternative genre

- Students' reflections on the project both in presentation to the class and in a cover memo describing their learning from the project.

- We have been, frankly, not only overwhelmed by the creativity that students showed in making the translation from scholarly to public genres, but by how that creativity has been bolstered by the production of their academic papers. Their creativity, rather than mere spectacle, reflected a deeper understanding of how the genre of delivery must not only suit the intended audience, but be undergirded by a body of knowledge of the topic that was developed through scholarly practices. Though the public genres included videos, brochures, websites, graphic novels, songs, lesson plans, poems, and many more formats, they all shared a common element: they were informed by earlier work within the processes of scholarship and peer review of the ivory tower.

CONCLUSION: THE PROGRAMMATIC ARGUMENT

If, in the end, our curriculum is making a programmatic argument, it is this: Amidst the various 21st century genres that exist, scholarly writing still provides enough value to both the academy and the larger polis that it warrants the time and effort of first-year writing programs. Rather than give up on the category of disciplinary/academic writing in favor of public genres, our programmatic efforts argue for the viability of building bridges between the two. Since writing programs interact with various publics within and beyond our campuses, this middle ground has real advantages for students and the programs that serve them. It can teach our students and our institutions that civic decision-making should be preceded by disinterested deliberation. It can provide students with both important tools for future academic research and an understanding of how that research can be reconfigured for the public good. [11] And it can fulfill civic obligations to educate active citizens while

11. In this, we have much to learn from Joann Campbell's historical study of the Mt.

at the same time suggesting to the wider public that the ivory tower is a space that is worth protecting for deliberations that serve the larger polis. Losing that protected space, that version of the ivory tower, would amount to an acceptance of a segmented world in which group ideologies taint—or even prevent—empirical research in favor of the vagaries of public opinion. Instead, our curriculum suggests that redefining what *we* mean by academic research and writing might be a more productive route, especially in a new media world in which the public intellectual has largely been displaced by the citizen journalist, to both positive and negative results.

The unfortunate side-effects of turning away from academic writing should not be underestimated. Doing so might be read by the public as a tacit acceptance that academic scholarship is self-indulgent and elitist, a perspective that is not only at the heart of the Wikipedia entry above, but also in attacks upon academe in many sectors of the media and public perceptions. That is, it would, at least to a degree, accept claims that research needs direct applicability and must be contained in perspicuous genres to have worth.

Thus, though we clearly need to consider the role of the scholar as public servant, we must also acknowledge the role of scholarship as a private act of inquiry, though never a cloistered one. Claims like that of Aaron Schutz and Anne Ruggles Gere that service learning is "unencumbered by disciplinary identity" (129) have merit; at the same time, they suggest that disciplinary identity can be an encumbrance. Though Schutz and Gere do in fact warn against any use of service learning that ends up "reinforcing ideologies and assumptions that we hoped to critique" (147) and do indeed provide models of service learning that are more engaged in communities as partners rather than merely bringing

---

Holyoke model, which offers a useful paradigm for considering how gender influences the purpose of academic work. In her study, she outlines two kinds of academic writing that existed in the mid 19th century: the male version that focused upon writing that demonstrated personal attainment of knowledge and participation in the learned world of "autonomous scholars," and the "culture of service" that demanded that women's writing also had practical purposes (while still valuing the goals of demonstrating one's abilities as an "autonomous scholar"). Since Campbell's study drew upon the academic atmosphere of a period in which what Dewey called a "distinctively learned class" still had cache—since college was still an elite affair, especially for men—this dichotomy was particularly pronounced. The female model, however, demonstrates school research can also reach fruition in service learning, and so overcome many of the problems associated with what Dewey called the disappearing "learned class" and the overall conception of the ivory tower as useless to the wider public.

a culture of unreflective "caring" to the work of service learning, their rhetoric retains an undertone of self-deprecation for the work of the academy that I have noted in other such depictions of our role. Such depictions tend to devalue positions of expertise in favor of positions of involvement; our curriculum suggests that neither is self-sufficient, and proposes instead that the ivory tower can inform, with genre translation, into the public sphere.

Our programmatic efforts also suggest that there is private value to students in retaining the category of the "academic" or "scholarly." As Nancy Sommers and Laura Saltz have suggested, students exposed to the rigors of academic research and deliberation benefit not only by their writing, but by the learning that accompanied their writing. And though they write as novices, and so lack full disciplinary expertise, these students are simulating and modeling expert discourse. As Sommers and Saltz note, "the enthusiasm so many freshmen feel is less for writing per se than for the way it helps to locate them in the academic culture, giving them a sense of academic belonging" (131). These students learned that a scholarly community is in fact a community, though one among many, in ways that Sommers and Saltz suggest: they write their way into expertise and they learn about the questions asked by various disciplines and the different sets of evidence used (134ff), with the key lesson of "learning to say something different than the source" (135). This type of learning can indeed inform active, activist citizens.

Further, in the use of the multi-modal approach to the public genre, the programmatic argument we are mounting acknowledges what Kathleen Yancey has called "a tectonic change" in literacy (298) and "a writing public made plural" (300). It has also helped us, as Yancey suggests, "think explicitly about what they [students] might 'transfer' from one medium to the next" (311). In our case, what we hope to transfer is academic rigor and methodologies, informed by disciplinary techniques, to civic work.

Living for a time in the ivory tower, then, can provide students the necessary expertise to go public with the knowledge base that informs the more narrowly rhetorical moment they have as academics. And finding and implementing the available means of persuasion within our program means finding solid, disinterested evidence within disciplinary communities and also finding appropriate genres for a public invested in multiple modes of delivery—not one or the other. In this sense, public genres provide an effective moment of civic engagement, while the research that precedes them dictates the reliability, and perhaps even the ethics, of that moment.

REFERENCES

Adler-Kassner, Linda and Heidi Estrem. 2003. Rethinking research writing: Public literacy in the composition classroom. *Writing Program Administration* 26 (3): 119-32.

Bergmann, Linda and Janet Zepernick. 2007. Disciplinarity and transference: Students' perceptions of learning to write. *Writing Program Administration* 31 (1-2): 124-149.

Brockliss, Laurence. 2000. Gown and town: The university and the city in Europe. *Minerva: A Review of Science, Learning and Policy* 38: 147-171.

Bruning, Stephen D. Shea McGrew, Mark Cooper. 2006. Town/gown relationships: Exploring university-community engagements from the perspective of community members. *Public Relations Review* 32: 125-130.

The Center for Information and Research on Civic Learning and Engagement. Available: *www.civicyouth.org/* (accessed 12 December 2009).

Crary, David. 2007. Study shows college kids growing more self-centered. *The Journal Times* February 26. Available: *www.journaltimes.com/nucleus/index.php?itemid=11122*

Cushman, Ellen. 1996. Rhetorician as an agent of social change. *College Composition and Communication* 47 (1): 7-26.

Davidson, S.L. 2007. Assessing university-community outreach. *Metropolitan Universities* 10: 63-73.

DelliCarpini, Dominic. 2005. *Composing a life's work: Writing, citizenship, and your occupation.* Pearson-Longman.

DelliCarpini, Dominic, Susan Campbell, and Joel Burkholder. 2007. Building an informed citizenry: Information literacy, first-year writing, and the civic goals of education. In *Information literacy collaborations that work*, ed. Trudi Jacobson and Thomas P. Mackey, 19-40. New York: Neal-Schuman.

Dewey, John. 1977. What pragmatism means by practical. In *Essays on pragmatism and truth*, ed. Jo Ann Boydston, 98-115. Southern Illinois UP.

———. 1958. *The school and society.* U of Chicago P.

Dively, Ronda Leathers and R. Gerald Nelms. 2007. Perceived roadblocks to transferring knowledge from first-year composition to writing-intensive major courses: A pilot study. *Writing Program Administration* 31 (1-2): 214-245.

Campbell, JoAnn. 1997. A real vexation: Student writing in Mount Holyoke's culture of service, 1837-1865. *College English* 59 (7): 767-788.

Corporation for National and Community Service. How do volunteers find the time? Evidence from the American time use study. July 2008. Available: *www.nationalservice.org/*

Downs, Douglas and Elizabeth Wardle. 2007. Teaching about writing, righting misconceptions: (Re)Envisioning "First-Year Composition" as "Introduction to Writing Studies." *College Composition and Communication* 58.4: 552-84.

Eakin, Emily. 2000. Professor Scarry has a theory. *New York Times Magazine* November 19, *query.nytimes.com/gst/fullpage.html?res=9506E3DA1138F93AA25752C1A9669C8B63.*

Eberly, Rosa. 2000. *Citizen critics: Literary public spheres.* Champaign: University of Illinois Press.

Ervin, Elizabeth. 2006. Teaching public literacy: The partisanship problem. *College English* 68 (4): 407-21.

Fishman, Stephen and Lucille Parkinson McCarthy. 1996. Teaching for student change: A Deweyan alternative to radical pedagogy. *College Composition and Communication* 47 (3): 342-365.

Kutney, Joshua P. 2007. Will writing awareness transfer to writing performance? Response to Douglas Downs and Elizabeth Wardle, "Teaching about writing, righting misconceptions." *College Composition and Communication* 59 (2): 276-79.

Mayfield, Loomis. 2001. Town and gown in America: Some historical and institutional issues of the engaged university. *Education for Health: Change in Learning and Practice* 14: 231-240.

National Commission on Writing. Writing: A ticket to work . . . or a ticket out: A survey of business leaders. *www.writingcommission.org/prod_downloads/writingcom/writing-ticket-to-work.pdf* (accessed 12 December 2009).

Schutz, Aaron and Anne Ruggles Gere. 1998. Service learning and English studies: Rethinking 'public' service." *College English* 60 (2): 129-49.

Sommers, Nancy and Laura Saltz. 2004. The novice as expert: Writing the freshman year. *College Composition and Communication* 56 (1): 124-49.

Wardle, Elizabeth. 2007. Understanding 'transfer,' from FYC: Preliminary results of a longitudinal study. *Writing Program Administration* 31 (1-2): 65-85.

WPA Outcomes Statement for First-Year Composition *http://wpacouncil.org/positions/outcomes.html* (accessed 12 December 2009).

Wells, Susan. 1996. Rogue cops and health care: What do we want from public writing? *College Composition and Communication* 47 (3): 325-341.

Yancey, Kathleen Blake. Made not only in words: Composition in a new key. *College Composition and Communication* 56 (2): 297-328.

Zukin, Cliff, Scott Keeter, Molly Andolina, Krista Jenkins, and Michael Delli Carpini. 2006. *A new engagement? Political participation, civic life, and the changing American citizen.* Oxford UP.

12

THE WPA AS ACTIVIST
Systematic Strategies for Framing, Action, and Representation

Linda Adler-Kassner

WPAs are often forced to make choices among an array of not particularly appealing options. Ann Feldman describes one such dilemma in the writing program she directs: Facing pressure to enact cuts that would, in part, preserve the 2-2 load taught by faculty (including Feldman), Feldman had to decide what case to pitch. Bigger classes? Large lectures with recitations? Cutting the second-semester research writing course? Ultimately, the program chose to "lower the ACT score that would allow more students to waive ... the first required course. This could reduce the number of students taking first-year writing courses," which meant that the English Department (and the program) could cut the number of writing sections offered, thus reducing costs (Feldman 2008, 88-89). Feldman's vignette illustrates the complicated choices facing WPAs. It raises questions with short- and long-term implications that are doubtless familiar: Who takes writing classes? What is the purpose of those classes in the university? Who teaches those classes and what is their status? The list goes on.

The responses that WPAs provide to questions like these comprise elements of larger stories about writing instruction. These stories lead to an identity for the WPA and/or the writing program that is developed over time within the local context of the institution. Across contexts, too, stories come to constitute an identity for our profession of writing instruction and our disciplinary identities as WPAs. These relationships come to exist within frames, which themselves lead to the perpetuation of particular ways of conceiving writing, writing instruction, and writers. As communication theorist Stephen Reese explains, frames are "organizing principles" that are constituted by and through individual and collective interpretation (Reese 2001, 11). Frames shape narratives, stories about "the way things are," which become linked to one another over time. For example, a story about what writers can or cannot do comes to be linked to one about what instructors do or do not teach, which then links to another about what schools do or do not do, and so on. Frames extend from the culturally-shaped signifiers associated with symbols, "code words" (Hertog and McLeod 2001, 139). As these code words are linked to greater numbers of meanings and concepts, they form increasingly elaborated structures—frames—that contain greater volumes of meanings and narratives (Hertog and McLeod 2001, 139-141; Lakoff 2004; Lakoff 2006). The greater the number of meanings and concepts within the frame, the more they reify dominant cultural values, becoming "commonsense" (see, e.g., Deacon et al 1999, 153).

One of the most pressing challenges that WPAs face in the current climate is figuring out just how to participate in this process of framing so that we can have some voice in—maybe even affect—the frames that surround stories about what writing teachers do, what students are, and what writing should be. As Mike Rose and Joseph Harris have separately noted, this requires us to step into public discussions in ways that might seem unfamiliar. (Rose 2006; Harris 1997). Elsewhere, I've called for WPAs to think of ourselves as activists of a kind for this work, borrowing from community organizers and media strategists who have long been involved in the work of shifting frames and changing stories (Adler-Kassner 2008). Their practices may enable WPAs to focus on one of the same activities that we so often stress to our students in our roles as writing instructors, that of making conscious choices among the various options that are available in communicative situations. Students' choices involve recognizing and choosing among the conventions they employ within various genres. Ours, too, involve making conscious choices when we navigate the tricky waters of discussions about curriculum, assessment, or any of the other issues that WPAs face on a regular basis. This choice-making involves understanding the ideologies surrounding the various options available and pursuing those options with a sense of their implications beyond our immediate actions.

Here, I'll focus on two of the big-picture choices that often exist at a level above the day-to-day ones that we face: Possibilities for personae that WPAs might enact should they decide to work on frame-changing, and potential ways that WPAs might develop alliances with others. Just as the genres and conventions that we talk about with students are suffused by the contexts, ideologies, and values of the communities in which they are situated, so the options for personae and alliance-building available

to WPAs are rooted in and reflect larger contexts surrounding education. The first step in exploring those choices, then, is to briefly explore
this context and the issues extending from it.

ANALYZING THE FRAME: HISTORICAL CONTEXTS FOR CONTEMPORARY DIALOGUE

Separately, linguists George Lakoff and Geoffrey Nunberg argue that
frame-changing must begin with a vision of what individuals, groups, or
causes *want,* not what they *do not want* (Lakoff 2004, 3; Nunberg 2006).
It's not enough, in other words, to focus on critique of what is not good,
useful, or important: to change frames, activist WPAs must put forward
alternative possibilities. Nunberg's and Lakoff's work, as well as Hertog
and McLeod's, also emphasizes that any vision of the possible must at
the very least take into consideration the broader frame that it reflects
(if not be situated within another frame entirely). For this reason alone,
WPAs who want to change frames need to understand the broad outlines currently surrounding stories about writing (and education), lest
we inadvertently perpetuate those outlines through stories that *seem* to
be alternative—but are not. For example: A WPA hears from her provost
that the campus would like to use the Collegiate Learning Assessment
to assess students' critical thinking and analytic writing. The frame surrounding such a decision could involve a number of stories (writing is
produced quickly, on demand and with little revision; the best expertise
on writing comes from outside of the campus; surface features are the
most important aspects of writing, and so on). The WPA responds that
a better assessment would be for faculty from other disciplines to assess
portfolios from the campus's writing courses.

While this alternative might seem more desirable, it also could perpetuate some of the same actions working against the interests of writing instructors and students. That's because both of these stories fall
within the same frame, one that says that the purpose of school is to
prepare students for participation in the democracy, which has shaped
conceptualizations of education from the mid-19th century forward.
This frame is rooted in an ideology most commonly associated with
the formative period around the beginning of the 20th century known
as the Progressive Era, and especially with the group of intellectuals
working during this period known as pragmatists. Progressive pragmatists believed that, as a nation, America was moving toward the achievement of a virtuous democracy, but that this progress was slowed by the

constant presence of instances when the nation encountered obstacles in the path of progress (referred to as declensions). But while these roadblocks seemed to interfere with the nation's progress, they were also important motivating factors for perpetuating it, as well. They forced Americans to gather their collective resources and develop new strategies, new methods, for overcoming these obstacles, thus contributing to the nation's collective wealth and furthering progress toward the virtuous democracy.

To participate in the collective action necessary for overcoming these obstacles, pragmatic Progressive ideology dictated that Americans needed to develop critical intelligence. This important quality, as they defined it, consisted of three essential characteristics: 1) the ability to engage in informed analysis and reflection; 2) the ability to demystify components of knowledge-making so that they are visible to all; and 3) the ability to apply processes of analysis, reflection, and demystification to declensions impeding the nation's progress toward virtuous democracy. The central purpose of education, then, was to foster the critical intelligence of the nation's young people in a controlled and structured environment.

But while Progressive pragmatists agreed that this intelligence was central to the development of American democracy, there was less consensus regarding how best to cultivate this quality, differences that were reflected in *approaches* to education. One group of Progressive pragmatists, referred to by historian Warren Susman as stewards, believed that all individuals had the capacity to be involved in this process of definition and management because each individual possessed the kernels of critical intelligence (Susman 1984, 90). Through education (as a form of communication), these kernels could be organically cultivated from within so that everyone could participate in the development of the democracy. In its ideal conception, this was a sort of utopian democracy of the critically intelligent people, all participating in the formulation and maintenance of collective community that was mutually beneficial to all, all invested in the nation's progress toward a virtuous democracy.

The other group, referred to by Susman as technocrats, believed that the development of critical intelligence was a more selective activity and that only certain individuals had the capacity to fully develop this important quality (Susman 1984, 90). Technocrats believe that those individuals should have the authority to manage systems and processes that would ensure the application of that intelligence to obstacles. Education was thus intended to sort out who was more and less suited for what kinds of development, to provide everyone with information about how to interact with information and intelligence managers, and to deliver educations appropriate to the roles that individuals were to occupy.

CONTEMPORARY IMPLICATIONS

While Progressive pragmatic ideology and questions about the purpose of education might seem remote to WPAs in the early 21st century, they are still very much with us. The stewardly and technocratic approaches outlined here imply different strategies for achieving a common goal. Specifically, they imply different responses to three key questions:

- What should students learn in school?
- Who should have the authority to determine that learning?
- What should be the relationship between both that learning and those doing the determining to the broader public?

Answers to these questions have implications for the larger issue of concern to Progressive pragmatists (and educators today, as well) that are illustrated in theorist James Carey's analysis of the relationship between communication and the broader idea of "democracy." "What we mean by democracy," Carey notes, "depends on the forms of communication by which we conduct politics. What we mean by communication depends on the central impulses and aspirations of democratic politics" (Carey 1997, 234). As the primary site where principles and values central to the development, perpetuation, and maintenance of American democracy are introduced to and cultivated in America's youth, education has long been understood as a key communicative practice (e.g., Dewey 1916). Using Carey's formulation, then, there is a dynamic tension between what is meant by "democracy" as the central principle through which America is imagined as a coherent, cohesive nation (Anderson) and "communication"—education—as the process through which principles and values central to the development and perpetuation of that democracy are maintained.

During the Progressive Era as now, these two approaches imply differences in the roles that schooling and teachers play in the development of the citizenry. Our field's scholarship, for instance, often reflects the stewardly idea that education is a central part of cultivating students' senses of themselves as citizens in a democracy. Tom Deans makes this case clearly in *Writing Partnerships* when he writes that:

> Throughout the history of U.S. higher education, service to the community - be it the local, national, or global community - has been integral to the missions of a wide range of colleges and universities, whether motivated by an ethic of public service, a mandate to extend research to the general public, or a commitment to particular religious beliefs.... Likewise ... [m]uch of our classroom practice is motivated by a commitment to prepare all students for reflective and critical participation in their personal, cultural, working, and civic lives. (Deans 10-11)

Mike Rose has long focused on a kind of circular relationship that exists around cognitive processes (developed by the individual within her culture), schooling, and the implications for culture of schooling processes, always with an eye toward broader implications, too. In "What We Talk About When We Talk About School" he suggests that:

> Safety, respect, expectation, opportunity, vitality, the intersection of heart and mind, the creation of civic space—this should be our public vocabulary of schooling—for that fact, a number of our public institutions. By virtue of our citizenship in a democratic state, we are more than economic and corporate beings. (Rose 2006, 423)

These examples, two among many, make the case that language education helps to prepare students for participation in democracy. Similarly, pragmatic Progressive conceptions of the development of critical intelligence stemming from the work of Dewey and other Progressive educators remain an influential paradigm in American schooling (e.g., Ozmon and Craver 1995, 149; Pulliam and Van Patten 2007, 48-49).

Elements of the technocratic approach to education are still present in contemporary discussions about education. They are reflected in concerns that educators (and school systems) no longer understand school's purpose, that the system has failed to fulfill its mission because it no longer understands the shape of the democracy and thus must be managed by experts who do understand that system. This narrative is everywhere in reports like *Ready or Not*, a document published by the American Diploma Project (ADP), an enormously influential group working to "reform" high school curriculum, that is aligned with Achieve.org and works in conjunction with the National Association of

Governors (among other partners). *Ready or Not* asserts that "The academic standards that states have developed over the past decade generally reflect a consensus in each discipline about what is *desirable* for students to learn, but not necessarily what is *essential* for them to be prepared for further learning, work, or citizenship after completing high school" (2006, 8). Among the recommendations in *Ready or Not* is the development of nationwide curriculum and national assessment; the report also intimates that in order to align secondary and post-secondary education, any assessment serving as the "ceiling" of secondary education could serve as the "basement" of post-secondary learning(2006, 15). It also asserts that since educators no longer understand the purpose of education (and the shape of the democracy for which it is preparing students), the "standards-based assessments" necessary for establishing these end- and beginning-points should be developed by external agents (for instance, ADP or ACT, another organization allied with ADP's efforts) who will have the authority to determine what students should learn. These are but brief illustrations of the contemporary manifestation of these narratives; however, they demonstrate the endurance of the stories that stem from them. While the Progressive Era may seem remote, our present situation is constructed in its long shadows.

CONSCIOUS CHOICE 1: HISTORICAL CONTEXT AND THE PERSONAE OF THE ACTIVIST WPA

These different approaches to the cultivation of critical intelligence also present some complicated implications for the personae that the activist WPA might adopt in order to enact decisions that reflect conceptions of democracy and education. A concern expressed by the editors of this collection in response to my proposal for it presents the opportunity to consider some of these issues. Bud and Shirley wrote to me, "We think it's especially important that reviewers of the proposal understand that you are discussing *strategies for activism on behalf of writing instruction and writing programs* (broadly defined) rather than *strategies for using writing programs as venues for activism.*" (Personal communication 12/17/07, emphasis added).

While I don't believe that Shirley and Bud intended their note to me to imply stark distinctions between two possibilities for enacting the dynamic tension between communication (including education) and democracy, I will take advantage of their language and repurpose it in order to explore these distinctions because they are important ones for WPAs to consider. These choices, too, are situated within the larger frame extending from the Progressive Era. It is useful, too, to understand that educators—WPAs—are not the only communicators engaged in processes of considering these choices. They are also central to discussions about (and debates over) the role of the journalist in contributing to and maintaining the democracy; their exploration in the literature of public journalism also highlights possible implication of these distinctions that are potentially useful for WPAs (and writing instructors) to extend to our own work.

In Carey's formulation, journalism (as another form of communication) and journalists also faced a choice extending from what are here identified as technocratic and stewardly approaches. The former, Carey says, came to constitute the dominant paradigm through which 20th century journalism developed, taking a shape that had concomitant implications for democracy. In this technocratic conception, journalism came to be understood as an entity that mediated between the powerful (primarily government) and the powerless (the citizenry). Journalists were to be "objective"—allied with neither interest, "conduits" of information from one to the other only—and media was to transmit, not cultivate, dialogue. Journalism and the press were thus:

> a true fourth estate that watched over the other lords of the realm in the name of those unequipped or unable to watch over it for themselves.... The truth was not a product of the conversation or debate of the public or the investigations of journalists. Journalists merely translate the arcane language of experts into a publicly accessible language for the masses" (Carey 1997, 245).

The "central weakness" of this approach, notes Carey, is that it systematically disempowered the citizenry, creating a system where citizens were "the objects rather than the subjects of politics" (Carey 1997, 246-247). The role of citizens in this conception, then, is to *react*, not to *act*, because they were positioned as "remote and helpless compared to the two major protagonists—government and the media" (Carey 1997, 250). More recently, civic engagement scholar Harry Boyte has referred to this model of participation as embodying "representative democracy," where citizens' roles are to select stand-ins who can advocate for their individual interests and citizens' responsibilities are to ensure the safeguarding of those interests (Boyte 2008, 1-2).

The alternative outlined by Carey and developed by advocates of the practice known as public journalism like Jay Rosen and Theodore Glasser outlines a different possibility. Here, journalism and journalists consciously acknowledge their roles as contributing to and participating in a public dialogue. Media scholar Jay Rosen, one of public journalism's most outspoken proponents, describes this conception in his "potential" definition of public journalism:

> Public journalism is an approach to the daily business of the craft that calls on journalists to 1) address people as citizens, potential participants in public affairs, rather than victims or spectators; 2) help the political community act upon, rather than just learn about, its problems; 3) improve the climate of public discussion, rather than simply watch it deteriorate; and 4) help make public life go well, so that it earns its claim on our attention. If journalists can find a way to do these things, they may in time restore public confidence in the press, reconnect with an audience that has been drifting away, rekindle the idealism that brought many of them into the craft and contribute, in a more substantial fashion, to the health of American democracy, which is the reason we afford journalists their many privileges and protections. (Rosen 1999, 22)

Here, "the task of the press is to encourage the conversation of the culture—not to preempt it or substitute for it or supply it with information from afar. Rather, the press maintains and enhances the conversation of the culture, *becomes one voice in that conversation,* amplifies the conversation outward" (Carey 1997b, 219). This vision of democratic action parallels Boyte's conception of a participatory democracy, which focuses on "rebuilding community, providing venues for citizen voice, and regenerating concern for the common good" (Boyte 2008, 1). While participatory democracy includes a broader and more active role for individuals in conceptualizing and coming together in collective action, it nevertheless also still implies direction by a technocratic elite who identify "problems" and orchestrate action to address those issues.

Again, while I don't believe that Bud and Shirley meant to imply that "acting on behalf of writing instruction and programs" was akin to the more passive and technocractic roles for the citizenry in Carey's and Boyte's notions of journalism and citizenship, their language becomes a useful device for exploring the possibilities for personae that activist WPAs might adopt in their attempts to change stories about writing and writers. If WPAs see the act of reframing as something done *on behalf of writing and writers* by a WPA, writing instructor, or a writing program, this choice *could* hearken a more technocratic approach where the WPA is seen as a member of an elite corps, better qualified and/or in a position of greater power to take action than others. This personae could be akin to the conception of the elite actor that has its roots in the Progressive pragmatic vision of technocratic action implied in what Boyte calls "representative" democracy and has been developed through the emergence of an academic culture that positions successful players as "mobile individualists" (Boyte 2008, 4) whose responsibilities are to act for themselves in alliances with others whose individual interests parallel their own, but do not necessarily share or form action rooted in a sense of the collective.

Alternatively, positioning ourselves as mediators or conduits in the academy—say, between students and administrators—might echo the same role that Carey outlines for journalists who see themselves as part of the "fourth estate," with the same mostly powerless positioning of students as that of the citizenry in Carey's formulation. Certainly, there is evidence in the WPA literature that this role is pragmatically necessary, too, as Richard Miller's work attests regarding the necessity for survival strategies within larger bureaucratic organizations (Miller 1998). Finally, as teachers and researchers who are grounded in a research-based tradition of best practices, we could certainly make the case that we *are* more informed and that our academic degrees (and positions as WPAs) qualify—even require—us to act "on behalf of writing instruction and writing programs."

To be sure, there are many reasons why it is not only a good idea, but in many instances strongly advisable, for WPAs to primarily inhabit a role that extends from these technocratic-tinged approaches to the cultivation of critical intelligence. The commandment for teacher-researchers to separate values (or "politics") from their work in the classroom or in scholarship is virtually sacrosanct, emerging straight from the pragmatic Progressive idea that neutral methods, not value-affiliated content, is the key to investigating problems and generating new knowledge. This is the scholar researcher who is engaged in research that can be replicated, aggregated, and disseminated (Haswell 2005) and that serves as a basis for action on behalf of the writing program. This personae is also an extension of the researcher that was developed in and through the work of Progressive pragmatists, who sought to develop and extend generalizable methodologies that could be applied to *any* obstacle (see

West 1989, 102; Adler-Kassner, 2008, 43-51; 181-185). Yet this approach, which Kristine Hansen notes dominates the academy, calls for a sometimes painful separation between personal convictions, often labeled "private," and public action (Hansen 2005, 27-28; see also Elbow 2000; Palmer 1998; and O'Reilley 2005 on their perceptions of the problematic separation between personal convictions and "objective" research).

On the other hand, "see[ing] writing programs as venues for activism" could reflect the more utopian, democratic possibilities inherent in the stewardly narrative. In Carey's formulation, it could put the writing program at the center of a larger discussion about writing and writers in public spaces—on the campus, in the community, and so on. Ideally, in this optimistic vision, students would also come to understand their roles as communicators (and therefore participants) in a democratic culture and come to develop a sense of their own authority and agency in this work. However, at the same time, it could require students and instructors to unwittingly participate in ideologies, values, and/or activities that do not reflect their own beliefs and principles. Nora Bacon has explored this dilemma in the context of another ostensibly democratic practice, service-learning, noting that while this practice seems to involve students in work that is in the best interests of their conceptualizations of themselves as democratic actors, sometimes that is not a role that students want to occupy (Bacon 1997).

The activist intellectual persona that can extend from the stewardly narrative is considerably more complicated than it might initially seem. Underneath its veneer of populism, the stewardly narrative held the potential to be quite paternalistic. Historian David J. Rothman notes that, "in their eagerness to play parent to the child, [Progressives] did not pause to ask whether the dependent had to be protected against their own well-meaning interventions" (Rothman, 1978, 72). Susman and West, working separately, note that central to stewardly Progressives' work was a desire to distance themselves from the material realities of their situations, a yearning, as Susman says, to be "*in* the world" but "not *of* the world" (Susman 95). Philosopher Cornel West notes that this desire led to an evasion of content in the work of Progressives, especially John Dewey—that is, an absence of attention to the specific materials (economic) conditions— which gave rise to Progressive/pragmatic thinking (West 227) and made it possible for two approaches as seemingly different as the stewardly and technocratic ones (both of which focused on method) to emerge from a common philosophy. These extensions of the stewardly approach might lead activist WPAs to conceive their work as an extension of participatory democracy, working *among* the community, but not *in* the community, working with but not alongside those with whom they have allied themselves. Additionally, the same separation between personal principles and public practice that is implied in research traditions extending from Progressive pragmatism are implied in this narrative.

A third possible persona for the activist WPA might stem from a revision of pragmatic Progressivism that extends from the work of philosophers like C. Wright Mills, and West himself, that West calls "prophetic pragmatism," which explicitly includes consideration of the material circumstances absent from the earlier approaches. As West identifies it, prophetic pragmatism reflects three elements that extend from the idea of critical intelligence rooted in the Progressive Era: 1) profound faith in, and advocacy for, the power of individuals to make a difference and improve democracy, balanced with acknowledgement that both of these efforts and the democracy is situated in and shot through with differences in power (West 227); 2) the importance of processes intended to forward the possibility of "human progress" that acknowledge and attempt to address profound differences in power among citizens coupled with "the human impossibility of paradise" (West 229); and 3) an acknowledgement that process is predicated on the adaptation of old and new traditions to "promote innovation and resistance for the aims of enhancing individuality and promoting democracy" (West 230). This instantiation of pragmatism parallels what Boyte identifies as "developmental democracy," which "focuses on the work of developing capacities for self-directed and collective action across differences for problem-solving and the creation of individual and common good" (Boyte 2008, 2).

With its explicit acknowledgement of and attention to power differences, the impossibility of a democratic utopia, and the desire to support individual diversity in the context of a broader democracy, prophetic pragmatism (and developmental democracy) opens up both possibilities for the WPA that are not present in the earlier traditions and which might not be contained in conceptions of the public or activist intellectual. Here, the WPA might be able to formulate a role incorporating both desirable and pragmatically important elements of the technocratic approach—such as the need to position ourselves within an existing, dominant, and valued research tradition and the value of our own research-based knowledge developed within that tradition—with the best elements of the stewardly approach, such as the belief that everyone in a writing program (students, instructors, every-one...) can actively participate in discussions about writing (communication) and democracy.

CONSCIOUS CHOICE 2: PERSONAE AND MODELS FOR FRAME- AND STORY-CHANGING WORK

These summaries outline the frames surrounding education that give rise to the kinds of questions and issues that WPAs might consider, as well as the personae that activist WPAs might choose as they navigate among these questions about communication (including education) and democracy. They also point to different ways that WPAs might approach the second set of choices associated with story- and frame-changing, those associated with building alliances. As Edward Chambers, Executive Director of the Industrial Areas Foundation (IAF, the nation's oldest community organization), explains, "Power takes place in relationships.... Seeing clearly that every act of power requires a relationship is the first step toward realizing that the capacity to be affected by another is the other side of the coin named power" (28). Three approaches to organizing—*interest-based organizing, values-based organizing,* and *issue-based organizing*—offer different possibilities for building alliances while considering the short- and long-term implications of the kinds of questions that WPAs face on a regular basis (about such things as course offerings, assessment, and curriculum staffing...) (also see Adler-Kassner 2008). These possibilities, similarly, have implications for the choices among personae available to WPAs. Of course, just as we might move among those choices of personae based on analysis of purpose(s), audience(s), and context(s), the same holds true for these models. Activist WPAs will likely move among them depending on the situation, "mix[ing] and phas[ing]," to employ a term used by organizers (quoted in Fleischer 2000, 83); to illustrate, following the discussion of each model I'll describe how we have used elements of each in ongoing assessment work of the First Year Writing Program (FYWP) at Eastern Michigan University (EMU) that I have directed for the last ten years.

Interest-based organizing, which developed out of the work of legendary organizer Saul Alinsky, is rooted in the utopian possibilities associated with the stewardly approach to cultivating critical intelligence. The end goal of interest-based work is to help people recognize and cultivate their own interests in and talents for change-making, because the assumption is that work is most effective, representative, and beneficial when everyone comes together around their shared common interests. This approach begins with learning about peoples' passions, because they hold the keys to involvement. Organizers learn about these stories by having one-on-one or small group discussions that help the organizer learn about what fires people up. The initial questions they ask are few, but important: What do you care about, and why? What motivates you to action around these issues? Once organizers have identified issues that people care about they move to the next step, connecting people around their interests: community jobs programs, the installation of lights on a dark street, even changing the size of the rocks next to a railroad bed that people needed to cross to get to work (e.g., Milroy in Adler-Kassner 2008, 101). The key here is for individuals to realize that when they come together around their passions and interests, they can affect change. As they realize they have this power, they become empowered to become more involved, affect more change. This change always stems from their interests and passions, though their motivations aren't especially relevant. Change by change, working person to person, the world becomes a better place as people work to improve their situations.

Using the interest-based organizing process that stems from Alinsky's work and that of the IAF as a starting point, the activist WPA's persona might also be aligned with the utopian elements of stewardship. His job is to discover peoples' self-interests—their passions—because in those passions lie motivations to action. These might include a desire to improve retention, streamline placement, cultivate technological literacy, or develop writing strategies necessary for employment. Whatever the interests are, through this model the activist WPA's role is primarily to unite people *around* shared interests in preparation for action. The organizer's primary agenda is to cultivate in people the realization that *they* can act, because empowering individuals to develop and participate in their own processes, not those of the WPA, is the key to maintaining and perpetuating the broader culture. Two additional issues are important here, too: 1) issues that are of central interest to the WPAs and the values that accompany them—like what assessment a university should use, how to cut a budget, what curriculum should be taught, and others that WPAs regularly face—take a back seat to the primary agenda of orchestrating others to act, 2) there is a presumption here that the issues identified among individuals will be for the social good, and that the short-term actions in which they will engage around these issues will ultimately lead to long-term benefit as individuals involved recognize their capacity for change-making. In this way the fundamental precepts of interest-based work parallel the Progressive pragmatic conception of declensions, which ultimately contribute to the development of the democracy because they help people develop their capacities for overcoming adversity. Using a *purely* interest-based model, then, the WPA's primary focus is mobilizing others, not in promoting particular positions regarding writing and writers; however, there is a presumption that the issues that others identify will ultimately contribute to the development of broader positions.

At EMU, using interest-based approaches has been a crucial part of our assessment work. In 2003, Heidi Estrem (then associate WPA) and I were presented with a question by our then-dean after we met with her to present results from an indirect assessment undertaken the previous year. In essence, she asked, "This is what students say. Who cares what students say?" We chose to understand this question as a statement about this administrator's passions, and to use it as an opportunity to learn about the passions of others on our campus. We wondered: What did members of our campus community identify as qualities of good writing? What made them passionate (in a good way) when they read something or wrote something? To learn about these passions, we convened focus groups of students, faculty, staff, and administrators to hear about their responses to these questions. We used transcripts of the focus groups as the basis for an assessment matrix which we then applied to portfolios from our second-semester research writing course, a general education requirement, to learn about how qualities associated with these community members' passions were evident in the work. (For more on this assessment see Adler-Kassner and Estrem, forthcoming.)

While interest-based organizing revolves around alliances built around shared interests, *values-based organizing* begins with cultivating shared values. As George Lakoff, whose work is often associated with this model, notes, "issues are secondary—not irrelevant or unimportant, but secondary. A position on issues should follow from one's values, and the choice of issues and policies should symbolize those values" (Lakoff 2006, 8). This approach is deeply rooted in linguistics and semiotics, resting on changing values associated with language and/or the language itself. Linguist Geoffrey Nunberg explains,

> [T]he symbol words of political discourse are different from specific symbols and cues... [t]hey don't simply encapsulate a particular issue, candidate, or

trend. They tell us how those specific symbols signify, so that we can group them as episodes in a greater political narrative that we evoke over and over again. Values stand in for an assortment of news items and running stories ... and connect them to an overarching narrative.... And for that reason, it's far more important to control the notion expressed by values than to control the more transitory symbols or catchphrases that stand in for a specific issue (Nunberg 2006, 30-31).

While interest-based organizing has its eye on short-term tactics, values-based work is focused first on long-term change. Success is achieved only when the *values* associated with an issue are addressed successfully. Michel Gelobter, Executive Director of Redefining Progress, illustrates this principle. Persuading California Assembly members to vote for legislation that included a system where polluters would have to pay for their emissions would be significant, he notes. "But if five years from now, we have to implement it and we still can't say 'gas tax' without being laughed out of the room," he asserts, "we're not winning the values battle" (Gelobter quoted in Adler-Kassner 2008, 109).

For the WPA working from a values-based model, identifying *her* values and those of the program is a crucial first step. What are the core principles, the things that are absolutely most important for and about writing and writers, and why are those principles core? Then the WPA can start identifying others who potentially share those values and begin to build alliances with them. Through alliance-building and discussion the WPA and allies eventually identify issues that they would like to address together. The organizer's role here is to make sure that her values (and those of her organization) remain primary; to do so requires her to endorse the importance of those values over others and to persuade others that they are more important.

The choices of persona and action extending from a doctrinaire values-based approach can present some challenging dilemmas. This approach means putting our values front-and-center and working from the presumption that they are better, more just, than ones held by others. This position might make WPAs who see themselves as democratic actors uncomfortable. And, to be sure, this approach reflects elements of the technocratic approach described earlier. Inherent in it is the belief that there *are* better and worse values, better and worse issues stemming from those values, and to some extent individuals who are more and less qualified (because of their beliefs) to advocate for these values. At the same time, many WPAs are passionate about the values we embrace and the practices that extend from them; those same WPAs sometimes struggle to sacrifice those principles and practices in the interests of developing alliances.

This was an issue that Heidi Estrem and I wrestled with in the focus groups described above. While we wanted to hear about peoples' passions, we recognized that without some boundaries, those passions could easily be expressed through statements about what they *didn't like* about (students') writing, not what they *did* like about writing. These positions contradicted some values that were at the core of our work, such as the idea that everyone can write, and that our role as educators was to cultivate peoples' abilities in positive ways. Thus, we were very careful to construct a structure for the focus groups that would privilege what we wanted. We asked participants to identify and bring with them specific pieces of writing from inside and outside school or work that they liked (not ones they didn't like), and we made sure that our questions focused on what they found to be beneficial about these pieces and why. We also kept track, on a whiteboard at the front of the room, of the language that people used when they described these pieces in an attempt to document a kind of shared vocabulary being used by, and emerging from, the groups. This activity reflected our belief that this language could reflect and perpetuate a sense of values about writing and writers shared among the groups.

Issue-based organizing, finally, represents a blend of the interest- and values-based models outlined here. Issue-based work is predicated on the idea that people can be *connected* around their immediate interests, but long-term social change will result only when these interests extend to and lead to action based on shared values. Issue-based organizing operates, then, along the boundaries of a three-sided triangle. On one side are individuals' passions as a starting point. As in interest-based work, the presumption here is that people can be inspired to action in and through these interests. But on the other side of the triangle are values, which are seen as an important part of the change-making equation. The presumption here, as in a values-based approach, is that change can only happen when long-term values are affected as well. Beginning with individual interests, then, the work here involves extending to collective, long-term action around these values. The connection between interests and values, then, forms the third side of the triangle.

For the WPA, the issue-based model makes possible a third persona and way of action that blends the stewardly and technocratic approaches and interest- and values-based approaches through which those personae are, to some extent, reflected. Like values-based organizers, WPAs working within an issue-based model certainly would identify their own values and principles, putting those on one side of a sort of conceptual triangle. Supporting these values would be both the WPA's interests and passions, as in interest-based work; and research-based practices that take into consideration long-term change, as in a values-based approach. Then the WPA might also engage in dialogue with others, as in interest-based work, to hear about *their* passions and interests. But where an interest-based approach would suggest that the WPA's stewardly persona should extend to fostering others' capacity for change-making, an issue-based persona would have the WPA consider questions of power and ideology that are wrapped up with these interests—the WPA's own, those associated with interests of others, and so on. Then the WPA would navigate among these different interests, along with their associated values and ideologies, to identify short-term, tactical actions that might represent both the WPA's interests (and values) and those of their potential allies. All the while, the WPA would also have an eye on the long-term, value-based, implications of these actions and make conscious decisions about how, when, and whether to take particular actions with these bigger-picture strategic values in mind. In this sense, the persona that the WPA might develop might reflect the principles involved in what West called prophetic pragmatism, with its fundamental faith in the power of individuals to make change, its belief in the never-perfect nature of American democracy, *and* its acknowledgement of the unequal power relationships that are inherent in both processes for change-making and results of those processes.

Our extended assessment process at EMU also reflects elements of issue-based organizing. In it, we attempted to create space for the passions and interests of those in our local community and use it to contribute to a shared frame to consider the work of writing (and writing instruction) on our campus. After we completed the initial draft of the assessment matrix from focus group transcripts, we brought it back to the groups to discuss what we had identified and learn about whether it reflected their interests and passions; we also shared with them key principles from our field—such as the idea that valid assessment is based in the principles of the discipline, and that good assessment is rooted in local contexts (Huot 2002)—to help them understand the broader frames through which we were operating. As we have undertaken curricular development using the results of this assessment (which we ultimately completed in 2006), we have continued to engage in conversations with constituencies outside of the First Year Writing Program who are passionate about and have a stake in the subject(s) of our work.

Two years ago we began a long-term collaboration with campus library faculty around issues related to information literacy and research processes; this winter we will take a draft of our program's outcomes, revised based on the 2004-06 assessment and additional research, to the campus community for input via a series of forums. In this way, we continue to try to "mix and phase" among these three models, accessing peoples' passions, working to advance our values, and cultivate capacity for shared action around issues related to writing and writers.

Each of these approaches, like the personae that extend from the stewardly, technocratic, and prophetic approaches to the cultivation of critical intelligence, exists along a spectrum. To change stories about writing and writers, what is most important is for WPAs and writing instructors to make conscious choices among these possibilities and to understand the implications of those choices. Each invokes a slightly different conceptualization of terms key to our work: communication and democracy. When we know what we mean by each and to what extent we want to privilege our own conceptions of these terms, we can begin to navigate among these personae, approaches, and decisions, acting consciously as activist WPAs to change stories about writing and writers.

REFERENCES

Adler-Kassner, Linda. 2008. *The activist WPA: Changing stories about writers and writing.* Logan: Utah State UP.

Adler-Kassner, Linda, and Heidi Estrem. 2009. The journey is the destination: The place of assessment in an activist writing program. *Organic writing assessment: Dynamic criteria mapping in action,* ed. Bob Broad, 14-36. Logan: Utah State University Press.

Anderson, Benedict. 2006. *Imagined communities: Reflections on the origins and spread of nationalism.* Rev. edition. London: Verso.

Bacon, Nora. 1997. Community service writing: Problems, challenges, and questions. In *Writing the community: Concepts and models for service-learning in composition,* ed. Linda Adler-Kassner, Robert Crooks, and Ann Watters, 39-55. Washington, D.C.: American Association of Higher Education.

Boyte, Harry. 2008. Civic driven change and developmental democracy. Civic driven change think tank project of the institute of social studies, The Hague, and Dutch development aid donors. Available at *www.hhh.umn.edu/centers/cdc/research.html* (accessed 25 October 2008.

Carey, James. 1997. The press, public opinion, and public discourse. In *James Carey: A critical reader*, ed. Eve Stryker Munson and Catherine A. Warren, 228-57. Minneapolis: U. of Minnesota Press.

Carey, James. 1997a. The communications revolution. In *James Carey: A critical reader*, ed. Eve Stryker Munson and Catherine A. Warren, 129-143. Minneapolis: U. of Minnesota Press.

Chambers, Edward and Michael Cowan. 2003. *Roots for radicals: Organizing for power, action, and justice.* New York: Continuum.

deCerteau, Michel. 1984. *The practice of everyday life.* Minneapolis: University of Minnesota Press.

Deacon, David, Michael Pickering, Peter Golding, and Graham Murdock. 1999. *Researching communications.* London: Arnold.

Deans, Tom. 2000. *Writing partnerships: Service-learning in composition.* Urbana, IL: NCTE.

Dewey, John. 1916. *Democracy and education.* New York: Macmillan.

Elbow, Peter. 2000. Premises and foundations. In *Everyone can write*, ed. Peter Elbow, 1-3. New York: Oxford University Press.

Feldman, Ann M. 2008. *Making writing matter: Composition in the engaged university.* Albany: SUNY Press.

Fleischer, Cathy. 2000. *Teachers organizing for change: Making literacy learning everybody's business.* Urbana: NCTE.

Gaylin, Willard, Ira Glasser, Stephen Marcus, and David Rothman. 1978. *Doing good: the limits of benevolence.* New York: Pantheon.

Glasser, Theodore, ed. 1999. *The idea of public journalism.* New York: Guilford Press.

Hansen, Kristine. 2005. Religious freedom in the public square and the composition classroom. In *Negotiating religious faith in the composition classroom*, ed. Elizabeth VanderLei and Bonnie Kyburz, 24-38. Portsmouth, NH: Boynton/Cook.

Harris, Joseph. 1997. *A teaching subject: composition since 1966.* Upper Saddle River, NJ: Prentice-Hall.

Haswell, Richard. 2005. NCTE/CCCC's recent war on scholarship. *Written Communication* 22 (2): 198-223.

Hertog, James and Douglas M. McLeod. 2001. A multiperspectival approach to framing analysis: A field guide. In *Framing public life*, ed. Stephen D. Reese, Oscar H. Gandy, and August E. Grant, 139-161. Mahwah, NJ: Lawrence Erlbaum.

Huot, Brian. 2002. *(Re) Articulating writing assessment for teaching and learning*, Logan, UT: Utah State Press.

Lakoff, George. 2004. *Don't think of an elephant! Know your values and frame the debate.* White River Junction, VT: Chelsea Green.

Lakoff, George. 2006. *Thinking points: Communicating our American values and visions.* New York: Farrar, Straus, and Giroux.

Miller, Richard. 1998. *As if learning mattered: Reforming higher education.* Ithaca: Cornell University Press.

Nunberg, Geoffrey. 2006. *Talking right: How conservatives turned liberalism into a tax-raising, latte-drinking, sushi-eating, Volvo-driving, New York Times-reading, body-piercing, Hollywood-loving, left-wing freak show.* New York: Public Affairs.

O'Reilley, Mary Rose. 2005. *The garden at night: Burnout and breakdown in the teaching life.* Portsmouth, NJ: Boynton/Cook.

Ozman, Howard, and Samuel Craver. 1995. *Philosophical foundations of education.* Upper Saddle River, NJ: Prentice Hall.

Parker, Palmer. 1998. *The courage to teach: Exploring the inner landscapes of a teacher's life.* San Francisco: Jossey-Bass.

Pulliam, John D and James J. Van Patten. 2007. *History of education in America.* 9th ed. Upper Saddle River, NJ: Prentice Hall.

Ready or Not: Creating a high school diploma that counts. 2004. American Diploma Project. Available at *www.achieve.org/files/ADPreport_7.pdf* (accessed 19 December 2009).

Reese, Stephen D. 2001. Framing public life: A bridging model for media research. In *Framing public life: Perspectives on media and our understanding of the social world,* ed. Stephen D. Reese, Oscar H. Gandy, and August E. Grant, 7-31. Mahwah, NJ: Lawrence Erlbaum.

Rose, Mike. 2006. *An open language: Selected writing on literacy, learning, and opportunity.* Boston: Bedford St. Martins.

Rosen, Jay. 1999. The action of the idea: Public journalism in built form. In *The idea of public journalism,* ed. Theodore L. Glasser, 21-48. New York: Guilford Press.

Susman, Warren. 1984. *Culture as history.* New York: Pantheon.

Rothman, David. 1978. The state as parent: Social policy in the progressive era. In *Doing good: the limits of benevolence,* ed. Willard Gaylin, Ira Glasser, Stephen Marcus, and David Rothman, 67-95. New York: Pantheon.

VanderLei, Elizabeth and Bonnie Kyburz. 2005. *Negotiating religious faith in the composition classroom.* Portsmouth, NH: Boynton/Cook.

West, Cornel. 1989. *The American evasion of philosophy: A genealogy of pragmatism.* Madison: University of Wisconsin Press.

13

WRITING PROGRAM ADMINISTRATION AND COMMUNITY ENGAGEMENT
A Bibliographic Essay

Jaclyn M. Wells

INTRODUCTION: COMMUNITY ENGAGEMENT AND WRITING PROGRAM ADMINISTRATION

A perusal of major composition journals from recent years reveals that community engagement is an increasingly common subject in the field's literature. Community engagement, as described in composition scholarship, comes in many forms, including course-based service learning, extension of university services to community members, and partnerships between community literacy organizations and university writing programs. Numerous articles and books debate the merits of writing-based community engagement projects, consider how different areas of the writing program can facilitate community-university cooperation, and examine specific examples of writing programs' community-based work.[1]

Even though administrative concerns reverberate throughout composition's community engagement literature, little of that literature directly connects community engagement with writing program administration. Candace Spigelman points to this in her *WPA* article, "Politics, Rhetoric, and Service-Learning" (2004). Spigelman writes: "To date, there is no body of literature that links writing-focused community outreach directly to writing program administration" (107). She calls for more work that creates this link: "As directors of first-year writing are likely to organize and oversee such [service-learning] initiatives, perhaps it is time for that scholarly work to begin" (107). Though Spigelman writes specifically

---

1. See Elenore Long's annotated bibliography, the final chapter in her recently published *Community Literacy and the Rhetoric of Local Publics*.

about service-learning in first-year writing, WPAs organize and oversee other forms of community engagement in writing programs. Examples include service-learning in professional and technical writing courses and partnerships between community literacy organizations and writing centers. Thus, Spigelman's call for scholarship that links community engagement with writing program administration applies to other forms of engagement—and other types of WPAs—as well.

In their *WPA* article, "Writing Program Design in the Metropolitan University: Toward Constructing Community Partnerships" (2002), Jeffrey T. Grabill and Lynée Lewis Gaillet address Spigelman's concern about the lack of scholarship connecting writing program administration with community engagement. Grabill and Gaillet argue that WPAs are fundamental to the design of university writing programs' community engagement work: "A community interface for writing programs, by which we mean the point of contact between the writing program and various communities, must first be imagined, designed, and constructed by WPAs" (64). Further, Grabill and Gaillet argue that research is essential to the process of administrative design:

> In order for a writing program to organize sustained community-based work, its partnership with "the community" must be under constant scrutiny. Framing community involvement as research is the best way we know to be both self-conscious about the community-based work of a writing program and useful to communities themselves. (66)

By urging WPAs to design "community interfaces" in their writing programs and to question these designs through research, Grabill and Gaillet are, like Spigelman, calling for a body of scholarship that links community engagement and writing program administration.

Nicole Amare and Teresa Grettano answer both Grabill and Gaillet's and Spigelman's calls for WPA scholarship about community engagement in their recent *WPA* article, "Writing Outreach and Community Engagement" (2007). Amare and Grettano refer directly to Spigelman's assertion that little scholarship connects writing program administration and community engagement (71). They work toward addressing this gap by describing Writing Outreach, a community engagement project at their writing program at the University of South Alabama. Amare and Grettano write: "We hope that theoretical and administrative support of programs like Writing Outreach will help create that link [that Spigelman calls for] and that WPAs...will consider this community engagement model as a service-learning option" (71). Additionally, because the Writing Outreach program was designed and revised using research, it answers Grabill and Gaillet's call for researched administrative design of community engagement. Specifically, two types of research were used: 1. Interviews of professors across the university before the program was implemented to help refine its focus (60), and 2. Evaluation forms that Outreach participants filled out to help assess the program's impact (65).

These three recent articles, all published in *WPA*, reveal the beginnings of a conversation about the connection between writing program administration and community engagement. Grabill and Gaillet's call for administrative design and research about those designs, as well as Spigelman's call for scholarship that links writing program administration and community engagement, are invitations for WPAs to think about how community engagement involves administrative work and how this work is scholarly. Amare and Grettano's answer to these calls provides one example of what scholarship that considers community engagement from a WPA perspective might look like.

The rest of this essay presents other scholarship that connects community engagement and writing program administration. The essays discussed here are not the only sources that link community engagement and writing program administration, but instead, represent a sample of this type of scholarship. Although some recent excellent books such as Eli Goldblatt's *Because We Live Here: Sponsoring Literacy beyond the College Curriculum* (2007), Jeff Grabill's *Writing Community Change: Designing Technologies for Citizen Action* (2007), Linda Adler-Kassner's *The Activist WPA: Changing Stories About Writing and Writers* (2008), and Ann Feldman's *Making Writing Matter: Redesigning First-Year Composition for the Engaged University* (2008) address the connection between writing program administration and community engagement, because reviews of the books are readily available, I have chosen to discuss only article-length work.

I considered three factors in choosing the scholarship I discuss here. First, and perhaps most importantly, I selected sources based on how directly they connect writing program administration and community engagement. In each article included in the essay, the connection between writing program administration and community engagement is a central issue, rather than merely an add-on or secondary concern. Second, I selected sources based on how recently they were published;

because this time period reflects the current interest in, and developing conversation about, community engagement and program administration. All of the articles in the essay were published since 1995. Third, I selected sources based on the perspective of the author. Though there is significant overlap between the sources presented, the articles I have chosen represent the three major perspectives related to writing program administration and community engagement. These are the perspectives of 1. WPAs who address community engagement, 2. community engagement practitioners inside composition who address writing program administration, and 3. community engagement practitioners outside composition who address administration. These three perspectives not only were a factor in choosing what sources to include, but also provide the organization for this essay.

These three perspectives are central to the field's understanding of how community engagement and administration are connected, but a failure to recognize the connections among scholarship from these three perspectives may contribute to what Spigelman notes as the lack of a "body of literature" that links administration and engagement (107). In other words, the perception that there is no body of administration-focused community engagement literature may be due to the fact that existing scholarship consists of somewhat disconnected arguments from these three different perspectives. After summarizing a sample of current scholarship from these perspectives, this essay concludes by arguing that more scholarship like the sources presented here and increased discourse among scholars who hold different perspectives (especially WPAs and community engagement scholars in and outside composition) will result in a more comprehensive and complete understanding of links between writing program administration and community engagement.

WPA SCHOLARSHIP THAT ADDRESSES COMMUNITY ENGAGEMENT

In this section, I return to, and describe more fully, Grabill and Gaillet's and Amare and Grettano's articles. These two articles, as well as the other sources described in this section, can be categorized as WPA scholarship because the authors are explicit about how writing program administration is central to their arguments.

As I mentioned in my introduction, Grabill and Gaillet argue that writing programs offer important sites for university-community collaboration, and that writing program administrators are key in creating and sustaining these sites (64). WPAs, Grabill and Gaillet recommend, should consider the context of their university and community to successfully create and sustain university-community collaboration. The authors draw on their experience as WPAs at Georgia State University in Atlanta to illustrate their ideas about university and community context in designing university-community partnerships. Georgia State, Grabill and Gaillet explain, is a "metropolitan university," meaning that it differs "from the traditional urban university in terms of mission, community leadership and partnerships, and (critical for WPAs) evaluation of traditional faculty responsibilities" (62). Specifically, the metropolitan university reconfigures the way faculty perceive the traditional categories of teaching, research, and service, asking them to "more fully merge these duties" and to "contribute to the metropolitan area's 'quality of life' while developing close partnerships with area enterprises in mutually beneficial ways" (63).

Grabill and Gaillet discuss program design that is based on this new reconfiguration within the metropolitan university, dividing their discussion into issues of administration, curriculum and teacher preparation, and building relationships with community organizations. Grabill and Gaillet's major point is that writing program administrators must thoughtfully work toward program design "to support community-based research and meaningful, sequenced curricular experiences" (74). Without critical, sustained program design efforts, the community and university continue to be separate; any community engagement projects in the university continue to be mere experiments or anomalies, and research, teaching, and service remain separate spheres. Grabill and Gaillet's consideration of the metropolitan university and how its circumstances influence program design and community partnerships, demonstrates their belief in establishing university-community partnerships that are sensitive to their contexts.

Like Grabill and Gaillet, Amare and Grettano argue that community engagement must be contextualized to the circumstances of the university and community and also that writing program administrators play a key role in achieving this. More specifically, the authors argue that community engagement projects must differ according to institution because of such issues as budgeting, the relationship between the institution and community, and student and faculty availability and commitment (57). The approach they propose, Writing Outreach, "is a type of service-learning program that may work well in a department interested in connecting or 'engaging' with community members for

a number of legitimate reasons while unable to implement a traditional course-based program" (59). The Writing Outreach program
at Amare and Grettano's university consists of free, weekly sessions
led by volunteer faculty members in which anyone in the university
and community can get help with particular writing skills. These skills
include MLA documentation, research strategies, the writing process,
writing cover letters and resumes, and more. Community members,
Amare and Grettano write, have consistently comprised around half of
the program's total participants, which demonstrates that interaction
among faculty, university students, and community members is occurring within the program.

The key difference between the Writing Outreach model of community engagement that Amare and Grettano describe and other
approaches to community engagement (classroom based service-learning programs, for example) is that faculty members are responsible for
performing the service. Amare and Grettano view this faculty participation as one of the program's major attributes. Because the responsibility
for service is the faculty members' instead of the students', the Writing
Outreach model offers a more sustainable and viable approach to community engagement for universities like that of the authors, where the
large number of commuter, nontraditional, and working-class students
makes community engagement projects in which students are primarily
responsible for the service difficult (71). Amare and Grettano's rationale for the Writing Outreach model demonstrates how writing program administrators should tailor community engagement projects to
the circumstances of their own university and community.

WPAs who write about community engagement may also compare
their administrative experiences in their writing programs with those
they encounter in community engagement activities. This scholarship
reveals how WPAs can use their administrative experience in other
areas to support their community engagement work. In "Writing Across
the Curriculum and Community Service Learning: Correspondences,
Cautions, and Futures" (1997), Tom Deans compares writing across
the curriculum (WAC) with community service learning (CSL). Like
the authors reviewed above, Deans draws on his own experience in this
article, discussing his work with a cross-disciplinary faculty group in his
university that was creating service-learning courses.

Deans identifies a number of correspondences between WAC and
CSL that he observed during his work. He argues that both movements:

1. Aspire to be "'modes of learning' (Emig 1977) and processes of discovery rather than trendy add-ons and quick fixes" (29);

2. Differ significantly from traditional teaching and learning, and therefore can "re-energize teaching" but also require significant planning (30);

3. Must be adapted contextually to suit a particular discipline, course, and instructor;

4. Push faculty "to adopt new perspectives on the values and conventions of their home disciplines" (30);

5. Are often viewed as "low-prestige activities" by faculty members (30); and

6. Have great potential to be "valuable site[s] of school-university collaboration" (30).

These correspondences are important for writing program administrators because knowledge about WAC can help to illuminate CSL (and vice versa), which can further help WPAs plan programs.

More specifically, Deans argues that those interested in CSL can draw upon WAC's strategies for gaining institutional acceptance. In addition to situating community engagement to the circumstances of the university and community—as Grabill and Gaillet and Amare and Grettano suggest—WPAs must gain institutional acceptance for community engagement projects if they are to be successful. Knowledge of how to foster institutional acceptance for projects and ideas is key for writing program administrators, whose greatest challenge is often gaining university and departmental support. After offering the correspondences between WAC and CSL, Deans suggests that CSL can learn from the history of WAC and imitate some of its strategies for institutional acceptance: "CSL advocates, by carefully reading the history of WAC and strategically working within our institutions, can help others discover its value for the academic disciplines" (35).

In their *College English* article, "Writing Beyond the Curriculum: Fostering New Collaborations in Literacy" (2000), Eli Goldblatt and Steve Parks also discuss how writing across the curriculum has gained institutional acceptance. Unlike Deans, however, Goldblatt and Parks are less interested in what community engagement can learn from WAC and more interested in how greater focus on the community can improve

WAC. They point out that WAC has gained acceptance partly because of its perceived potential for preparing students for their own fields, but that this approach to WAC may not endure in the new century:

> . . . the deal WAC struck with departments and disciplines—to train students in the major and forward the move to specialized education—may not generate and sustain the sort of literacy instruction necessary for students in universities of the next century. (585)

Parks and Goldblatt call for an expanded notion of WAC in which "compositionists reframe WAC to reach beyond university boundaries" to schools and community programs (585). They write that, "An alliance among university instructors and teachers both in K-12 and adult basic education is particularly crucial" (587). Collaboration with the community, Goldblatt and Parks argue, can allow for the cross-disciplinary conversations about knowledge that compositionists often envision WAC as fostering.

The article contains three major sections. In the first, Goldblatt and Parks review recent calls for an expanded notion of WAC and discuss the conflict between the traditional structure of writing programs and new demands on them. In the second section, Goldblatt and Parks discuss an example of school/community/university partnership, The Institute for the Study of Literature, Literacy, and Culture, which they describe as "an alliance of university, public school, and community educators" (593). In the third section, Goldblatt and Parks consider the advantages and disadvantages of these types of partnerships. Goldblatt and Parks demonstrate how writing programs—and common areas within them, like WAC—must respond to the changing university. Writing program administrators are fundamental to guiding this response. Goldblatt and Parks' reframing of WAC to include community collaboration demonstrates for WPAs the theoretical connections between these two composition movements and how they can develop cooperatively. The authors' discussion of The Institute for the Study of Literature, Literacy, and Culture models for WPAs the type of community partnerships that they are proposing.

COMMUNITY ENGAGEMENT SCHOLARSHIP IN COMPOSITION THAT ADDRESSES ADMINISTRATION

The administrative questions addressed by the sources I discuss in this section include how to sustain community engagement, where to locate it within the writing program, and what outcomes demonstrate the success of a community engagement project. In this scholarship, the authors' main focus is on community engagement. Though administrative issues reverberate throughout these sources, the authors are less explicit than the authors in the previous section about the relevance of writing program administration to their arguments.

Wayne Campbell Peck, Linda Flower, and Lorraine Higgins' *College Composition and Communication* article, "Community Literacy" (1995), describes the Community Literacy Center (CLC), a university-community collaboration between Pittsburgh's Community House and The National Center for the Study of Writing and Literacy at Carnegie Mellon University. Peck, Flower, and Higgins use the term "community literacy" to describe the evolving discourse they witness during the collaboration: This discourse, they write, "has emerged from the action and reflection between residents in urban communities and their university counterparts" (220). An example of such discourse is a newsletter written by fifteen-year-old Mark and ten of his teenage peers entitled "Whassup with Suspension." The newsletter, which became "required reading for teachers and students in Mark's high school," was one product of an eight-week project in which Mark and the other teenagers investigated why student suspension was on the rise in public schools (200). Peck, Flower, and Higgins offer the major principles that have emerged after six years of the CLC's existence, as well as the problems that arise in such university-community collaborations. Throughout the article, the authors refer to examples from the CLC that support their ideas about university-community collaboration, community literacy, and conversations among diverse populations.

Peck, Flower, and Higgins' discussion of the Community Literacy Center addresses two key areas of administration. The first is the site for community engagement. One of the CLC's major strengths, the authors argue, is that it is a partnership between two existing programs. These two programs—Pittsburgh's Community House and Carnegie Mellon's National Center for the Study of Writing and Literacy—are established within their community and university respectively, which contributes to the CLC's sustainability and influence. The second key area of administration addressed by Peck, Flower, and Higgins is the relationship between the university and community partners. The nature of the relationship between Pittsburgh's Community House and Carnegie Mellon's National Center for the Study of Writing and Literacy is fundamental to the CLC's success.

The authors explain that the CLC draws on the settlement house movement in the early 1900s in America and Britain. This movement, "with its twin footholds in the community and the university, enabled people to cross boundaries, allowing them to work together to improve the educational practice and cultural climate of their neighborhoods" (202). The CLC reinvents the settlement house model, and focuses on "collaborative problem solving and the appreciation of multiple kinds of expertise" (203). Peck, Flower, and Higgins show that by fostering collaboration between the university and community partners and drawing on each partner's expertise, the CLC is a sustainable, mutually beneficial university-community partnership.

Writing centers offer another potential site in university writing programs for program based community engagement. In "Professional Development and the Community Writing Center" (2006), published in *Praxis*, James Jesson describes the community outreach efforts of the Undergraduate Writing Center at the University of Texas at Austin. Specifically, he discusses the Carver Library project. Like the CLC, the Carver Library project is a partnership between a university partner—the Writing Center—and a community partner—the George Washington Carver branch of the Austin Public Library. Writing center consultants go to the library to provide free writing assistance to community members. Like many community engagement projects, the Carver Library project centers on the belief that it is mutually beneficial to both participant groups, namely, the university tutors and the community tutees. The mutually beneficial nature of the project is evident in Jesson's discussion of how the Carver Library project addresses two of the Writing Center's major goals. First, it "satisfies specific community needs and solidifies relations between the university and Austin residents" (par. 3); second, the project "further[s] undergraduate consultants' professional development" (par. 4). Jesson also acknowledges many of the challenges raised by extending the Writing Center's services to members of the community. These challenges include: the wide variation in clients and writing tasks that tutors encounter in the Carver Library; the lack of amenities, like frequently used reference works and a reception desk that are available in the university Writing Center but not in the library; and the unfamiliar—and sometimes less friendly—environment of the library's space. Despite these challenges, however, Jesson concludes that "the community outreach project has granted the public entry into the writing center while providing a bridge for consultants into the community" (par. 12). Importantly, Jesson not only demonstrates how his university's writing center offers potential for community engagement, but also shows how the community's public library provides a ready-made, already established community site for engagement. Jesson's discussion of the Carver Library project demonstrates that identifying sites for engagement in the university and community can allow for sustainable, mutually beneficial university-community partnerships, and it also models how writing centers and public libraries can operate as sites for engagement.

Frankie Condon's article, "The Pen Pal Project" (2004), describes another community engagement project that is located in a university writing center, the Saint Cloud State University Pen Pal Project. The Pen Pal Project connects university writing center tutors with inner-city elementary school children. Throughout the course of a semester, the pen pals exchange letters that discuss their interests, friends, lives, and communities. Toward the end of the semester, the tutors travel to the children's school to collaborate with them on a writing project; at the end of the semester, the elementary school students travel to the university writing center for a celebration. Condon makes an important point for writing program administrators when she explains the pragmatic circumstances that allowed her to plan and implement this project. Specifically, Condon explains that she knew an interested teacher from the elementary school, and the school's proximity to the university made it accessible to the writing center tutors. Condon focuses on the pragmatic planning of this project—including explanation of how her writing center served as a site for program-based community engagement—and that focus is quite helpful to WPAs (perhaps writing center administrators in particular) who are embracing university-community partnerships.

Another administrative issue raised by Condon's article is tutor training, specifically the benefits for the writing center tutors, who were also students in her writing center theory and practice course. She writes that, "The quality of relationships forged in and through the Pen Pal Project seems to me to have helped my students to grow as tutors in ways that I could not have taught them in any classroom or staff meeting" (par. 10). The tutors, she writes, began reflecting more thoughtfully on their role as university writing center tutors, thinking more compassionately about student writers, and considering the ways that material conditions and inequalities shape the students who come to the writing center. Condon's essay offers writing center administrators a rationale for community engagement as a method of training tutors.

While program-based community engagement projects like the Community Literacy Center, the Carver Library Project, and the Pen Pal Project are common, course-based service learning offers another form of community engagement for writing program administrators interested in doing community work. In "Rhetoric Made Real: Civic Discourse and Writing Beyond the Curriculum" (1997), published in *Writing the Community: Concepts and Models for Service-Learning in Composition*, Paul Heilker acknowledges problems with course-based service learning, but also argues that—when conducted appropriately— service learning in composition offers many potential benefits. Among these benefits is the potential for providing students with real rhetorical situations for their writing: "Writing teachers need to relocate the where of composition instruction outside the academic classroom because the classroom does not and cannot offer students real rhetorical situations in which to understand writing as social action" (Heilker 71). Heilker points out that service learning can provide composition students with real rhetorical situations for their writing while simultaneously benefiting the community.

The problem with many course-based service learning projects, Heilker warns, is that they separate community service from student learning so that the two are "'connected only superficially by some writing assignment'" (qtd. in Heilker 73). To address this problem, Heilker proposes an approach to writing-based service learning in which students "actually complete essential writing tasks for the nonprofit agencies in which they are placed" (74). Whereas many writing-based service learning projects ask students to perform a service activity and then write about it, in this approach to service learning, the writing actually *is* the service that students perform. Heilker writes that, "This version of service-learning thus offers students real rhetorical situations in which to work: real tasks, real audiences, real purposes for writing" (75). These real tasks, audiences, and purposes move writing outside of the academy, which benefits both the student writers and the community organizations. For WPAs who are interested in how the composition course can serve as a site for mutually beneficial community engagement, Heilker offers one approach.

Like Heilker, Ellen Cushman points to the potential problems with course-based service learning in writing programs, but also argues that

service learning can be beneficial to university and community participants when it is conducted appropriately. In her *College Composition and
Communication* article, "Sustainable Service Learning Programs" (2002),
Cushman argues that lack of sustainability is a common problem in service learning. She writes, "...despite all the best intentions, I fear that
some service learning initiatives still replicate a hit-it-and-quit-it relation
with communities" (41). Engagement projects that end abruptly after a
semester—or, sometimes, only a unit in a semester—can result in community members' mistrust of the university because of the implication
that the university's interest in the community is fleeting or even self-
interested. Additionally, Cushman argues that community members can
become understandably frustrated by inconsistencies among different
university members with whom they collaborate (41). These inconsistencies relate directly to sustainability because, instead of working with one
university participant or group over a long period, community members may find themselves working with a variety of university members
in shorter projects. Finally, the most fundamental problem created by
lack of sustained community engagement is the quality of the work performed. In some cases, community participants may reasonably expect a
community engagement project to result in high-quality work, but in reality, the project is not sustained long enough to produce this quality work.

   To address the issue of sustainability, Cushman proposes that faculty
have a consistent presence in service learning projects: "Professors in
service learning initiatives garner trust from community members...
when they show a consistent presence in the community" (58). The
professor's involvement in service learning also benefits the writing
class: "When the service learning teacher is on site with students, the
kinds of tasks assigned and integrated into the classroom can be carefully weighed, mutually informative, appropriately demanding, and
responsive to community needs" (49). In addition to having a greater,
consistent presence in service learning projects, Cushman argues, professors who are involved in service learning initiatives can work toward
sustainable service learning programs by integrating their teaching,
service, and research in the service learning project (41). Even though
Cushman's main focus is on the professor's, rather than the administrator's, role in service learning, her argument is quite relevant to writing program administrators, who are often responsible for initiating
and overseeing service-learning programs. By encouraging professors
in service learning to use the strategies Cushman explains—and by

supporting the professors who already do—WPAs can facilitate more successful, sustainable service learning projects in the writing program.

COMMUNITY ENGAGEMENT SCHOLARSHIP OUTSIDE COMPOSITION THAT ADDRESSES ADMINISTRATION

The third set of sources I discuss includes community engagement scholarship outside composition studies that directly addresses administrative issues. This scholarship is relevant to writing program administration because it offers a broader perspective on higher education that WPAs must consider if they are to situate community engagement in the university context. The sources described in this section are particularly relevant to WPAs because they directly address the role of administration in community engagement.

Many sources described earlier in this essay emphasize the importance of gaining institutional acceptance for community engagement. Deans, for example, proposes that community engagement proponents can—and should—gain acceptance across the academic disciplines for engagement work by employing strategies that have been used to gain acceptance for writing across the curriculum. In addition to acceptance across the university, the success of community engagement is also dependent upon departmental support. Brian Conniff and Betty Rogers Youngkin's article, "The Literacy Paradox: Service-Learning and the Traditional English Department (1995), published in the *Michigan Journal of Community Service Learning*, addresses the role of community engagement in traditional English departments (those which focus primarily on literature). Specifically, they describe the Dayton Literacy Project, a service-learning literacy course whose success "suggests some of the ways that the discipline of English can be re-envisioned to integrate academic study in the humanities with literacy instruction" (86). Conniff and Youngkin offer an important perspective to writing program administrators, and particularly to those WPAs who are struggling to gain departmental support for community engagement projects in traditional English departments that may be unreceptive to their composition-focused work in general.

Unlike many of the other community engagement projects described by other sources in this essay, the Dayton Literacy Project involves literature. The course at the center of the Dayton Literacy Project is a semester-long service-learning undergraduate course in which students simultaneously "study literacy in the classroom...and serve as literacy mentors to women who were receiving Aid to Families with Dependent Children in the Dayton area" (87). These women, who the authors describe as Adult Basic Education (ABE) women, were "welfare mothers, reading at a fifth to eighth grade level, working toward a General Equivalency Degree (GED)" (87). Each week, the course convened for one conventional classroom session, in which only the undergraduate students and professors met and discussed readings in the area of literacy; Mike Rose's *Lives on the Boundary* and Walter Ong's *Orality and Literacy* were among the readings (88). The class then met a second time during the week, this time with the ABE women. During these meetings, the class would discuss selected poetry and fiction that had been assigned that day; Maya Angelou's *I Know Why the Caged Bird Sings* and passages from Walt Whitman's *Leaves of Grass* were among the selections. In addition to discussing literature, the ABE women wrote each week and revised their writing with the help of the undergraduate students during class time. Often, this writing related to the day's reading, like when the students wrote poems about their own families after reading the Alice Walker poem "To My Sister Molly Who in the Fifties" (91).

Conniff and Youngkin report that the project was a success overall, proving mutually beneficial for all of the university and community participants involved:

> The Dayton Literacy Project was successful on just about every level. In fact, what seems most surprising, in retrospect, is just how little difficulty we had in reconciling the various goals and ambitions of everyone involved: undergraduates, faculty, Adult Basic Education students, social services administrators, and graduate students. (91)

English departments can benefit from projects like the Dayton Literacy Project, the authors argue, because "literacy work can provide a department like ours—both the faculty and the students—with an entirely new range of opportunities" (91). Conniff and Youngkin's article is important for writing program administrators because it models how community engagement can work in a traditional English department by drawing on the department's expertise in literacy—including literature that some writing-focused community engagement projects may exclude. Finally, Conniff and Youngkin's description of the methods they used to evaluate the program's success are useful to WPAs who are interested in assessment of community engagement. This discussion of assessment supports the article's more general ideas about how to gain departmental support for community engagement: Positive assessments of engagement programs are fundamental to gaining support for projects like the Dayton Literacy Project.

While Conniff and Youngkin offer a brief discussion of assessment, Barbara A. Holland's "A Comprehensive Model for Assessing Service-Learning and Community-University Partnerships" (2001), published in *New Directions for Higher Education*, focuses exclusively on assessment. Holland writes that, "as new initiatives in higher education, service-learning programs and community-university partnerships depend on effective assessment strategies to generate the evidence that will sustain internal and external support and document impacts" (53). Holland's argument that assessment is fundamental to gaining support for community engagement aligns with many sources included in this essay that also focus on gaining acceptance and support for community work.

Central to Holland's model of assessment is that the impacts on all participants in the service-learning project must be assessed: "For service-learning to be sustained, the institution, faculty, students, and community partners must see benefits of shared effort" (53). Holland's assessment model's attention to all service-learning participants aligns well with the mutually beneficial aims of most service-learning projects. Her assessment framework "is based on a goal-variable-indicator-method design" in which the researcher should raise four major questions:

- Goal: What do we want to know?

- Variable: What will we look for?

- Indicator: What will be measured?

- Method: How will it be measured? (55)

Exploring these questions will aid researchers in designing assessment, but Holland also argues that researchers should not design assessment in isolation. Instead, she writes, participants in the service-learning project should be involved in the design of the project's assessment: "The translation of goals and objectives into a set of specific variables whose impact can be measured for each participant group requires consultation with those constituents in the design phase" (58). After describing her model, Holland cautions readers about some common challenges to assessment. Most of these challenges, Holland argues, result from lack of planning; and the model she presents, with its careful exploration of goals, variables, indicators, and methods, may minimize many of these challenges. In addition, Holland advises that those conducting assessment should carefully consider the available resources and expertise for assessment. Even though Holland does not write specifically about writing-based service learning, the model of assessment that she presents is useful to writing program administrators. Because the model is so flexible, it can provide WPAs with a general framework for assessment that can be used with many different types of service learning and community-university partnerships.

CONCLUSION: DEVELOPING A BODY OF ADMINISTRATION-FOCUSED ENGAGEMENT LITERATURE

The purpose of this essay has been to present a sample of scholarship that links writing program administration and community engagement. As the essay's organization suggests, this scholarship generally falls into one of three types: WPA scholarship that addresses community engagement, community engagement scholarship in composition that addresses administration, and community engagement scholarship outside of composition that addresses administration.

The discussion presented here demonstrates that scholarship does connect writing program administration and community engagement. Though this discussion contradicts Spigelman's assertion that "there is no body of literature that links writing-focused community outreach directly to writing program administration," it is understandable why she would make this claim (107). First, the amount of scholarship that *directly* links writing program administration with community engagement *is* relatively small. The scholarship discussed in this essay is only a sample, but even an exhaustive list of this type of scholarship would not be huge. Second, scholarship that connects writing program administration with community engagement is from disparate perspectives, including WPAs and non-WPA community engagement practitioners in and outside of composition. Our previous failure to make connections among these perspectives may make it seem as though there is no body of scholarship about the topic.

Bringing together the three perspectives presented in this essay demonstrates that there is a greater body of literature linking writing program administration and community engagement than may be immediately apparent. As more university writing programs search for ways to make community engagement an integral part of their work, the need for a body of literature that considers engagement from an administrative standpoint grows more pressing. This body of literature will be developed as more writing program administrators produce scholarship that connects their administrative expertise and experience with their community engagement work. Such scholarship would answer calls for composition scholars to connect their research and service (see Cushman, "The Public Intellectual, Service Learning, and Activist Research," for example). Additionally, increased communication from scholars with different perspectives—specifically, WPAs interested in community engagement and community engagement practitioners in and outside of composition—may result in a body of scholarship that better acts as an ongoing conversation about how administration and community engagement are linked.

REFERENCES

Adler-Kassner, Linda. 2008. *The activist WPA: Changing stories about writing and writers.* Logan, UT: Utah University UP.

Amare, Nicole and Teresa Grettano. 2007. Writing outreach as community engagement. *WPA: Writing Program Administration* 30 (3): 57-74.

Condon, Frankie. 2004. The pen pal project. *Praxis: A Writing Center Journal 2* (1). projects. uwc.utexas.edu/praxis/?q=node/38.

Conniff, Brian and Betty Rogers Youngkin. 1995. The literacy paradox: Service-learning and the traditional English department. *Michigan Journal of Community Service Learning* 2 (1): 86-94.

Cushman, Ellen. 2002. Sustainable service learning programs. *College Composition and Communication* 54 (1): 40-65.

Deans, Tom. 1997. Writing across the curriculum and community service learning: Correspondences, cautions, and futures. In *Writing the community: Concepts and models for service-learning in composition*, ed. Linda Adler-Kassner, Robert Crooks, and Ann Watter, 29-37. Washington, D.C.: American Association for Higher Education, 1997.

Emig, Janet. 1977. Writing as a mode of learning. *College Composition and Communication* 28 (2): 122-128.

Feldman, Ann M. 2008. *Making writing matter: Redesigning first-year composition for the engaged university.* Albany, NY: SUNY Press.

Goldblatt, Eli and Steve Parks. 2000. Writing beyond the curriculum: Fostering new collaborations in literacy. *College English* 62 (5): 584-606.

Goldblatt, Eli. 2007. *Because we live here: Sponsoring literacy beyond the college curriculum.* Cresskill, NJ: Hampton Press.

Grabill, Jeffrey T. and Lynée Lewis Gaillet. 2002. Writing program design in the metropolitan university: Toward constructing community partnerships. *WPA: Writing Program Administration* 25 (3): 61-78.

Grabill, Jeffrey T. (2007). *Writing community change: Designing technologies for citizen action.* Cresskill, NJ: Hampton Press.

Heilker, Paul. 1997. Rhetoric made real: Civic discourse and writing beyond the curriculum. In *Writing the community: Concepts and models for service-learning in composition*, ed. Linda Adler-Kassner, Robert Crooks, and Ann Watter, 71-77. Washington, D.C.: American Association for Higher Education.

Holland, Barbara A. 2001. A comprehensive model for assessing service-learning and community-university partnerships. *New Directions for Higher Education* 114: 51-60.

Jesson, James. 2006. Professional development and the community writing center. *Praxis: A Writing Center Journal* 4 (1) projects.uwc.utexas.edu/praxis/?q=node/134.

Long, Elenore. 2008. *Community literacy and the rhetorics of local publics*. West Lafayette, IN: Parlor Press and WAC Clearing House.

Peck, Wayne Campbell, Linda Flower, and Lorraine Higgins. 1995. Community literacy. *College Composition and Communication* 46 (2): 199-222.

Spigelman, Candace. 2004. Politics, rhetoric, and service-learning. *WPA: Writing Program Administration* 28 (1/2): 95-114.

ABOUT THE AUTHORS

SHIRLEY K ROSE, Professor of English and Director of Writing Programs at Arizona State University, also teaches graduate courses in writing program administration. Her publications include two previous collections on writing program administration research and theory, also co-edited with Irwin Weiser, along with articles and chapters on writing teacher preparation and issues in the professionalization of graduate students in rhetoric and composition. She has been a member of the Executive Committee of the Conference on College Composition and Communication and is a Past President of the Council of Writing Program Administrators. She regularly serves as a consultant-evaluator for national and international college writing programs and she is an experienced Peer Reviewer for the Higher Learning Commission of the North Central Association of Colleges and Schools.

IRWIN WEISER, Professor of English at Purdue University, has served as Director of Composition and Head of the Department of English. In 2009-2010, he served as Interim Dean of the College of Liberal Arts. He teaches graduate courses in contemporary composition theory, writing across the curriculum, composition research methods, and writing assessment, as well as undergraduate composition courses. In addition to two previous collections on writing program administration co-edited with Shirley K Rose, he co-edited, with Kathleen Blake Yancey, *Situating Portfolios* (1997, Utah State UP) and has published articles and chapters on the preparation of teachers of writing and portfolio assessment. Weiser has been a member of the Executive Board of the Council of Writing Program Administrators and of the Executive Committee of the Conference on College Composition and Communication and has been a member of the editorial board of *WPA* and *CCC*. He has co-led the WPA annual summer workshop in 2004 and 2005, and will co-lead the 2010 and 2011 summer workshops.

LINDA ADLER-KASSNER is professor and director of the Writing Program at University of California, Santa Barbara. From 2000 to 2010, she taught and directed the first-year writing department at Eastern Michigan University. She is the author, most recently, of *The Activist WPA: Changing Stories about Writing and Writers* (USUP) and is currently completing *Reframing Writing Assessment to Improve Teaching and Learning* with Peggy O'Neill (forthcoming from USUP). Her books, chapters, and articles focus on rethinking and advocating for broadened ideas about writing, writers, and the teaching of writing.

LINDA S. BERGMANN is associate Professor in the English department at Purdue University and director of the Purdue writing lab. She recently published a textbook, *Academic Research and Writing: Inquiry and Argument in College*, and was coeditor of the collection, *Composition and/or Literature: The End(s) of Education*. She has published articles on writing and learning in such journals as *Journal of the Council of Writing Program Administrators, Composition Studies*, and *Language and Learning Across the Disciplines* and in numerous edited collections.

COLIN CHARLTON is assistant professor of rhetoric and composition at the University of Texas-Pan American in South Texas. He is currently in the final stages of co-writing a text with four colleagues and fellow WPAs, *GenAdmin: Theorizing WPA Identity in the 21st Century*.

JONIKKA CHARLTON is an assistant professor of rhetoric and composition at the University of Texas-Pan American. She is currently at work on two books, *GenAdmin: Theorizing WPA Identity in the 21st Century* (co-authored with Colin Charlton, Tarez Graban, Kate Ryan, and Amy Ferdinandt Stolley) and *The WPA's Progress* (co-authored with Shirley K Rose), (both under advance contract with Parlor Press). She has recently published in *WPA* and *Praxis: A Writing Center Journal.*

DIANE CHIN is associate director of the Chicago Civic Leadership Certificate Program, a sequence of civic engagement courses for undergraduates at the University of Illinois at Chicago. Her doctoral dissertation, *Inadvertent Alienation* (2007), analyzes service-learning rhetoric that tends to create a negative image of service-learning in academia.

DOMINIC DELLICARPINI is associate professor of English and writing program administrator at York College of Pennsylvania. His books include *Composing a Life's Work: Writing, Citizenship, and Your Occupation, Issues: Readings in Academic Disciplines,* and *Conversations: Readings for Writing.* His research and publications focus upon writing programs' role in developing informed, engaged citizens. He has served on the Executive Board of the Council of Writing Program Administrators and is co-founder of the *National Conversation on Writing* initiative.

ANN MERLE FELDMAN is professor of English at the University of Illinois at Chicago. She directs the first-year writing program and the Chicago Civic Leadership Certificate Program (CCLCP). Her scholarly interests include genre and rhetorical theory, e-learning, civic engagement, and higher education. Her recent book, *Making Writing Matter: Composition in the Engaged University* (SUNY Press, 2008) argues that teaching writing as a situated, civic activity must be a core intellectual activity in the engaged metropolitan university.

CHRIS FOSEN is an associate professor of English at California State University, Chico and teaches courses in composition, writing pedagogy, and rhetorical theory. He has written chapters for the *Dictionary of Literary Biography* and several edited collections in composition studies, and is currently collaborating with Thia Wolf and Jill Swiencicki on a book about first-year writing, inquiry, and public sphere pedagogy.

ELI GOLDBLATT is professor of English at Temple University. His 2007 Hampton Press book, *Because We Live Here: Sponsoring Literacy beyond the College Curriculum,* won the Best Book award from the Council of Writing Program Administrators. His center at Temple, New City Writing, supports literacy-related projects in schools and neighborhood centers in North Philadelphia. In addition to his composition and rhetoric work, he has also published three books of poetry and two books for children.

CAROLINE GOTTSCHALK-DRUSCHKE is a Ph.D. candidate in the department of English and a fellow in the Landscape, Ecological and Anthropogenic Processes (LEAP) program at the University of Illinois at Chicago. Her dissertation project is a quantitative and qualitative study of the rhetorics and practices of watershed-based agricultural conservation efforts.

JEFF GRABILL is a professor of rhetoric and professional writing and co-director of the Writing in Digital Environments (WIDE) research center at Michigan State University. His research focuses how to communicate with diverse audiences with respect to technical and scientific issues. Grabill has published two books on community literacy and articles in journals like *College Composition and Communication, Technical Communication Quarterly, Computers and Composition,* and *English Education.*

TIMOTHY HENNINGSEN is about to complete a PhD in literature from the University of Illinois at Chicago. His dissertation identifies and analyzes the influence of 19th century American literature on Caribbean novelists, poets, and critics in the colonial and early post-colonial era. His interest in teaching and rhetoric has evolved from his participation as an instructor and curriculum developer in UIC's Chicago Civic Leadership Certificate Program. Tim currently lives in Seattle.

DAVID A. JOLLIFFE is professor of English and curriculum and instruction at the University of Arkansas at Fayetteville. His most recent work examines the transition in reading demands and abilities from high school to college and the development of literacy programs in rural schools and communities.

EILEEN E. MEDEIROS is an associate professor at Johnson & Wales University where she teaches courses in composition, public speaking and food writing.

JESSIE L. MOORE is an assistant professor at Elon University, where she teaches professional writing and rhetoric, and TESOL. She also coordinates the university's first-year writing courses. Her current research focuses on preparing future teachers to support K-12 ESL students, integrating digital literacies into a multi-section first-year writing course, and supporting faculty writers.

TOM MOSS is the associate director of the first-year writing program at University of Illinois–Chicago. Previously, he was the assistant director of composition at Columbia College in Chicago. He received his MFA in Creative Writing from Ohio State University, where he also taught composition and tutored in the OSU writing center.

SUSAN WOLFF MURPHY is Associate Professor of English at Texas A&M University-Corpus Christi. She is director of the First-Year Learning Communities, First-Year Writing, and First-Year Islanders Programs. She is co-editor of *Teaching Writing with Latino/a Students: Lessons Learned at Hispanic-Serving Institutions.* Her work on writing program administration, writing centers, and civic engagement appears in *The Journal of Border and Educational Research, Civic Engagement in the First Year of College,* and *Writing Center Journal.*

MICHAEL H. NORTON, M.A. is the Assistant Director of the Community Learning Network @ Temple University and a doctoral candidate in the Sociology Department. He has been active in the field of campus-community partnerships and community-based learning since 2006 at Bryn Mawr College, Temple University, and for Pennsylvania Campus Compact.

NADYA PITTENDRIGH is a Ph.D. candidate at the University of Illinois at Chicago, working on a dissertation in rhetoric, punishment and activism.

STEPHANIE TURNER REICH is a Ph.D. candidate in English studies with a concentration in gender and women's studies at the University of Illinois at Chicago. Her dissertation project focuses on genre shifts in recent transnational literature.

LINDA K. SHAMOON, professor of writing and rhetoric at the University of Rhode Island, is co-editor and contributing author of *Coming of Age: The Advanced Writing Curriculum*, named Best Book for 2000 by WPA: The Council of Writing Program Administrators. Her textbook, *Public Writing*, is forthcoming from Longman. Her work on writing program and curriculum development appears in *College English, CCC,* and *WPA: The Journal of the Council of Writing Program Administrators.*

Michael Strickland is associate chair of the English department and a member of the environmental studies department at Elon University in North Carolina. He was formerly director of writing across the curriculum at Elon, and coordinator of the professional writing and rhetoric program. He teaches courses from first-year writing to travel writing, as well as the rhetoric of environmental issues and conservation writing.

Jill Swiencicki, formerly associate professor of English at the California State University, Chico, is currently visiting assistant professor at Rochester Institute of Technology, where she teaches courses in rhetoric, writing, and women's studies. Her articles have appeared in *College English, Rhetorical Education in America, Multiple Literacies for the Twenty-First Century,* and *Rhetoric, the Polis, and the Global Village.*

Jaclyn Wells is a doctoral candidate at Purdue University. Her dissertation, *Online Writing Labs as Sites for Community Engagement,* addresses the intersection of community engagement, public rhetoric, and community-based research. Her work appears in the *Writing Program Administration Journal* and *Reflections: A Journal of Writing, Service-Learning, and Community Literacy.*

Thia Wolf is the director of the First-Year Experience Program at CSU, Chico and Professor of Composition Studies. Her current research focuses on the relationship between civic development and identity formation in first-year students. She has published most recently on writing center administration and on the CSU, Chico Town Hall.